S0-BVF-124

Youth Against Age

To John Bender, mentor
with thanks
for playing Piers
to my Cuddie (p. 224)

Affectionately,

Steven

American University Studies

Series IV
English Language and Literature

Vol. 21

PETER LANG
New York · Berne · Frankfurt am Main

Steven Marx

Youth Against Age

Generational Strife in Renaissance Poetry

with special reference
to Edmund Spenser's *The Shepheardes Calender*

PETER LANG
New York · Berne · Frankfurt am Main

Library of Congress Cataloging in Publication Data

Marx, Steven
Youth Against Age.

(American University Studies. Series IV, English Language and Literature; vol. 21)
Bibliography: p.
1. Spenser, Edmund, 1552?–1599. Shepheardes Calender. 2. Conflict of Generations in Literature. 3. Age Groups in Literature. 4. Youth in Literature. 5. Old Age in Literature. 6. Pastoral Literature – History and Criticism. I. Title. II. Series.
PR2359.M28 1985 821'.3 85-15994
ISBN 0-8204-0183-8
ISSN 0741-0700

CIP-Kurztitelaufnahme der Deutschen Bibliothek

Marx, Steven:
Youth Against Age: Generational Strife in Renaissance Poetry; with special reference to Edmund Spenser's *The Shepheardes Calender* / Steven Marx. – New York; Berne; Frankfurt am Main: Lang, 1985.
(American University Studies: Ser. 4, English Language and Literature; Vol. 21)
ISBN 0-8204-0183-8

NE: American University Studies / 04

Printed by Lang Druck, Inc., Liebefeld/Berne (Switzerland)

To JHM: Patron, Wife and Friend

Preface

I started this project many years ago. As a young graduate student, I was attracted by the pastoral tradition in literature because it expressed some of the joys, longings and regrets I shared with my contemporaries. I wanted to write about how pastoral combined a quest for innocence with the disillusionment of experience and issued in a vision of life alternative to that of established society. I wanted to validate and test my own attitudes by matching them with a vital strain of western sensibility.

As it turned out, I was not ready to carry the study beyond its preliminary state without undertaking some field work. After a period of research and full-time teaching in New York, I left the city to go with my wife in search of a real Arcadia. I found it at the end of the road on the coast of British Columbia. There we encountered a community of like-minded emigrants. We bought an old homestead and started raising goats, vegetables, and children. In summer we doffed clothes and played songs on pipe and tabor. In winter we slaughtered animals and gathered round the stove, at times sick or cold or hungry. Together with neighbors, we established a summer camp, a theatre troupe, and a farmer's co-op.

After eight years, the pastoral ideals that had drawn me to the country—ideals of both a soft and a hard life outside of civilization—began to lose their hold. Instead, I felt myself aspiring toward new ideals of involvement, responsibility, recognition and reward, ideals represented by the image of the city. Leaving the peripheries and going back to the center by affirming my imperial citizenship appeared as the inevitable next step of personal growth. And yet, saying farewell to the stream that tumbles out of the forest and meanders through the pasture, to the nannies and their kids browsing on maple shoots, to the garden fenced against the deer, to the heavy log house, the ancient apple trees and the big rock, I knew that some day, after my children had grown, I would be ready to return there again for good.

While living in the wilderness I had no expectation of continuing my scholarly project, but I never stopped puzzling about the question of innocence and experience. I couldn't reconcile two contrary views of rustic life: how could it be both paradise and purgatory? The answer came to me as I left the pastoral world behind and reentered civilization. Though contraries, innocence and experience were also complementary. Both states involved extremes of refusal to engage the dominant social reality on its own terms. I saw that innocence was like the youth I was leaving behind and experience was like the old age I would some day encounter; they all excluded the middle ground I was entering—the stage of adulthood which maintains the nonpastoral, historical world and passes it on to future generations. When I later went to the texts, the hypothesis was confirmed: I found the conspicuous absence of pastoral herdsmen of middle age and the repeated presence of a dramatic vignette depicting "a young man and an old in solemn talk." (*As You Like It*, II, iv, 20)

Though the critical approach of this study stems from my own experience, it would never have reached completion without the advice and support of others. I wish to express gratitude to S. K. Heninger, whose close reading and heartening comments about parts of this work encouraged me to offer the whole for publication, to Martin Evans, who criticized my first attempts, to Bliss Carnochan, Anne Mellor and Seth Schein, who read and discussed several chapters with me, to Herbert Lindenberger, who perused the whole manuscript, and to Ron Rebholz, who scrutinized more than one draft. I am especially indebted to John Bender for many kinds of help, including shepherding my search for theses. I also want to thank Joe Montgomery and Claire-Elise Grace for putting up with an absent-minded father who stole one of their rooms for his dusty books and noisy typewriter. Finally, to Jan Howell Marx, who kept faith in this project during the years I abandoned it, who urged me to take it up again when I was ready, and who made it financially possible for me to carry it through, what can I say but, "it's done!"

Sections of chapter three, "*Fortunate Senex*: The Pastoral of Old Age," have appeared in *Studies in English Literature, 1500-1800* 25 (1985). The author wishes to thank the Dean of Humanities and Sciences and the English Department at Stanford University for a joint publication grant.

Contents

List of Illustrations

Introduction

Pastoral Ideals and the Life Cycle

"Genres de vie" is the French term for what English speakers call "the stages of life." This book concerns itself with the fundamental connection between *genres de vie* and literary genres, between chronological categories of human existence and traditional kinds of poetic discourse. Its central focus falls upon the debate of youth and age, a verse convention which sets a boy and an old man in a rustic landscape and pits them in generational combat. It argues that this neglected Renaissance commonplace distills the thematic and formal essence of the larger mode of pastoral. While offering a rhetorical, historical and anthroplological analysis of the particular sub-genre, the book proposes a new way of reading all pastoral, based on a study of the life cycle.[1]

Pastoral is usually regarded as an idealized vision of rustic life generated by a rejection of the city or the court. This book develops the theory that pastoral is generated by a rejection of adulthood and middle age. The Arcadian world, situated spatially at the peripheries of civilization, represents stages of development situated temporally at the peripheries of human life. This thematic preoccupation with rejecting the middle finds appropriate expression in the formal structure underlying most Renaissance pastoral works—the verbal contest or debate. The book discovers the source of this generic form in the medieval predecessor of the eclogue known as *conflictus* or *debat*. By delineating the schematic components and affective strategies of this generic source, the book prepares an approach to later pastoral writings. The final proof the book's thesis emerges in its application to a single major work. Reading *The Shepheardes Calender* as an example of the pastoral debate of youth and age discloses the poem's hidden unity and reveals how Edmund Spenser employed the resources of kind to achieve his own novel purposes.

This book arrives at the interpretation of a single poem by way of investigating the generic convention to which that poem belongs. And it examines the convention itself in light of a more general discussion locating the pastoral mode within the universe of literary kinds. Such a discussion begins with an essay at definition. What, in the first place, do we mean by "pastoral"? Many writers have applied themselves to this question; their collective effort yields a discouraging lack of consensus. The sixteenth-century critic, George Puttenhame, defined it as an allegorical screen behind which poets can take liberties "to glance at greater matters" of state and evade responsibility for criticism.[2] Alexander Pope claimed that pastoral was "a representation of Innocence," while Dr. Johnson saw it as a decadent affectation of crudeness.[3] Some modern critics have reacted to the untidy variety of theories and manifestations of pastoral by evading the question altogether, preferring either to speak of different "versions of pastoral" which share no common identity, or to recognize pastoral simply by the presence of the "pastor" or shepherd motif.[4] Though such nominalistic approaches avoid the pitfalls of pedantic disputation and over-restrictive classification, they deny us the fruitful use of a uniquely significant, emotionally laden and time-honored concept.

My own sense of the core idea of pastoral derives from its usage in common parlance rather than in literary discourse. I arrive at the meaning of "the pastoral" by asking what is meant by "a pastoral," or "pastoral," the adjective. To me, a "pastoral" suggests something very like "an idyll"—the word Theocritus, "the father of pastoral," used to label his poems. As an adjective, "pastoral" is synonymous with "idyllic." I understand it to mean some place or state that is distant from and more desirable than the place or state from which I regard it. "The pastoral," or plain "pastoral," I define as a mode of literature that envisions an ideal world.

For the Renaissance writer and his audience, this is indeed what all fiction does; it depicts life not as it is, but as it might be. In his *Defence of Poesy,* Sir Phillip Sidney declares that the poet achieves godlike stature because of his ability to rise above mere reality and to create ideal worlds of the imagination:

> Nature never set forth the earth in so rich tapestry as divers poets have done; neither pleasant rivers, fruitful trees, sweet-smelling flowers, nor

> whatsoever else may make the too-much-loved earth more lovely; her world is brazen, the poets only deliver a golden.[5]

Sidney argues for the idealistic quality not of a single mode but of all literature. Yet in choosing the example of a verbal tapestry that portrays the beauties of nature and in referring to the poet's creation as a "golden world," he equates the whole realm of the imagination with the familiar landscape of pastoral, where men "fleet the time carelessly, as they did in the golden world."[6]

No matter what he actually thought of the idea of a peaceful rustic existence, the Elizabethan poet could not disengage the notion of "a better world"—that is, an alternative way of being—from traditional pastoral conventions. He often mixed the vision of a remote heroic age of warriors with that of the Golden Age when all was peace and harmony. Indeed, though Sidney himself frequently expressed aversion for the shepherd's life and for the natural setting, he situated his epic romance glorifying prowess, courage and striving in a perfect rural landscape, and titled it *Arcadia*.[7]

Despite the frequent combining of modes, the ideal qualities of the pastoral world remain distinct from those of the heroic. The world of Faerie traversed by the knight of epic is in fact usually a darker, wilder and more treacherous place than the actual environment of the audience. What makes his world "golden" is the quality of effort and accomplishment it elicits from its inhabitants in their struggles to triumph over nature and one another. In pastoral, on the other hand, the environment itself, rather than the people and their deeds, has the golden shimmer. The setting, both as landscape and as social structure provides a place that absorbs the individual isolated identity into its surroundings. The ideal life here is a function not of being good but of being in the good place. "The good place" translated into Greek is "Eu-topia," and forms the title of Sir Thomas More's vision of a golden world—a vision that Sidney approves as a "way of patterning a commonwealth most absolute."[8] In its portrayal of the golden world as a good place which guarantees the good life to its inhabitants, pastoral is a kind of utopian fiction.

While the author of epic or romance makes us forget our literal surroundings by transporting us to his legendary setting, the pastoralist, like his utopian counterpart, emphasizes the juxtaposition of golden and brazen worlds in order to demonstrate the superiority of the other place to here. He may do this with a homiletic disquisition, as in this typical passage from Richard Barnefield's, *The Shepheard's Content* (1594):

> Thus have I showed in my Countrey veine
> The sweete Content that Shepheards still injoy;
> The mickle pleasure, and the little paine
> That ever doth awayte the Sheepheards Boy. . .
>
> Who would not then a simple Shepheard bee,
> Rather than be a mightie Monarch made?
> Since he enjoyes much perfect libertie,
> As never can decay, nor ever fade:[9]

Or he may imply the contrast through a catalog of rustic delights available only to those who have discovered the perfect place—as does Theocritus:

> Here are oaks and galingale; here sweetly hum the bees
> about the hives. Here are two springs of cold water. ..

and Vergil:

> Here are cool springs; here are soft meadows, Lycoris;
> here woods; here with you only time itself would slowly waste me away.

and Milton:

> Here dwell no frowns, nor anger; from these gates
> Sorrow flies far. See, here be all the pleasures. . .[10]

With such self-conscious evocations of the beauties of the other world, the pastoralist often attempts to move his mistress to "come away" from brazen reality to a land of heart's desire:

> Come liue with me, and be my loue,
> And we will all the pleasures proue,
> That Vallies, groues, hills and fieldes,
> Woods, or steepie mountaine yeeldes.
>
> And wee will sit vpon the Rocks,
> Seeing the Shepheards feede theyr flocks,
> By shallow Riuers, to whose falls,
> Melodious byrds sings Madrigalls.[11]

In such conventional poems of "Invitation," the remote and enviable quality of the bucolic setting is meant to seduce the listener into imaginative or physical surrender. But the other world of pastoral also shares with the utopian fiction a critical and philosophical function. The vision of a place free from the economic, political and social evils of the present system supplies a point of view from which the status quo can be judged and faulted. On these grounds, Sidney defends pastoral as a form of utopian satire:

> Is the poor pipe disdained, which sometimes out of Meliboeus' mouth can show the misery of people under hard lords and ravening soldiers, and again, by Tityrus, what blessedness is derived to them that lie lowest from the goodness of them that sit highest? Sometimes under the pretty tales of wolves and sheep, can include the whole considerations of wrong-doing and patience.[12]

Whether sensuous or moral, the ideal worlds of utopian fictions lend themselves to classification by the values they embody. In the aristocracy of Plato's *Republic,* these are the values of justice: everyone gets what he deserves—from visionary contemplation to hard labor—according to talents determined by birth and innate capability. In More's *Utopia,* the good is the temperate pleasure of prosperity and peace, equally distributed to everyone. In Huxley's *Island,* the best of all possible worlds provides its inhabitants with a variety of mystical revelations.

Pastoral versions of utopia share a specific set of values.[13] They envision the good life as one lived in accord with some conception of "nature." The ideals of such a natural existence take shape largely by contrast to the competitive, complex and artificial life of court and city. Bucolic life is imagined as humane, simple and spontaneous. Though often physically strenuous, the human condition in Arcadia is admirable because it is easier in a mental, an emotional, a moral and a spiritual sense. This kind of admiration for a "natural" life is described by A. O. Lovejoy and George Boas as a product of "civilized man's misgivings with civilization," and it is classified in their history of ideas as the ideology of primitivism.[14] In the golden world of pastoral, primitivist values are reified in specific poetic conventions.[15]

The most prevalent of these are the figure of herdsman and the setting of the natural landscape. In the shepherd, man is portrayed as vigorous and pure, uncorrupted by the degeneracy of polite society. In the groves, forests and fields of Arcadia, the person finds surroundings that are beautiful, fresh and open to the four elements and to other forms of life. The shepherd's harmony with these surroundings symbolizes the harmony and integration of his inner nature, a lost human wholeness. Sidney's old herdsman Dorcas, for example, describes his life as liberated from the toils of ambition, "neither subject to violent oppression, nor servile flattery." Among his flocks, "it is lawfull for a man to be good if he list. . .there where the eye may be busied in considering the works of nature and the hart quietly rejoyced in the honest using them."[16]

From the urban perspective of poet and audience, all rural environments may appear similar. But in fact, Arcadia is not only a place of perpetual spring and flowered banks. A significant proportion of bucolic poetry praises the rugged and rocky features of country life. The natural world of poverty, of labor, of winter and rough weather is also an ideal environment, for it nourishes the simple virtues of hardiness, health and honesty, and it provides an opportunity for those who are alienated from civilization to discover how "sweet are the uses of adversity." There, in the words of Duke Senior in *As You Like It*, they may find a life" . . .exempt from public haunt. . . tongues in trees, books in the running brooks/ Sermons in stones, and good in everything." (II,i,15-17)

A number of scholars have remarked upon the presence of two pastoral landscapes and the correlation of these landscapes with the two varieties of philosophic primitivism.[17] "Soft" primitivism glorifies the natural life for its freedom from civilized restraint and for the ease and pleasure it provides. "Hard" primitivism is a response to the corruption and lack of restraint of civilized life and praises nature for the strictness and discipline it confers. But little notice has been paid to a corresponding polarity in the second essential pastoral convention, the figure of the rustic. Whether that character is male or female, whether a tender of sheep, goats or cattle, whether a farmer, a forester or even a fisherman has little direct bearing on the sentiments he expresses or on the ideals he embodies. The determining factor is the person's age. There are essentially two kinds of pastoral characters, young and old. One rarely finds a shepherd of middle age.

The association of idealized conceptions of youth with pastoral conventions was familiar long before William Empson wrote about childhood as a "version of pastoral" in the 1930's.[18] But discussions of this association have been brief, peripheral or have centered on late 18th and 19th century adaptations of pastoral conventions to the Romantic myth of childhood. Yet both ancient and renaissance pastorals are also engaged with the ideal of childhood innocence, especially as that ideal condition is brought into relief by the imminence of its departure during the stage of adolescence.

The mode's concern with youth is complemented by its concern with old age. Whether it be in eclogues by Theocritus, Vergil, Garcilaso, Marot, Mantuan, or Jonson, in pastoral romances like *Rosalynd* or *Diana,* in collections of lyrics like *England's Helicon* or Davison's *Poetical Rhapsody,* one consistently finds herdsmen of advanced years playing important dramatic roles and representing a distinct cluster of attitudes and ideas. The aged shepherd is not, as one of the few scholars who have noticed his generic presence maintains, a minor intruder from neighboring genres who actually has no place in the bucolic world.[19] He is native to it, and an understanding of his part is essential to any definition of the genre as a whole. Just as both soft and hard landscapes together comprise the setting of pastoral, so both youth and age are the pastoral stages of life.[20]

What accounts for this threefold connection between pastoral conventions, a golden world of primitivistic ideals and the life stages of youth and age? The answer to this question is based on the polarity of center and periphery. All three represent remoteness from the hub of the dominant socially defined reality. The pastoralist invites the listener to come away from his normal haunts in city and court to a place that is better than "the world." "The world" is the creation and the possession of the worldly, to whom primitivists always feel superior. And who are the wordly? To be sure, they are the members of the sex, race, class and party that is privileged with wealth and power in any particular society at a given time. But in a more general sense, the wordly are those in *every* society who are designated by Hindu sacred texts to "maintain the world": adults.[21] Adults are people who have finished growing up—"L *adultus,* past participle of *adolescere,* to grow up." Adult concerns are specifically those of procreation, custodianship, ambition, wealth and power. Renaissance critics located such concerns within the purview of the "life of action"—the *vita activa*—and specifically excluded the *vita activa* from the ideals of Arcadia.[22] In visual schemata of the ages of man, adulthood is represented by the highest step on a staircase that descends in both directions.[23] Like Oedipus while he was king, the adult stands tall on two legs at noon. Youth is still in the process of growing—*adolescens*—while the elderly descend, shrink or walk on three legs. Both youth and age reside on the peripheries of the adult world, and for this reason are pictured in pastoral as inhabitants of its green and golden fringes.

The question of why youth and age have such prominent roles in pastoral can also be answered by reference to the life cycle itself. Youth and age are polar phases of that cycle and draw our attention to its importance as a way of organizing information and understanding reality. This orderly sequence of developmental changes is the place of strongest contact between the human and the natural world. The person who has never smelled new mown hay or shivered on a frosty morning will nevertheless experience the force of nature in the thickening of his beard or the wrinkling of his hands. Even the most refined urban dweller is aware of the inner changes that are brought on by the same "force that through the green fuse drives the flower." And the periods of youth and age are the times in everyone's life when the natural forces of growth and decline make themselves most strongly felt. During those periods, the realities of the self and "the world" which dominate the less mutable being of the adult may more often be questioned.[24]

Not only is the life cycle the civilized person's strongest and most intimate confrontation with nature, that cycle has always appeared as a particularly "primitive" topic of concern. It is the source of myths, rituals and patterns of design in the most widespread and aboriginal of cultures; and it is likewise, the most fundamental standard for the distribution of duties and privileges.[25] A modern anthropologist has declared that "the simpler the organization of a society the more influential age will be as a criterion for allocating roles."[26] Like singing contests or seasonal festivals, then, an emphasis on stages of the life cycle and particularly on the contrast of youth and age provides poets with a touch of real rusticity to authenticate their pictures of the pastoral world. The intrinsic connections between pastoral's thematic ideals and the schema of the life cycle make it only natural that Shakespeare should have reserved his Seven Ages of Man speech for declaration in the Forest of Arden.[27]

Since youth and age are both marginal in relation to middle age and the metropolitan world, they share many of the same counter-cultural ideals. But insofar as they are situated on opposite boundaries of adulthood, their ideals are polarized. In his own pastoral writings, William Blake suggested the opposing yet complementary relationship of these ideals in his categories of "Innocence and Experience: Contrary States of the Human Soul."[28]

Blake's terms govern the organization of the next three chapters of this study. In all of them I continue to plait the strands that together constitute pastoral's thematic braid: traditional bucolic conventions, idealized conceptions of the good place, and the extreme stages of the life cycle.

Chapter one deals with innocence, the pastoral of youth. It presents evidence for the association of youth and pastoral rusticity in the mind of the Renaissance reader and poet. First, the traditional Vergillian pattern of the writer's career demanded that the youthful apprentice poet adopt the persona of shepherd-pastoralist. Second, the essential pastoral setting of Eden or the Golden Age was described as the childhood of the human race and as a projection of the individual's own childhood. Third, custodianship of the rural seasonal festivals depicted in pastoral literature was entrusted entirely to institutionalized groups of young people throughout Europe during the early modern period.

The pastoral of youth represents the shepherd as *puer eternus*—the eternal boy. His physical beauty, his cleansed doors of perception, his unjaded sensitivity, and his access to the energies of the unconscious endow him with special artistic and spiritual gifts. But most important, the young swain incarnates some nostalgic vision of prelapsarian eroticism. Like Feste's song in *Twelth Night,* the pastoral of youth ". . .dallies with the innocence of love/ In the old age." (II,iv, 47-9) The good life here affords the joys of love without its pains. For this reason, several critics have said that pastoral itself is a projection of the Freudian Pleasure Principle. During the Renaissance, the ideal of the life of pleasure—the *vita voluptatis*—represented an alternative to the life of action, the *vita activa*. Also known as the life of love (*vita amoris*), the life of pleasure was often symbolized in images of youthful frolics in fields and groves.

The innocent ideal of love without pain or guilt underlies several bucolic motifs. It appears as prepubescent affection unstained by the poison of sexual desire, or as polymorphous sexual play undeflowered by the fall of orgasmic coitus, or as the reign of the spirit of Free Love, when "whatever pleased was lawful." All of these sexual ideals locate the innocence of love some time in the lost past; all describe it by contrast to norms of adult sexuality; and all of them exemplify typical adolescent attitudes and yearnings.

The landscape of the pastoral of youth is the *locus amoenus*—the pleasureable spot of trees, grass and flowers. Not only does that spot provide an enticing site for making love, the very landscape frequently appears as a figuration of the beloved's body. Such an erotic geography is the ultimate extension of the utopian ideal of the good place and of the Pleasure Principle's dream of infantile gratification. Within the larger, adulthood-oriented universe of epic, the pastoral landscape of the body functions as an "oasis." In the Bible, in the *Odyssey*, in the *Divine Comedy* and *The Faerie Queene*, such bowers of bliss have the recreative allure of childlike absorption in pleasure, but for the epic hero striving to realize his manhood, the *locus amoenus'* promise of eternal childhood eventually is unmasked as a threat.

Like all utopian ideals, the pastoral of youth is generated by a "negative formula." Innocence is defined by the absence of the constraints and burdens of adult reality. A similar contrast to the central, middle-aged world informs the pastoral of old age. In some instances, bucolic poetry envisions youthful and aged shepherds living in harmony, exchanging the joys and rigors of the mean estate. But more often, pastoral emphasizes the secondary contrast between the two equally peripheral states. Chapter two, "*Fortunate Senex*: The Pastoral of Old Age," explores the hard and wintry setting inhabited by elderly shepherds and outlines the ideals of the good life they voice and embody. Formulations of such ideals of old age appear in classic oriental schemata of the life cycle, in anthropological descriptions of old age in primitive communities, and in the writings of present-day gerontologists. A source of many of the old shepherd's ideals is Cicero's *De Senectute*, where they are expounded by the hero, Cato the Elder. Cato praises self knowledge, moderation, vigor, the feeling of fulfillment, and freedom from both sexual desire and from ambition as the virtues of age, and he links them with retirement from the active life and with the adoption of a rustic existence.

Usually conveyed by exhortation rather than invitation, the values of the old shepherds are gounded in an autumnal or wintry nature, a nature of harvest, reckoning, judgment and stark unmasking. These values commend looking toward the future rather than the past; they prize self-restraint, consideration of consequence, thrift and work. The ideals of age are usually associated with the soul and mind rather than the body. Ultimately the wisdom of age is not only practical but transcendental. Old rustic characters tend to become hermits, philosophers and magicians. In this guise, they embody the last of the three traditional ways of life, the *vita contemplativa.*

The same negative formula or dialectical logic that generates the pastoral world as a utopian alternative to the actual one, when applied to Arcadia itself, leads to the widespread phenomenon of "anti-pastoral." A speaker in the landscape takes an anti-pastoral stance, not when he attacks the values of an opponent (and thereby affirms his own), but when he expresses pain or internal conflict. In this case he no longer fades into the setting, either hard or soft, no longer represents an ideal either of innocence of experience. Instead, he severs himself from the landscape and also from the conditions of his age, and accentuates the isolation of his individual identity. The melancholy swain represents the denial of pastoral ideals because he no longer inhabits the good place, where simply to be is to be happy, or at least content. And his complaint, which is among the most popular of pastoral forms, usually denies the very landscape conventions which define his setting.

Chapter three, "The Shepheardes Sorrow," shows how the repudiation of pastoral ideals is related to the rejection of both youth and age. It follows the logic of reversal in different forms of poetic complaint, providing background for the later discussion of Colin Clout's mysterious presentation of himself in *The Shepheardes Calender* as a *puer senex*: an unripe, prematurely aged young-old man. There are a number of causes for the melancholy shepherd's rejection of pastoral ideals: youth's disappointment in love, or its dismay at the triumph of mutability and death and old age's despair at the failure of long years' experience to provide contentment and wholeness. That rejection often is accompanied by an affirmation of a wholly different kind of ideal, one that moves out of the rustic landscape and out of the natural cycle encompassing youth and age. The new ideal is either a transcendental vision of the "greener fields and pastures new" of life beyond the grave, or an ethos of aestheticism which elevates the voice and the verse that chants its own despair into imperishable monuments. Finally, while bidding adieu to the bucolic setting and the ideals it represents, the anti-pastoral of melancholy will sometimes turn from the past and look forward to a glorious future in the epic quest, the *vita activa,* and the adult stage of life.

Having completed this mapping of pastoral themes in terms of the positive and negative ideals of youth and age, the study continues with an examination of the relationship among those four terms. They constitute the poles upon which a structural paradigm of all pastoral poetry can be suspended. Chapter four, " 'Youthe and Elde are often at Debaat,' " focusses upon such a paradigm: the allegorical verse debate—a specific "kinde" or subgenre especially popular among Renaissance pastoralists.

Though it has distant analogs in the Theocritean amoebic singing contest, the Renaissance pastoral debate is the survival of a medieval rather than a classical convention. The chapter's title quotes a comment of Chaucer's Miller which reveals the familiarity of the kinde of *debaat* during the middle ages. Known by a variety of names—including *altercatio, respuesta,* and *Streitgedicht*—and dealing with a whole range of topics, the medieval debate frequently portrayed the conflict of youthful and elderly principals, for example in "The Parlement of the Thre Ages," and Robert Henrysson's "Ressonyng Betuix Aige and Yowthe." The prevalence of this otherwise almost extinct medieval kinde in Renaissance pastoral calls attention to the interchangeability of eclogue and debate forms throughout the middle ages.

An analysis of complete verse debates in this chapter emphasizes the way habits of classical rhetoric and medieval disputation affect the pastoral poet's practise and the reader's response. The formal structure of the verse debate is dualistic; it is designed to present, though not to resolve, the conflict of two opposing points of view. Such a structure is particularly suited to articulate philosophical and mythical systems of polarities. In the case of youth and age, the pastoral debate airs not only the opposition of generic pastoral ideals, but also the more concrete conflicts of generational strife, of identity crises at both life stages, and of the self-contradictions experienced by the individual moving from one stage to the next.

As a consciously rhetorical design, the debate of youth and age also elucidates the way ideals are conditioned by their contexts. First, it shows how the principles and the reasoning processes of both speakers depend on their places in the life cycle. And second, repeated references to the landscape and weather of the natural setting subordinate the dialectical shifting of the weight of the argument to the oscillation of the diurnal and seasonal cycles. This framing of discourse generates a relativity of perspective consistent with the traditional rhetorician's prescription to look at all questions from both sides—*in utramque partem*—without coming to a final determination. The same relativity that Aristotle's *Rhetoric* teaches in its lengthy elaboration of the contrasting mentalities of youth and old age emerges as a characteristic Renaissance habit of mind. It finds expression not only in literature but in the illusionistic feats of perspective painters, in Cartesian dualism, in Leibnitz' metaphysics of the point of view, and in the ethical scepticism of Montaigne, who chose a pair of balances for the emblem on his escutcheon.

Pastoral's yoking of idealistic theme with relativistic structure typifies the Renaissance concept of fiction. Sidney declares that though he projects golden worlds, ". . .the poet. . .never affirmeth." In its very name, the genre of pastoral debate suggests this *concordia discors*. For all its suggestions of visionary utopianism and idyllic escape, "pastoral" can never evade the skeptical, searching and conflict-laden intellectuality of "debate." The most luscious of bowers and the most pious of homesteads are "places" of rhetoric—*loci* and *topoi*—as well as geography.

There is no more comprehensive compendium of pastoral dichotomies than *The Shepheardes Calender*. Here Spenser treats the debate of youth and age as the central feature of Arcadia. In "Februarie," he presents a strict reproduction of the medieval *debat*, and, without becoming repetitious, sounds variations of the paradigm in all eleven remaining eclogues. He unifies the whole collection by balancing the six eclogues of the old year against the six eclogues of the new. Spenser also vastly expands the antithetical possibilities of his genre. He tempers pastoral's allegorizing and mythologizing tendencies with a drive toward mimetic realism. He uses the interplay of utopian ideals to disclose the inner life of individuals at a particular stage of psychological development in a particular historical circumstance. The last chapter of this study asserts that Spenser molds the pastoral debate of youth and age into a forerunner of the modern *Bildungsroman*. By presenting a number of such debates, he dramatizes the conflicts of attitudes that complete within the mind of the young person suspended between childhood and majority. By placing those debates in a certain phased sequence, he allows the reader to experience the gradual reversal of perspective from youth *to* age that signals the person's unconscious emergence into maturity. And by revealing "Immerito" as a central integrating consciousness who mediates between author, fictional characters and reader, Spenser illuminates the way the contrary energies and multiple personae of adolescence can coalesce into the unified identity of the adult self.

NOTES

[1] Despite the steady flow of scholarly studies on pastoral during the last twenty years, this particular topic merits further research. Discussion of pastoral works, like Judy Zahler Kronenfeld's 1970 Stanford Dissertation, "The Treatment of Pastoral Ideals in *As You Like It*: A Study of Traditional Renaissance Dichotomies" and Patrick Cullen's section on *The Shepheardes Calender* in *Spenser, Marvell and Renaissance Pastoral* (Cambridge: Harvard University Press, 1970) have analysed individual examples of the pastoral debate of youth and age; and a number of writers have noted its recurrence as a "minor pastoral *topos*," e.g. Thomas Rosenmeyer, *The Green Cabinet: Theocritus and the European Pastoral Lyric* (Berkeley: University of California Press, 1969), p. 57. Hallett Smith has observed the larger significance of the convention, but with no more than a passing remark:

> The conflict of youth and age is very common in the pastoral mode. It is simply another form of the central problem which makes pastoral—the problem of the values inherent in the good life. (*Elizabethan Poetry* [Cambridge: Harvard University Press, 1952], p. 42).

My hypothesis that these pastoral "values inherent in the good life" are themselves conditioned by one's place in the life cycle, and that pastoral's thematic ideals are necessarily related to *both* stages of youth and age has been noticed only by one other student of the mode. In "The Aging Boy: Paradise and Parricide in Spenser's *SC*," *Poetic Traditions of the English Renaissance*, ed. Maynard Mack (New Haven: Yale University Press, 1982), pp. 25 ff, an essay that came to my attention after this study was completed, Harry Berger Jr. argues that youth and age have a special relation to the "Paradise Principle" that he sees generating all pastoral. His reading of "Februarie" and "Nouember" has several elements in common with that presented in chapters four and five of this study. But Berger makes no mention of the genre of *debat*, nor does he elaborate the connection between old age and pastoral in general. Recent criticism has concurred that a dialectical structure is common to most pastoral poetry. See Harold Tolliver, *Pastoral Forms and Attitudes* (Berkeley: University of California Press, 1971), pp. 1-20, and Paul Alpers, "The Eclogue Tradition and the Nature of Pastoral," *CE* 34, 1972, pp. 353-371; also *The Singer of* The Eclogues: *A Study of Virgilian Pastoral* (Berkeley: University of California Press, 1979), pp. 97 ff. Yet although the word "debate" crops up frequently in the consideration of particular bucolic works, the term is used loosely rather than in reference to a specific genre. To my knowledge there have been no studies of the pastoral debate *per se*.

[2] *The Arte of English Poesie*, ed. Gladys Doidge Wilcock and Alice Walker (Cambridge: Cambridge University Press, 1963), Chapter XVIII, p. 38.

[3] Alexander Pope, *Guardian #40* (1713) in *The Tatler and The Guardian Complete in One Volume* (Edinburgh: William P. Nimmo & Co., 1880), p. 59. Samuel Johnson, "Pastoral Poetry I," *Rambler #36*, July 21, 1750, in *Eighteenth Century Critical Essays*, ed. Scott Elledge (Ithaca: Cornell University Press, 1961), II, 579.

[4] William Empson, *Some Versions of Pastoral* (London, 1935; rpt. New York: New Directions, 1960). See also, W. W. Greg, *Pastoral Poetry and Pastoral Drama* (London: Sidgewick and Jackson, Ltd., 1906. rpt. New York: Russell & Russell, 1959), p. 417:

> It cannot be too emphatically laid down that there is and can be no such thing as a "theory" of pastoral. . .pastoral is not capable of definition by reference to any essential quality; whence it follows that any theory of pastoral is not a theory of pastoral as it exists, but as the critic imagines that it ought to exist. "Everything is what it is, and not another thing," and pastoral is what the writers of pastoral have made it.

This empiricist dogma accounts for the weakness of Greg's still standard reference work on pastoral. Rather than a history of a tradition unified by some idea, it is a mere chronicle of particular works selected and described because they happen to include references to shepherds. When he insists on the tautology that pastoral is nothing but what poets have made of it, Greg ignores the fact that a literary convention is not the fabrication of later scholars but a pattern that the poet chooses *before* starting to compose.

[5] *The Prose Works of Sir Phillip Sidney*, ed. Albert Feuillerat (Cambridge: Cambridge University Press, 1962), III, 8.

[6] *As You Like It*, I, i, 111. *The Complete Works of William Shakespeare*, ed. George Lyman Kittredge (Boston: Ginn & Co.). All later citations are to this edition. To clarify the often-blurred distinction between the better world of pastoral escape—the green world—and the better world of the work of art that imaginatively represents this green world, see Harry Berger, "The Renaissance Imagination: Second World and Green World," *CR*, IX, 1965, pp. 36-79.

[7] On Sidney's hostility to pastoral ideals, see chapter four, below, and David Kalstone, *Sidney's Poetry: Contexts and Interpretations* (Cambridge: Harvard University Press, 1965), pp. 9-40.

[8] "Defence of Poesie," *Prose Works*, III, 15.

[9] In *English Pastoral Poetry from its Beginnings to Marvell*, ed. Frank Kermode (New York: Barnes and Noble, 1952), p. 179.

[10] Passages from Theocritus, *Idyll* 5, 45-7; Vergil, "Eclogue 10," 42-3, and Milton, *Comus*, 2, 194, cited by Ellen Zetzel Lambert, *Placing Sorrow: A Study of the Pastoral Elegy Convention from Theocritus to Milton* (Chapel Hill: University of North Carolina Press, 1976), p. xiv.

[11] Christopher Marlowe, "The Passionate Sheepheard to his Love," in *England's Helicon*, ed. H. E. Rollins (Cambridge: Harvard University Press, 1935), I, 184.

[12] "Defence of Poesie," *Prose Works*, III, 22.

[13] The approach to pastoral as an idealizing and critical literary mode has recently been questioned by more than one scholar. Paul Alpers has warned us not to allow philosophical analysis to obscure our apprecation of "the verve of the poetry," and he

has urged us to remember that the poet and poetry itself is the central pastoral theme. See "The Eclogue Tradition. . ." p. 363 and *Singer*, pp. 6 f. True, and worth repeating, yet the study of pastoral ideals is necessary to elucidate obscure designs and ambiguous logic in major literary works, as has been demonstrated by Cullen and Kronenfeld. Others have questioned the idealizing tendency of pastoral by claiming that the mode is defined by certain stock motifs such as the *locus amoenus* or the shepherd. (See Ernst Robert Curtius, *European Literature and the Latin Middle Ages*, trans. Willard Trask [New York: Pantheon Books, 1953], p. 187, and Kronenfeld's nominalistic introduction). But what explains the persistence of these *topoi* is their identification with perennial human states and desires. Pastoral conventions project thematic ideals—Smith's "values inherent in the good life"—and by so doing draw together a timeless work of the collective imagination. W. W. Greg, one of the least philosophically-oriented of pastoral's critics, noted the connection of "pastoral" and "ideal."

> I noticed that I have used the expression "pastoral ideal," and the phrase, which comes naturally to the mind in connexion with this form of literature, may supply us with a useful hint. It reminds us, namely that the quality of pastoralism is not determined by the fortuitous occurrence of certain characters but by the fact of the pieces in question being based more or less evidently upon a philosophical conception. (*Pastoral Poetry and Pastoral Drama*, pp. 2-3.)

[14] A. O. Lovejoy and George Boas, *Primitivism and Related Ideas in Antiquity* (Baltimore: Johns Hopkins Press, 1935; rpt. 1965), p. ix.

[15] This general description of pastoral ideals requires immediate qualification. Throughout the history of the genre, the meaning of pastoral's norm of "nature" has been complicated by variations and discrepancies. "Nature," like "primitive," can have connotations both negative and positive, can be red in tooth and claw as well as Edenically serene. Pastoralists often mock or reject the ideals of primitivism as soon as they invoke them. Sometimes they praise nature only insofar as it resembles art. Usually, the poet's vision of nature rather than nature itself constitutes the pastoral ideal. See Edward William Tayler, *Nature and Art in Renaissance Literature* (New York: Columbia University Press, 1964).

[16] "The Lady of the May," *Prose Works*, II, i, 335. Seen as a projection of ideals of the good life, pastoral is a kind of utopia. But the divergence between the two genres are as instructive as their similarities. Utopia is a philosophical treatise clothed in a literary fantasy. Pastoral is literature with a philosophical substratum. Literary ideals are conveyed and held differently from philosophical ones, despite Sidney's repeated assertions to the contrary in his *Defense*. The names of the genres themselves hint at the nature of the contrast: "utopia" is technical and theoretical; it suggests street plans and tours with official guides. "Pastoral" is melodious and concrete; it evokes "pleasant rivers, fruitful trees, sweet-smelling flowers." Utopia is set in the future tense or the conditional mood. It argues for the way things shall or should be. Arcadia is set in the past; it sings of the way things were before the present decline. The pastoralist calls us *back* to Eden, to the place where we once belonged; and he bases his appeal on the submerged power of nostalgia. See Laurance Lerner, *The Uses of Nostalgia: Studies in Pastoral Poetry* [New York: Schocken Books, 1972], pp. 41-63).

[17] Judy Zahler Kronenfeld, pp. 239-279; Paul Alpers, "The Eclogue Tradition. . .," pp. 352-3; Patrick Cullen, pp. 1-29.

[18] see Samuel Johnson, "Pastoral Poetry I," in *Rambler* #36 July 21, 1750, *Eighteenth Century Critical Essays*, 11, 579 and *Some Versions of Pastoral, pp. 85-112.*

[19] Thomas Rosenmeyer, *The Green Cabinet: Theocritus and the European Pastoral Lyric* (Berkeley: U. of Cal. Press, 1969), pp. 58-9.

[20] My assumption here that a person's biological state of life conditions his ethical ideals, his philosophical stance and his social role reflects observations about the Ages of Man so common throughout the western tradition and in primitive cultures that anthropologists speak of them as universals. However, some of the specific traits I attribute to childhood, youth, adulthood and old age, have been suggested by the developmental psychology of Erik Erikson and may therefore be time and culture bound. Mitigating this proviso is the fact that Erikson based a number of his studies of the life cycle on Renaissance literary and historical characters—in particular Hamlet and Martin Luther.

[21] Subhir Kakar, "The Human Life Cycle: The Traditional Hindu View and the Psychology of Erik H. Erikson," *Philosophy of East and West*, XVIII: 3 (1968).

[22] Hallet Smith, "Pastoral Poetry" in *Elizabethan Poetry* (Cambridge: Harvard University Press, 1952), pp. 4-13; also Kronenfeld, pp. 13-54.

[23] Hans v.d. Gabelentz, *Die Lebensalter u.d. Menschliche Leben in Tiergestalt* (Berlin, 1938), p. 8; Samuel C. Chew, *This Strange Eventful History* (New Haven and London, 1962).

[24] For this reason medieval schemata of the ages of man associate each of the stages with a different animal.

[25] Andre Varagnac, *Civilisation Traditionelle et les Genres de Vie* (Paris: Editions Andre Michel, 1948).

[26] S. N. Eisenstadt, "Archetypal Patterns of Youth," in *Youth: Change and Challenge*, ed. Erik H. Erikson (N. Y.: Basic Books, 1963), p. 29.

[27] Such emphasis on the life cycle is part of traditional culture's concern with unifying the individual's life with that of others in the tribe as well as with the observed life of the universe around him. Primitive life, according to Mircea Eliade is "the ceaseless repetition of gestures initiated by others." *The Myth of the Eternal Return* (New York: Pantheon, 1954), p. 5.

[28] Support and documentation for the material in the summaries of the next five chapters are omitted here, but are found later.

1

Puer Eternus: The Pastoral of Youth

Ambo florentes aetatibus, Arcades ambo[1]

Though pastoral presents itself as a celebration of rural over urban, the bucolic fiction of another, better world has always served as a vehicle to glorify more than country life. The very persistence of this fiction results largely from its ability to disguise longings too subversive of dominant social values to be straight-forwardly expressed. The most prevalent of such Arcadian aspirations is the ideal of innocence. In the words of Alexander Pope:

> The first rule of pastoral [*is*] that its idea should be taken from the manners of the Golden Age and the moral be formed upon the representation of innocence.[2]

Itself a charged and problematic notion, "innocence" has inspired painters, musicians and poets, as well as preachers, hucksters and pornographers to depict worlds that "represent" its meaning. The Arcadian realm overlaps with the Garden of Eden, the Golden Age, the Elysian Fields and with many early accounts of the New World as an elaboration of that ideal, a vision of a natural utopia free of the corruption of historical civilization. Whether or not they are inhabited by shepherds, all these places are pastoral in that they project a world of innocence.

The representation of innocence invokes the spectre of a lost past. Eden and the Golden Age lie buried in prehistory. The happy savages of the New World preserve the departed way of life of the ancestors of Europeans. The atmosphere of bitter-sweet longing which suffuses the groves and meadows of Arcadia conveys a sense of former beauty destroyed by the passage of time. The landscape and the type of culture that pastoral memorializes has suffered the encroachment of ruthless historical forces: war, urbanization, economic development, exploitation, enclosure, absentee landlordism and ecological disaster. In this respect the mode expresses a valid social concern for the decline of rural values and the destruction of nature. But in fact, the good old days before the demise of country life elegaically recalled by the pastoralists usually turn out to be the days of their own youth—whether they transpired in the twentieth, the sixteenth or the first century.[3]

Until the present era, many writers and readers of pastoral grew up in rural areas before moving to cosmopolitan centers to find colleagues, stimulation and non-rustic means of support. They therefore tended to equate their sense of the golden years of childhood with idealized memories of country life:

> Whilome in youth, when flowrd my ioy full spring
> Like Swallow swift I wandred here and there:
> For heate of heedlesse lust me so did sting,
> That I of doubted daunger had no feare.
>   I went the wastefull woodes and forest wyde
>   Withouten dreade of Wolues to bene espyed. . .
>   For ylike to me was libertee and lyfe.[4]

The lost past celebrated and mourned in pastoral is in fact what Renaissance writers often called the Golden Age: "the Worldes Childhoode."[5] For, as Sir Walter Ralegh noted in his *History of the World*:

> . . . our younger yeares are our golden Age; which being eaten up by time, we praise those seasons which our youth accompanied: and (indeede) the grievous alternations in our selves, and the paines and diseases which never part from us but at the grave, make the times seeme so differing and displeasing: especially the qualitie of man's nature being also such, as it adoreth and extooleth the passages of the former, and condemneth the present state how just soever.[6]

Following Ralegh's observation, this chapter argues that pastoralists' idealizing of innocence—their exaltation of rural over urban, nature over art, simple over sophisticated—expresses a preference for the life stages of childhood and youth and a consequent antipathy toward the condition of adulthood. The pastoralists' revolt against civilization is largely a rejection of the demands and the compromises of maturity; their utopian counterculture is in fact a youth culture; and their nostalgia for a more primitive state of society often disguises a longing for their own lost childhood. This thesis implies a corollary interpretation of the most common pastoral conventions. The shepherd swain represents the figure of youth itself, the central theme of love represents specifically young love, and the dominant pastoral setting of the *locus amoenus,* the pleasant spot of eternal springtime, represents a vision of childhood that will never pass.

Assertions similar to these have been made before. Other writers have observed the convergence between the pastoral ideal of innocence and the glorification of childhood. However, no one has proposed, as I do here, to use the Protean concept of "youth" to illuminate the web of relations connecting pastoral conventions with various systems of thought—systems of literary genre, psychic archetypes, developmental stages and social stratification. Perceiving that web can deepen an understanding of what pastoral is all about and can enrich readings of many individual works. It can also refine knowledge of cultural history. During the last twenty five years, interest in the ideals of youth and childhood has flourished among researchers in a variety of fields. A historian of ideas has written a book on *The Cult of Childhood* as one strain of philosophical primitivism; a social historian has written about *Childhood and Cultural Despair,* and a large bibliography of work by psychohistorians has analyzed changing conceptions and roles of youth during the period 1500 to 1800. And yet, among all these writers, mention of the pastoral mode remains conspicuously absent.

Perhaps the overlooked connection is attributable to the tendency to exaggerate periodization and discontinuity in both social and literary history. Like the author of *The Image of Childhood,* most people associate the apotheosis of childhood exclusively with the Romantics and their descendants:

> Until the last decades of the eighteenth century, the child did not exist as an important and continuous theme in English Literature. . .With Blake's "Chimney Sweeper" and Wordsworth's Ode on "Intimations of

> Immortality," we are confronted with something essentially new, the phenomenon of major poets expressing something they considered of great significance through the image of the child.[7]

It is true, as George Boas points out, that the primitivism that equates the artist with the child and sets both in opposition to the philistine bourgeois adult is a leitmotif from Blake to Lawrence, from Schiller to Rilke:

> Die Kindheit ist das Reich der grossen Gerechtigkeit und der tiefen Liebe. . .Entweder es bleibt jene Fuelle der Bilder unberuehrt hinter dem Eindringen der neuen Erkenntnisse, oder die alte Liebe versinkt wie eine sterbende Stadt in dem Aschenregen dieser unerwarteten Vulkane. Entweder das Neue wird der Wall, der ein Stueck Kindsein umschirmt, oder es wird die Flut, die es ruecksichtslos vernichtet, d.h. das Kind wird entweder aelter und verstaendiger im buergerlichen Sinn, als Keim eines brauchbaren Staatsbuergers, es tritt in den Orden seiner Zeit ein und empfaengt ihre Weihen, oder es reift einfach ruhig weiter von tiefinnen, aus seinem eigensten Kindsein heraus und das bedeutet, es wird Mensch im Geiste *aller* Zeiten: Kuenstler.[8]

But both Coveny and Boas ignore the fact that pastoralists have expressed ideas like these since the time of Theocritus. Most of his herdsmen are youths, and the sensibility in all the *Idylls* is pointedly childlike.[9] Many of the singers of Vergil's eclogues are adolescents, and even his old shepherds are referred to as *pueri*—boys. During earlier times, "The Cult of Childhood" has in fact a literal as well as figurative meaning, since the *puer eternus*—the boy god—often dominates fertility rituals which identify his eternal rejuvenation with the rebirth of the spring.[10] The central pastoral themes of youth and vegetation combine to draw this literary tradition within the orbit of initiation rites, occult symbols and millenarianism. The orbit extends from the Eleusinian predecessors of Theocritus' Daphnis to the medieval mystic, Joachim of Flora's vision of the end of history as the transfiguration of all humanity into the state of boyhood.[11] It also includes Renaissance neoplatonists who used the figure of the young swain to represent an initiate into spiritual-erotic mysteries.[12] The shepherd boy is the child of the imagination that the Romantics and the moderns equate with the spirit of the artist. As David Wagenknecht has insisted, ". . .pastoralism is the great unexplored link between Romantic and Renaissance ideas."[13] It is largely through the vision of innocence that this link is forged.

In what follows, I expand that vision of innocence by plaiting the three thematic strands mentioned in the introduction: a) recurrent pastoral motifs, b) primitivistic ideals of the good life in a better world, and c) concepts of childhood or youth as an admirable human state. Beginning with customs extrinsic to the poetry itself, I show how literary tradition stipulates pastoral to be the poet's youth-work, while the pastoral theme of rustic festivity coincides with the social practise of rural youth groups in Renaissance England. Then, moving into the texts, I delineate the essential conventions of bucolic character, theme and setting which project ethical, aesthetic and erotic ideals associated with childhood. I conclude the chapter by demonstrating that when adult writers include pastoral interludes in the larger context of epic or drama, they are generally portraying a regressive return to the state of childhood innocence—a return regarded as both solace and threat.

Within the overall plan of my study, this exploration of pastoral innocence supplies thematic background for my later examination of the pastoral debate of youth and age—a literary convention which provides a key to interpret Spenser's *The Shepheardes Calender*. The present chapter therefore leads into the next chapter's parallel treatment of the contrary ideals of experience in the pastoral of old age. But the pastoral of youth also rewards attention for its own sake, not only as a link between the Renaissance and Romanticism, but as a universal strain of sensibility. The ideal of childhood remains an archetypal theme, as timeless as the celebration of the garden. The holy child, in the words of C.G. Jung, is "bigger than big, smaller than small." It appears in the earliest and most widespread of religious myths as the bearer of special powers and as the symbol of the transition between the secular world of the conscious adult self and the unknown but intuited world that lies beyond:

> The "child" is therefore *renatus in novam infantiam.* It is thus both beginning and end, an initial and a terminal creature. The initial creature existed before man was, and the terminal creature will be when man is not. Psychologically speaking, this means that the "child" symbolizes the preconscious and the post-conscious essence of man. His preconscious essence is an anticipation by analogy of life after death. . .The child had a psychic life before it had consciousness. Even the adult still says and does things whose significance he realizes only later, if ever. And yet he said them and did them as if he knew what they meant. Our dreams are continually saying things beyond our conscious comprehension. . .We have intimations and intuitions from unknown sources. Fears, moods, plans, and hopes come to us with no visible causation. These concrete experiences are at the bottom of our feeling that we know ourselves very little; at the bottom too, of the painful conjecture that we might have suprises in store for ourselves.[14]

* * *

The young Elizabethan poet started his career by writing pastorals. He did so not only because his grammar school study of Latin and his first exposure to literature was by way of the *Eclogues* of Mantuan and the *Bucolics* of Vergil.[15] Any writer who aspired to join the illustrious company on the heights of Parnassus knew that his ascent should start in the vales of Arcady. An ancient decorum demanded that the first fruits of literary labor take the form of pastoral. In the introduction to his first published work, Spenser thus addresses *The Shepheardes Calender*:

> Goe little booke: they selfe present,
> As child whose parent is unkent. . .
> And asked who thee forth did bring
> A shepheards swaine say did thee sing. . .[16]

The humble pose of shepherd swain symbolized both rusticity and youth. The budding poet, "who for that he is

Unkouthe. . .is unkist, and unknowne to most men. . .," affects the diffidence equally appropriate to bumpkin and debutant. In the commendatory epistle, E.K., Spenser's apologist and commentator, provides a full explanation of the connection:

> Which moved him rather in Aeglogues, then otherwise to write doubting perhaps his habilitie. . .following the example of the best and most ancient of Poetes, which deuised this kind of wryting, being both so base for the matter, and homely for the manner, at the first to trye theyr habilities; and as young birdes, that be newly crept out of the nest, by little first to prove theyr tender wyngs, before they make a greater flyght.[17]

The posture of rustic humility displays the prudence and caution of the petitioner and at the same time the young man's anything but humble claim to a noble lineage:

> So flew Virgile, as not yet well feeling his winges. So flew Mantuane being not full somd. So Petrarque. So Bocace; so Marot, Sanazarus, and also diuers other excellent both Italian and French Poetes, whose footing this Author euery where followeth,. . .So finally flyeth this our new Poete, as a bird whose principals be scarce growen out, but yet as that in time shall be able to keepe wing with the best.[18]

By adhering to the Vergilian "Perfecte Pattern" of a poet's career, the pastoralist undertakes the youthful apprenticeship that may eventually permit him entry into the guild. Following the generic models established by past masters, his first work falls within strict limitations of scope, length, subject matter, diction and tone. Implicitly, however, the writing of pastoral expresses the poet's intention to address himself to some "higher argument" at a future time. The pastoral product itself can be regarded as a kindof "inaugural dissertation"—a proof of ability to proceed.

In this sense, pastoral juvenilia form the literary equivalent of their creator's youth. Once the initial offering is accepted, the writer sloughs off the bucolic role like a snakeskin and looks back upon it as an earlier phase of his own development:

> And even as up to this point you have fruitlessly spent the beginnings of your adolescence among the simple and rustic songs of shepherds, so hereafter you will pass your fortunate young manhood among the sounding trumpets of the most famous poets of your century, not without hope of eternal fame.[19]

Thus predicts the seer in Sannazaro's *Arcadia,* though its author never did go on to write epic or drama. Spenser, on the other hand, like Milton, Pope, Blake and Wordsworth followed the curriculum faithfully. At the end of *The Shepheardes Calender,* Spenser's pastoral persona, Colin Clout, hangs up his oaten reed and bids the herdsman's world adieu. At the opening of *The Faerie Queene*—the major accomplishment of his majority—Spenser announces his own metamorphosis:

> Lo I the man, whose Muse whilome did maske,
> As time her taught, in lowly Shepheards weeds,
> Am now enforst a far vnfitter taske,
> For trumpets sterne to chaunge mine Oaten reeds,
> And sing of Knights and Ladies gentle deeds.[20]

Though the writer at this point still feels himself "unfit" for the task ahead, he accepts his Muse's command to renounce the pastoral role "enforst" by his youth, and resolutely steps forward to accept the part of courtier and epic poet.

The "Knights and Ladies' gentle deeds" that the adult poet will sing are performed in a broader and more consequential arena than the rural landscape of the shepherd swain. Rather than the natural world of cyclical recurrence or the private world of thoughts and feelings, it is the public sphere of grand personages, heroic acts and cataclysmic events. The distinction between the setting and subject matter of the major genres and the world of pastoral corresponds to a difference in the actual concerns and experiences of maturity and youth. By its very nature the public, active life is adult, while the private, natural world is a protected domain of the young.

Pastoral's affirmation of nature and rustic life also converges with youth in the social institutions of holiday festivity. Among the features of rural existence eroded by the growth of mercantile civilization, the decline of seasonal celebrations evoked some of the strongest nostalgia from the poets and their audiences:

Happy the age and harmelesse were the dayes
For then true love and amity was found
When every village did a May Pole raise
And Whitson-ales and MAY-GAMES did abound.[21]

The urban readers of Elizabethan poetry went back to the country for holiday escape from the rigors or the boredom of everyday routines.

Hey ho, to the green wood now let us go
Sing heigh and hey ho.[22]

Come away, come sweet love, the golden morning brekes
All the earth, all the ayre of love and pleasure speaks.[23]

The "other world" to which they came away for a feeling of rejuvenation lay beyond the city walls, outside civilized matrices of order and meaning. The natural wilderness teemed with the vitality of youth:

Every bush now springing
Every bird now singing,
Merily sate poore Nico
Chanting tro li lo

Lo lilo li lo

Till her he had espide,
On whome his hope relide

Down a down a down
Down with a frown
Oh she pulled him down.[24]

The poetic motif of *reverdie*, or regreening, which introduces so much Middle English poetry and retains its popularity in Tudor pastorals, expresses the unity of natural and human rhythms. The flowing of the water and warming of the earth in the mineral world correspond to the movement of sap and swelling of buds in the vegetal world and to the stirring of the animal spirits in the creatures of the field and in the hearts of "Yonge folke":

> The merrymakers took to the woods as foresters, returning thence with the May Pole. A King and Queen of the Forest, or Lord and Lady of the May, were chosen to impersonate Robin Hood and Maid Marion. This couple presided over the pastimes on the village green. . .The sports—the archery contests, bouts at quarterstaff, wrestling for the ram—culminated in a ritual of initiation. To join the band of merry men and to wear Lincoln green was to renew one's contact with nature. To give a lass "a green gown" was to tumble her in the grass. The may-games, with their morris dances and hobby horses could be not only rough but frankly carnal.[25]

In European peasant societies of the sixteenth and seventeenth centuries, adolescents were designated as the custodians of these rural festivities.[26] People of all ages who participated in the revels of May were permitted to act childishly, but the young folk were in charge:

> Is not thilke the very moneth of May
> When love lads masken in fresh aray?. . .
> For thilke same season, when all is ycladd
> With pleasaunce; the grownd with grasse, the Woods
> With greene leaves, the bushes with bloosming Buds.
> Yougthes folke now flocken in every where,
> To gather may buskets and smelling brere:[27]

The organization was carried out by institutionalized youth groups known as Charivari or Abbeys of Misrule.[28] Such parish institutions sponsored the rituals which expressed unruly youthful instincts—on the one hand giving them vent and allowing them to kindle and energize the rest of the community, and on the other, containing and restricting them within broadly acceptable limits.

The rural festive periods were characterized by Saturnalian reversals of all sorts. Masters would exchange authority with their servants and youth would take dominance over age.[29] In Spenser's "May" eclogue, Palinode describes how the Church hosted pagan ceremonials and the saints themselves got slightly tipsy:

And home they hasten the postes to dight,
And all the Kirke pillours eare day light,
With hawthorne buds, and swete Eglantine,
And girlonds of roses and Sopps of wine.
Such merimake holy Saints doth queme
(11-16)

These festivities did not elicit universal admiration, however. Piers replies to this invitation with a dose of cold water and tells his crony to grow up:

For Younkers, Palinode, such folies fitte
But we be men of elder witt.
(18-19)

In rebuking his friend's nostalgia for the unrestrained liberty of the revellers, Piers helps define the pastoral of youth by arguing the contrary perspective of age. The conflict between the two observers exemplifies a continuing public controversy about holiday festivity during the sixteenth and seventeenth centuries. Piers' reply reflects a widespread Puritan disapproval of such Maying practises:

> Against May, Whitsunday, or other time all the young men and maids, old men and wives, run gadding over night to the woods, groves, hills, and mountains, where they spend all the night in pleasant pastimes. . .And no marvel, for there is a great Lord present amongst them, as superintendent and Lord over their pastimes and sports, namely Satan, prince of Hell. . .I have heard it credibly reported (and that *viva voce*) by men of great gravity and reputation, that of forty,

three score, or a hundred maids going to the wood over night, there have scarcely the third part of them returned home again undefiled. These be the fruits which these cursed pastimes bring forth.[30]

The Puritan attitude rested partly on objections to the release of animal instincts and partly on their aversion against the playful and hence childlike elements of both pagan and Catholic ritualism.[31] The Puritans also objected because such regressive ventures into pastoral *otium*—holiday leisure—took valuable time away from the dutiful conduct of every-day business. Piers continues his invective:

> Those faytours little regarden their charge. . .
> Passen their time that should be sparely spent,
> In lustyhede and wanton meryment. . .
> I muse what account both these will make. . .
> When great Pan account of shepherds shall aske.
> (39-54)

He prefers the sensible, modern and *adult* routine of the urban merchant.

By the late sixteenth century, the youth groups that organized holiday misrule and regreening festivals were already an archaic country phenomenon. In the city, their social function died out with the rise of professional and guild associations structured along class and status, but not age-grade lines. According to N.Z. Davis, this persistence in the countryside of youth groups which united people across the borders of economic and social rank helps explain "how the peasant community defended its identity against the outside world."[32]

Thus, during the Tudor period, pastoral's vision of the country took on connotations of holiday escape and the aura of a declining way of life preserved in youth and by youth. But the association of the bucolic herdsmen with the child runs deeper than this historical circumstance; it permeates the texture of the poetry. The protagonist of English pastoral, who, in Sidney's words, "pipes as though he should never be old," invariably carries the epithet of "swain."[33] The multiple denotations of this word—"rustic," "shepherd," "young suitor," and "boy," build the identification of rural life and youth into the very language of the poet. For Vergil, whose eclogues Viktor Poeschl characterized as the expression of "a pure, childlike poet's soul," the equivalent term to "swain" is *puer*.[34] This word signifies "herdsman," "menial laborer," and "boy." The shepherd thus represents the eternal boy, a stereotype of youth itself, which in other contexts has become known as the *puer eternus*.

This term originated with Ovid's address to Iacchus, the child-god of the Eleusinian mysteries. C.G. Jung and his disciples used it to name an indispensable and compelling "archetype of the collective unconscious":

> The child personifies the transcendant powers of the collective unconscious itself. . .(it is) an avatar of the self's spiritual aspect. . .The *puer eternus* figure is the vision of our first nature, our primordial golden shadow, our affinity to beauty, our angelic essence as messenger of the divine, as divine message.[35]

James Hillman expands this definition of the *puer* ideal by adducing the analogy of horizontal and vertical axes. The *puer's* prospensity is for flying and falling. Like E.K.'s poet-bird, or Icaros or Phaethon, he oscillates between the heights and depths of his "labile moods":

> He is weak on earth, for he is not at home on earth or the horizontal space-time continuum we call reality. The puer understands little of work, of moving back and forth, left and right, in and out, which makes for subtlety in proceeding step by step through the labyrinthine complexity of the horizontal world.[36]

This account of the *puer's* emotional volatility, his alienation from "the world," and his capacity for spiritual transcendance complements descriptions of the figure of the pastoral swain. In his essay on *Peter Pan* and *Alice in Wonderland* as nineteenth century versions of pastoral, William Empson identifies the herdsman with a similar conception of the child, the human being as yet uncorrupted by the repressive and distorting influences of custom and culture. The pastoral swain as child is also, according to Empson, the poet, the artist, the original genius whose access to natural instincts and to unconscious fertility provides a steady flow of creative inspiration. The notion is based on a feeling

> . . .that no way of building up character, no intellectual system, can bring out all that is inherent in the human spirit and therefore there is more in the child than any man has been able to keep. . .the world of the adult made it hard to be an artist. . .they kept a taproot going down to experience as children. . .

The child, according to this line of thought, "possesses the right relation to nature which poetry and philosophy seek to regain."[37]

The constellation of shepherd and child plays a central role in traditional Christian iconography. In the gospels, the good shepherd Jesus portrays the innocence of his flock as an analogue for grace: those who would enter the kingdom of heaven must become like little children. Medieval mystics like Joachim of Flora, Meister Eckhart and St. Francis of Assisi described their own transfigured consciousness as that of a babe's at the breast, a milennial return to the Edenic garden. As the cult of childhood gained popularity in devotional literature during the seventeenth century, Nativity songs like Milton's "Ode," emphasized the traditional juxtaposition of baby Jesus, shepherds and livestock, and adopted the tone, imagery and diction of literary pastoral. In the poetry of Marvell, Crashaw, Traherne and even Robert Herrick, the lamb, the good shepherd, the Edenic Adam, and the *puer eternus* are superimposed in the figure of the bucolic swain playing his oaten flute:

> Go prettie child, and beare this Flower
> Unto thy little Saviour;
> And tell Him, by that Bud now blown,
> He is the Rose of Sharon known:
> When thou hast said so, stick it there

Upon his Bibb, or Stomacher:
And tell Him, (For good hadsell too)
That thou hast brought a Whistle new,
Made of a clean straight oaten reed,
To charme his cries, (at time of need:)[38]

Once again, this pastoral of youth is set into relief by the response of the Puritans. Just as they opposed the ideal of innocence in holiday festivity, they had little patience with the notion of a holy primitive state. Like Calvin, who condemned unbaptized babies not to Purgatory or Limbo, but to Hell, and like Augustine, who dwelt on the malice of the newborn child, they believed more in original sin than original innocence. To Jesus' invitation, "Come little ones," the Puritans preferred St. Paul's injunction: "When I was a child I spake as a child, I understood as a child, I thought as a child: but when I became a man, I put away childish things."[39]

Renaissance Neoplatonists also idolized youth in the figure of the shepherd, but they found in him an adolescent rather than an infantile quality of innocence: "It is the mentality of this age, the so-called aesthetic stage of life, that pastoral celebrates. Socrates calls it the 'beauty of the young, over whom the god of love watches'."[40] Under the influence of the school of Ficino, Italian writers like Poliziano and Tasso used bucolic conventions to symbolize membership in an esoteric brotherhood of initiates. Whether or not, as Richard Cody claims, most Renaissance pastoral is really a cipher of hermetic doctrines of transcendance, the idealistic, passionate and agonizingly sensitive adolescent heroes of *Aminta, Orphee,* Sannazaro's *Arcadia,* and Garcilaso's *Eclogues* see the world from the *puer's* "Aesthetic point of view. . .the world as beautiful images or as a vast scenario. . .life become literature."[41] Their home in the woods represents no rustic crudeness, but a higher refinement, a world of feelings and ideas displaced from city and court. In their aetherial vulnerability, their humorless sincerity, and their cultivated alienation, these characters prefigure the *Sturm und Drang* heroes of nineteenth century romanticism.

Many of the spiritual ideals of the pastoral of youth reappear in Wordsworth's "Immortality Ode." As part of the narrator's meditation on the meaning of his own life cycle, the poem alludes to most of the themes considered thus far: the pattern of the poet's growth, nostalgia for a lost past, rural festivity, Christian devotion and Neoplatonism. The speaker begins with recollections of his early childhood as the pastoral stage of his life:

> There was a time when meadow, grove and stream
> The earth, and every common sight,
> To me did seem
> Apparelled in celestial light,
> The glory and the freshness of a dream. . .
>
> . . .And all the earth is gay;
> Land and sea
> Give themselves up to jollity
> And with the heart of May
> Doth every Beast keep holiday;
> Thou child of Joy
> Shout round me, let me hear thy shouts, thou happy
> Shepherd-boy.[42]

There follow the recognitions that he must leave this paradise behind as he takes roles on the "humorous stage" of adult social life, that he must travel inland from the immortal sea that brought him hither, that he must bear the earthly freight that custom loads on his soul. These recognitions bring on depression, which is then relieved by another episode of bucolic nostalgia. But after revelling in the fantasy of young lambs, the sound of pipes and the rejoicing of the Maying, the speaker concludes by affirming, or at least asserting, his faith in the value of adulthood. The mature person's "philosophic mind," he insists, not altogether convincingly, will console him for losing the childhood vision of "splendor in the grass and glory in the flower."

In "Auguries of Innocence," Blake also speaks of the capacity "To see a world in a Grain of Sand/And a Heaven in a wild

Flower." He attributes childhood's heightened power of sensation to the cleansed doors of perception that have been the gift of the shepherd since Theocritus:

> Come sit we under this elm tree, facing
> The nymphs and Priapus there by the rustics'
> seat and the oaks. If you sing as once
> . . .I'll give you
> to milk three times a she-goat with twins;
> although she's two kids, she fills up two pails
> Plus an ivywood bowl fragrant with wax,
> two-handled, new made: you can still smell the chisel. . .[43]

According to Thomas Rosenmeyer, Theocritus' herdsmen ". .if not children, are protected by the same patterns that make the child's world familiar and pleasureable. The shepherd's range of understanding and reason is limited. . .he is a perceiver of concrete sensations and beautiful things."[44] This freshness of perception graces the Renaissance bucolic song:

> And we will set upon the Rocks
> Seeing the shepheardes feede theyr flocks
> By shallow Rivers, to whose Falls
> Melodious birds sing Madrigalls.
>
> And I will make thee beds of Roses,
> And a thousand fragrant poesies,
> A cap of flowers, and a kirtle,
> Enbroydred all with leaues of Mirtle.
>
> A gowne made of the finest wooll,
> Which from our pretty Lambes we pull,
> Fayre lined slippers for the cold:
> With buckles of the purest gold
>
> A belt of straw, and Iuie buds
> With corall clasps and Amber studs. . .[45]

Theocritus invented the inventory genre, "the single most effective and congenial device in the pastoral lyric. . ." in order to "document the discreteness of the herdsman's sensory experience and his detachment-in pleasure."[46] The primitive pleasure of the senses associated with childhood presents as significant a pastoral ideal as the spiritual innocence ascribed to it by Christians and Platonists. Arcadia is a landscape of the body as well as of the mind.

Renaissance writers and painters found a favorite mythological motif in the Judgement of Paris. They depicted the future abductor of Helen of Troy in the guise of a shepherd awarding the golden apple to Aphrodite and turning his back on Hera and Athena. Mythographers saw in this motif a symbol of pastoral's identification with the *vita voluptatis,* the life of erotic pleasure, and its rejection of the lives of action and contemplation.[47] In fact, sensual love comprises the most common of bucolic themes.

It is appropriate that the poetic mode which praises nature over art celebrates the biological drive that human beings share with plants and animals. The Renaissance critic Julius Caesar Scaliger theorized that herdsmen made love their chief occupation because of their scanty dress, their healthy and plentiful food and their proximity to beasts.[48] Others have attributed pastoral's emphasis on love to the absence of competing concerns. In a world like the shepherd's, free from want, war, politics and social climbing, there is not much else to do. Pastoral *amor,* as Greg observed, is love *in vacuo,* love removed from its usual social context.[49] Poggioli saw Arcadia itself as an erotic utopia projected and ruled by the Freudian Pleasure Principle, and W.H. Auden spoke of "Arcadian Cults of Carnal Perfection."[50]

As the expression of an outlook on life that is characteristically adolescent, the pastoral ideal exalts a particular kind of eroticism: Young Love. It excludes the complexities of social courtship, the domesticated and exploratory love of long-term relationships, the contractual-sacramental love of marriage, and the procreative, nurturing love of parenthood. Instead, it proposes the pleasure of the body as the state of innocence—a natural, simple condition of salvation that is itself childlike. The pastoral ideal of young love takes a number of contradictory forms: a utopia of licentiousness, or one of chastity or a paradoxical combination of the two. But all the varieties of the ideal share the faith that such pleasure once existed in the original unfallen condition of humanity remembered with nostalgia and regret.

This reading of pastoral relies upon the modern psychological tenet that erotic pleasure itself is a type of release from the constraint of civilization achieved only through a temporary reversion to an earlier state of consciousness:

> The proper carrying out of the sexual act and the enjoyment of it involves an ability to give way to the irrational, the timeless, the purely animal in one: it includes loss of individuality in a temporary fusion with another. It contains the potentiality of leaving behind the tensions of civilization as one loosens the bonds of reality to float again in the purely sensuous. . .The sexual act contains a definite and direct relationship to infantile relatedness to the mother, with a renewed interest in sucking, in odor, in skin eroticism and a reawakening of old forbidden desires to explore and play with orifices. So very much that has been forbidden and kept unconscious. . .needs to be released. The very good sexual adjustment demands such abilities to reverse the socialization process–and yet to permit the individual to be secure in the feeling that the regression and reversal will be only temporary and not reclaim the self.[51]

A number of pre-Freudian precendents substantiate this view of sexuality. From Hellenistic and Roman times, the god of love was pictured in Cupid as a wanton and fleshly baby; and paintings of the Golden Age show the dalliance of naked couples encouraged by the ministrations of teasing *putti.* "Know that love is a careless child," says the narrator of Ralegh's "Walsingham."

However, most earlier writers thought of the erotic age not as infancy but as adolescence. Medieval preachers, noting the correspondence between the seven ages of man and the seven deadly sins, equated lust with youth.[52] In the seven acts of Jaques' pageant in *As You Like It,* the lover, "Sighing like a furnace, with a woeful ballad/Made to his mistress' eyebrow," takes his part between schoolboy and soldier (II, vii, 148-9) "In youth is pleasure/In youth is pleasure," repeats the refrain of a popular Elizabethan ballad.[53] The categorization rests largely on physiological fact: puberty heightens the differences between the sexes and brings on an acute increase of desire.[54]

As much as the intensity, it is the aesthetic quality of adolescent sexuality that makes it an ideal of the pastoral youth. This quality of freshness, delicacy and wonder distinguishes *Fruelingserwachen,* the spring awakening of the erotic, from the more familiar, self-aware and bounded sexuality of the adult. Spenser illustrates the distinction in his description of the beauty of the flower, the sexual organ of the plant:

Ah see who so faire thing does faine to see
In springing flowre the image of thy day
Ah see the Virgin Rose, how sweetly shee
Doth first peepe forth with bashfulf modestee
That fairer seemes, the lesse ye see her may
Lo see soone after, how more bold and free
Her bared bosom she doth broad display
Loe see soone after, how she fades, and falles away.[55]

In the curl of its unfolding but still involuted shape resides the particular beauty of the closed rose. Its perceptible form reveals loveliness, yet hides an imminent mystery. To the beholder, the early stage conveys an experience of pure potentiality in the promise of even greater pleasure. This is the aesthetic of pastoral innocence, and it can be translated into one of the meanings of the archetype of the *puer*: "an anticipation of something desired and hoped for."[56] Once the flower opens and "bold and free/Her bared bosom she doth broad display," that particular quality is lost. The complete revelation reaches a limit; mystery and wonder dissipate; in sets decay. From the perspective of the pastoral of youth, it is irrelevant that the fall of the petals brings on the ripening of the fruit.

The aesthetic of youthful eroticism dominated the culture of the Renaissance, which often defined itself as a period of freshness and rebirth.[57] It is manifest in painting: Botticelli's

Primavera and *Birth of Venus;* in music: the song books of Dowland, Campion and Morley; as well as in the lingering adoration of youthful bodies that permeates pastoral literature:

> I saw one that I judged among these beauties the most beautiful. Her tresses were covered with a veil most subtly thin, from under which two bright and beautiful eyes were flashing, not otherwise that the clear stars are wont to burn in the serene and cloudless sky. Her features. . .fill with desire the eyes that looked upon them. Her lips were such that they surpassed the morning rose; betwixt them, every time that she spoke or smiled, she showed some part of the teeth, of such an exotic and wondrous beauty that I would not have known how to liken them to anything other than orient pearls. From there descending to the delicate throat as smooth as marble, I saw on her tender bosom the small girlish breasts that like two round apples were thrusting forth the thin material; midway of these could be seen a little path, most lovely and immoderately pleasing to look upon, which inasmuch as it terminated in the secret paths was the cause of my thinking about those parts with the greater efficacy.[58]

Inventories like this one from Sannazaro's *Arcadia* were often condemned by British moralists as typical Italianate lasciviousness. But most English poets embraced the southern influence Hallett Smith notes that the quasi-pastoral genre of "Erotic-mythological" Elizabethan poetry gains much of its appeal from similar highly charged pictorial descriptions of adolescent beauty.[59] The opening passage of Marlowe's *Hero and Leander* blasons the bodily charms of its heroine, "Venus' Nun," and concludes with an evocation of infantile bliss:

> Some say for her the fairest *Cupid* pyn'd
> And looking in her face, was strooken blind.
> But this is true, so like was one the other.
> As he imagyn'd *Hero* was his mother
> And oftentimes into her bosome flew,
> About her naked necke his bare armes threw.
> And laid his childlish head upon her brest,
> And with still panting rockt, ther tooke his rest.[60]
> (I, 37-44)

The most precious jewell of Hero's beauty resides in her maidenhead, the badge of innocence. Though wholly in love, she hesitates to surrender the instrument of restraint:

> Ne're king more sought to keepe his diademe,
> than *Hero* this inestimable gemme. . .
> No marvell then, though *Hero* would not yeeld
> So soone to part from that she deerly held.
> Jewels being lost are found againe, this never,
> 'Tis lost but once lost, lost for ever.
>
> (II, 77-86)

This rhetoric of adoration doesn't discriminate between the erotic attraction of girls and boys. Instead it plays on the distinctly hermaphroditic flavor of young love:

> Amorous *Leander*, beautiful and yoong,
> . . .
> His dangling tresses that were never shorne,
> Had they beene cut, and unto *Colchos* borne,
> Would have allur'd the vent'rous youth of *Greece*,
> To hazard more, than for the golden Fleece. . .
> His bodie was as straight as *Circes* wand,
> *Jove* might have sipt out Nectar from his hand
> Even as delicious meat is to the tast,
> So was his necke in touching, and surpast
> The white of *Pelops* shoulder. I could tell ye,
> How smooth his brest was, and how white his bellie,
> And whose immortal fingars did imprint,
> That heavenly path, with many a curious dint,
> That runs along his backe, but my rude pen,
> Can hardly blazon foorth the loves of men,
> Much lesse of powerfull gods. . .
>
> (I, 51-71)

Such descriptions place the reader in a position of a voyeur, who, reminiscent of the guests at Pelops' feast, figuratively devours flesh with his hungry eyes. The emotional distance between observed and observer accentuates the contrast between innocence and experience, ignorance and knowledge. The watcher's pleasure is that of King Neptune, the *senex amans,* whose aged coldness is inflamed by the heat of Leander's passion and who steals delight from watery contact with the helpless youth:

> The god. . .
> . . .clapt his plumpe cheekes, with his tresses played,
> And smiling wantonly, his love bewrayed.
> He watch his armes, and as they opend wide,
> At every stroke, betwixt them would he slide,
> And steale a kisse, and then run out and daunce,
> And as he turnd, cast many a lustfull glaunce,
> And throw his gawdie toies to please his eie
> And dive into the water, and there prie
> Upon his brest, his thights, and everie lim,
> And up againe, and close beside him swim,. . .
> (II, 181-90)

Pastoral often exhibits young bodies bathing—in the sea, in a fountain, or in a stream—to extend that contrast between the sensual cleanliness of the child and the degeneracy of the dirty old man peeking from the bushes. Sannazaro, for instance, introduced this description of bathing sherpherdesses between the blason of the young girl and an account of the old god Priapus' rape of a nymph:

> But seeing the sun mounted high and heat grown every intense, they (the group of shepherdesses) turned their steps toward a cool hollow, pleasantly chattering and jesting amongst themselves. Being arrived there shortly and finding living springs so clear that they seemed of purest crystal, they began to refresh with the chill water their beautiful faces, that shone with no ingenious artifice. By pushing their trim sleeves back to the elbow they displayed all bare the whiteness of their arms, which added no little beauty to their tender and delicate hands. For this reason we, grown yet more desirous of seeing them, without much delay drew near to the place where they were, and there at the foot of a great tall oak we took our seats in no determined order.[61]

The vision of innocent sexuality not only governs the aesthetic sensibility of the pastoral of youth, it generates a set of ideologies. The most common of these is the ideology of Free

Love—the theory that the good life is achieved in a utopia of unrepressed libido, a golden age of liberated pleasure when, in Tasso's words, "S'ei piace ei lice"—whatever felt good was right.[62] This is a juvenile philosophy in a number of senses. It expresses a desire for sexual freedom typical of the frustrated adolescent shackled by taboos on premarital sex or by lack of a willing partner. His desire tends to be more generalized than individualized, and he has yet to experience any bitter consequence of promiscuity.

Pastoral's advocacy of free love is also youth-oriented insofar as it locates sexual contentment in the social arrangments of the childhood of the race. For the sexual primitivist, the development of civilization is a Fall from Paradise, a history of suppression of the native desires of the body. He finds a prelapsarian state in the archaic ways of non-urban societies where natural instinct is allowed to rule. The medieval eclog form of Pastourelle is plotted on the assumption that any peasant lass by definition is receptive to the proposal of country pleasures.[63] The Elizabethan lyric that celebrates the outriding to the green world reflects actual Maying practises but also gives vent to the fantasy of rural licence:

> Come shepherds, come!
> Come away
> Without delay,
> Whilst the gentle time doth stay.
> Green woods are dumb,
> And will never tell to any
> Those dear kisses, and those many
> Sweet embraces that are given;
> Dainty pleasures, that would even
> Raise in coldest age a fire,
> And give virgin-blood desire.
> Then, if ever
> Now or never,
> Come and have it:
> Think not I
> Dare deny
> If you crave it.[64]

In the "quest for Paradise" that Renaissance adventurers embarked upon in their voyages of discovery to the New World, they found primitive societies whose apparent sexual freedom confirmed the myth of Edenic innocence.[65] From Montaigne's "Essay on Cannibals" to Diderot's *Supplement au Voyage de Bougainville,* old world commentators perceived in native cultures a way of life where love was unhampered by guilt or restraint:

> . . .au moment où le mâle a pris toute sa force, où les symptômes virils ont de la continuité. . .au moment où la jeune fille se fane s'ennuie, et d'une maturité propre à concevoir des desirs, à en inspirer et à les satisfaire avec utilité,. . .L'un peut solliciter une femme et en être sollicité; l'autre se promener publiquement le visage découvert et la gorge nue, accepter ou refue les caresses d'un homme;. . .C'est une grande fête. . .Si c'est une fille, de la cabane, et l'air retentit pendant toute la nuit du chant des voix et du son des instrumens. . .On déploie l'homme un devant elle sous toutes les faces et dans toutes les attitude. Si c'est un garçon, ce sont les jeunes filles qui font en sa présence les frais et les honneurs de la fête et exposent à ses regards la femme nue sans réserve et sans secret. Le reste de la ceremonie s'acheve sur un lit de feuilles. . .[66]

This dream of an original condition wherein what Blake called "an improvement in sensual enjoyment" brings a restoration of the state of innocence has repeatedly been translated from pastoral myth into the reality of chiliastic social and religious movements. From the twelfth until the eighteenth century, the "Brethren of the Free Spirit" established secret pantheist congregations throughout Europe whose members claimed literally to return to Eden through the practise of nudism and promiscuous sex.[67] Wilhelm Fraenger has convincingly argued that the vision of legions of blissful orgiasts cavorting in the groves, pools and watercourses of Hieronymus Bosch's painting known popularly as "The Garden of Earthly Delights," illustrates the doctrine of this Arcadian cult.[68] At the center of the garden flows the Fountain of Youth.

The pastoral ideology of free love has also found expression in a more secular libertinism. In what Frank Kermode refers to as "Jouissance poetry,"[69] seventeenth century writers like St. Amant, Thomas Stanley, John Wilmont and Thomas Carew uttered their nostalgia from the primitive state "when all women were for all men, and all men were for all women" with an undertone of rakish cynicism:

Thrice happy was that Golden Age
When compliment was constru'd Rage,
  And fine words in the Center hid;
When cursed *NO* stain'd no Maids Blisse,
And all discourse was summ'd in *Yes*
  And nought forbad, but to forbid.[70]

The cavalier poet inverts the ideal of natural purity with a self-ironic sarcasm. But no matter how sophisticated his tone, the sexual adventurer too is driven by the thirst for innocence, for a resting place that will satisfy the infantile yearnings of the *puer* inside him. Witness the title and the selling points of a publication like *Playboy,* it is evident the fantasies of Arcadia and of pornotopia often overlap. Members of Fanny Hill's Swinger's club called themselves "restorers of the Golden Age," and many a present day "adult entertainment center" goes by the name of "Garden of Eden."

The most effective and influential statement of the ideology of free love occurs as a chorus in Tasso's pastoral drama *Aminta*:

O happy Age of Gould; happy houres;
Not for with milke the rivers ranne,
And hunny dropt from ev'ry tree;
Nor that the Earth bore fruits, and flowres,
Without the toyle or care of Man. . .

. . .
  But therefore only happy Dayes,
  Because that vaine and ydle name,
That couzning Idoll of unrest,
Whom the madd vulgar first did raize,
And call'd it Honour, whence it came
To tyrannize oe'r ev'ry brest,
  Was not then suffred to molest

Poore lovers hearts with new debate;
More happy they, by these his hard
And cruell lawes, were not debarr'd
Their innate freedome; happy state;
The goulden lawes of Nature, they
Found in the brests; and them they did obey.
Amidd the silver streames and floures,
The winged *Genii* then would daunce,
Without their bowe, without their brande;
The Nymphes sate by their Paramours,
Whispring love-sports, and dalliance,
And joyning lips, and hand to hand;
  The fairest Virgin in the land
Nor scornede, nor flor'yed to displaye
Her cheekes fresh roses to the eye,
Or ope her faire brests to the day,
(Which now adayes so vailed lye,)
But men and maydens spent free houres
In running River, Lakes, or shady Bowres.[71]

To symbolize sexual innocence, Tasso here uses the same cluster of metaphors—Virgin/Rose/Breast—that Spenser later adapted to convey the aesthetic attraction of youthful eroticism. But there is a discrepancy between the two rhetorical figures. The veiled, suggestive beauty of the budding rose, whose allure Spenser's singer heightens to the detriment of the exposed bloom, represents teasing sexual decadence to the speakers of Tasso's chorus. Their ethos finds healthy, carnal affirmation in a bosom bared to the sunshine and nothing positive in coyness, withdrawal, and hesitancy.

This descrepancy reflects a difference between the aesthetics of primitivism and its ideology. The beauty of sexual innocence depends on unfulfilled desire. It is born, as Plato said of love itself, from the union of Poverty and Plenty. The liberation of Free Love, on the other hand, postulates a Gratified Desire that tends to disappear by very virtue of its fulfillment. Indeed, by the end of the *Aminta,* Tasso's protagonist has grown up enough to learn the value of the honor and the chastity that was earlier rejected.

The pastoralist often conflates the diverging aesthetic and ideological affirmations of sexual innocence into a logically unstable but nevertheless compelling ideal: the free love of youth itself. Such an ideal superimposes the dichotomy of nature and civilization upon the dichotomy of youth and age, assuming no distinction whatever between the stages of adulthood and old age, treating them both as a single "other," hostile to youthful energy. The Age of Gold becomes the perfect state when the awakening sexuality of youth is neither controlled nor exploited by adults and their social order, but instead is allowed to flower freely in its own natural setting:

A Little GIRL Lost

Children of the future Age
Reading this indignant page;
Know that in a former time,
Love! sweet Love! was thought a crime.

In the Age of Gold
Free from winters cold:
Youth and maiden bright,
To the holy light,
Naked in the sunny beams delight.
Once a youthful pair
Fill'd with softest care:
Met in garden bright,
Where the holy light,
Had just removed the curtains of the night.
There in rising day,
On the grass they play:
Parents were afar:
Strangers came not near:
And the maiden soon forgot her fear.

They agree to meet,
Tired with kisses sweet
When the silent sleep
Waves o'er heavens deep;
And the weary tired wanderers weep.
To her father white
Came the maiden bright:
But his loving look,
Like the holy book,
All her tender limbs with terror shook.
Ona! pale and weak!
To thy father speak:
O the trembling fear!
O the dismal care!
That shakes the blossoms of my hoary hair.[72]

Blake's version of the Golden Age includes both the attraction of purity and the release of freedom. Free love is the innocence of the child. Freedom and innocence are destroyed together by the aged man whose holy book signifies the repressive law of civilization—a law which in other *Songs of Experience* takes the form of chartered streets, urban blight, and whip-wielding schoolmasters. Tasso's "Honore" here has become the grey-beard father and the priests who turn the garden of love into a cemetery.

> I went to the Garden of Love
> And saw what I never had seen:
> A Chapel was built in the midst,
> Where I used to play on the green.
>
> And the gates of this Chapel were shut,
> And Thou shalt not, writ over the door;
> So I turned to the Garden of Love,
> That so many sweet flowers bore,
>
> And I saw it was filled with graves,
> And tomb-stones where flowers should be:
> And Priests in black gowns, were walking their rounds,
> And binding with briars, my joys and desires.[73]

In setting lusty youth against crabbed age, Blake adopts the convention of pastoral debate which he is likely to have first discovered in his reading of *The Sherpheardes Calender,* but which originates in the medieval *conflictus.*[74] In his later prophetic writings, affected by the experience of the American and French revolutions, Blake extended the debate over sexuality to a larger mythical framework. The young figure of Orc, representing revolutionary energy itself, grows out of the pastoral motifs of child, sex and nature. Orc wars perpetually against the aged Urizen, who represents the Priests and Beadles of Civilization and their authoritarian, rationalistic Newtonian order. The ultimately epic struggle between innocence and experience, *puer* and *senex,* energy and order, eros and civilization germinates as the central drama in the garden of pastoral.

One might expect longing for the past and sexual attraction for innocence to appeal primarily to older people whose youth has left them. But in fact, this kind of pastoral has always been most popular among "the younger sort," as Gabriel Harvey observed in his report of the immense interest shown in *Hero and Leander* and *Venus and Adnonis* at the beginning of the seventeenth century.[75] Indeed, adolescence is the most nostalgic of ages. The young man in his teens and early twenties has the greatest appreciation for innocence because he is in the midst of losing it. At one moment he may feel like the victim, at the next like the mourner; he is both pristine maiden and dirty old man, both coltish stud and prudish parson. This ambivalence stems from the developmental process itself, especially the process of sexual maturation. On the one hand desire signals growing up: aggressiveness, self-confidence, status, the power to beget children. On the other, the emergent sexual drive stimulates regressive longings for dependence, passivity, and all-enfolding bodily pleasure, for it reopens the possibility of infantile gratification forgotten during the latency period of late childhood.

And yet the nostalgia for a state of untrammelled sexual freedom can modulate abruptly into its opposite: a nostalgia for asexuality, for the very departing condition of childhood which prevailed before desire ever reared its seductive and threatening head. To the adolescent, the prepubertal age also appears as a lost paradise, for it is free of the emotional and moral conflicts of sexual maturity and because it antedates the coarsening of the skin, the growth of the beard and the deepening of the voice. The pastoral of youth projects a green Edenic world to signify chastity as well as liberty. From the perspective of adolescence, either provides a "better world"—an innocent alternative to its own dilemmas.

The same garden of love that Blake's speaker sees spolied by a thorny hedge and a barricaded chapel, according to Christian iconography, betokens the ideal of the *Hortus Conclusus* or "Enclosed Garden" of the Virgin Mary's pristine body:

> . . .I speake not of the Garden of *Hesperides*. . .nor yet of *Tempe*, or the Elizian fields. I speake not of Eden, the Earthlie Paradice. . .But I speake of Thee, that GARDEN so knowne by the name of HORTUS CONCLUSUS, wherein are al things mysteriously and spiritually to be found, delicious in winter, then in Summer, in Autumne, then in the Spring. . .where are al kinds of delights in great abundance. . .where are Arbours to shadow her from the heats of concupiscence; flowrie Beds to repose in, with heavenlie Contemplations; Mounts to ascend to, with the studie of Perfections. . .[76]

But the bond between pastoral nature and virginity is broader and more ancient than this; it goes back to priesthoods, vestals and fertility rituals. By the time of Ovid, the literary association of the pastoral Golden Age with the virgin goddess Astraea had become firmly established. In Vergil's apocalyptic fourth eclogue, Astraea ushers in the return of the Golden Age, and in Spenser's fourth eclogue, Astraea is identified with the Virgin Queen Elizabeth, "The queen of shepheardes all":

> Ye shepherds daughters, that dwell on the greene,
> Hye you there apace:
> Let none come there but that Virgins bene,
> To adorne her grace
> And when you come, whereas shee is in place
> See that your rudenesse doe not you disgrace:
> Bind your fillets faste
> And gird in your waste,
> For more finesse, with a tawdrie lace.
>
> (128-35)

The tight-laced virgin rose remains closed, self-protecting, immune from time, thereby retaining her integrity, her power over herself and her eternal youth. Artemis, the virgin sister and rival of Aphrodite, ranges the woodlands but also protects childbirth and childhood:

> Whatever is coming to be and is not yet mature is under the care of this virgin Goddess. In Greece, young girls nine years of age were consecrated to her, and young men too, prayed for her protection. The very virginal intactness of the psyche protects what is immature and unripe;

Artemis takes care of the *puer*, for the young man is an image for the defenselessness and vulnerability of incipient developments in the psyche.[78]

Virginity is not exclusively a female attribute. For the young male, freedom from sexual desire itself appears like a pastoral condition, while its onset is experienced as a fall:

How happie were a harmless Shepherd's life
If he had never known what love did meane;
But now fond love in every place is rife
Staining the purest soule with spots uncleane[79]

Like Richard Barnefield's Shepherd, Spenser's Thomalin is a devotee of Artemis, out on a playful holiday hunt, delighting in the woods and the early springtime: "It was upon a holiday/When shepheardes groomes han leaue to playe,/I cast to go a shooting. . .". Unknowingly, he comes upon Cupid disguised as a brilliant peacock, and suddenly the childishness of the shepherd boy's playing turns to earnest:

So long I shott, that al was spent:
Tho pumie stones I hastly hent,
And threwe: but nought availed:
He was so wimble and so wight,
From bough to bough he lepped light,
And oft the pumies latched.
Therewith affrayd I ran away:
But he that earst seemd but to playe,
A shaft in earnest snatched,
And hit me running in the heele:
For then I little smart did feele:
But soone it sore encreased.
And now it rranckleth more and more,
And inwardly it festreth sore
Ne wote I how to cease it.
("March," 61 ff.)

The male adolescent experiences puberty as an encounter with an infantile energy in the guise of a splendid male sexuality. He assumes that he can both conquer and play heedlessly with this force, but it quickly overwhelms him. Androgens spread through his body like poison. First they affect his physical and emotional equilibrium; then they begin to change his intellectual awareness and to pervert his social relationships.

Shakespeare presents the same idea of puberty as a fall in *The Winter's Tale*:

> *Hermione*: . . .you were pretty lordings then
> *Polixenes*: We were, fair Queen,
> Two lads that thought there was no more behind
> But such a day to-morrow as to-day,
> And to be boy eternal.
> *Her.*: Was not my lord
> The verier wag of the two?
> *Pol.*: We were as twinn'd lambs that did frisk i'th' sun
> And bleat the one at th' other. What we chang'd
> Was innocence for innocence; we knew not
> The doctine of ill-doing, (no) nor dream'd
> That any did. Had we pursu'd that life,
> And our weak spirits ne'er been higher rear'd
> With stronger blood, we should have answer'd Heaven
> Boldly, "not guilty"; the imposition clear'd
> Hereditary ours.
> *Her.*: By this we gather
> You have tripp'd since.
> *Pol.*: O my most sacred lady,
> Temptations have since then been born to's; for
> In those unfledg'd days was my wife a girl;
> Your precious self had then not cross'd the eyes
> Of my young play-fellow.
>
> (I, ii, 63-68)

This anti-sexual attitude belongs to the rabbinical and patristic tradition of virulent mysogyny which identifies all women with Eve and sees them as the agency by which sin, guilt, mortality and time itself were introduced into a previously perfect and static world. Only in the happy prepubescent garden state was true friendship possible; or, as Marvell would have it, only before the advent of women could boys maintain their intimate communion with mother nature.

In the series of "Mower" poems, Marvell chronicles the process of sexual maturation as the alienation from the green world of childhood innocence. Damon is first discovered in perfect sensual rapport with the rural environment:

> I am Damon the Mower known
> Through all the meadows I have mown.
> On me the corn her dew distills
> Before her darling daffodils:
> And, if at noon my toil me heat,
> The sun himself licks off my sweat;
> While going home, the evening sweet
> In cowslip-water bathes my feet.[80]

The first encounter with Juliana and with the pangs of hetero-sexual passion spoils the idyllic sensuousness of his joyful solitude by introducting desire, jealousy and despair:

> How happy mought I still have mowed,
> Had not Love here his thistles sowed!
> But now I all the day complain,
> Joining my labor to my pain. . .
> (65-69)

Juliana not only pollutes the Mower's happiness by summoning desire in the first place, she then has the audacity not to respond to his advances: "How long wilt thou, fair Shepherdess/Esteem me and my presents less?/. . .thou un-grateful hast not sought/Nor what they are, nor who them brought." However, the fault ultimately resides not in the woman, but in the fated course of the Mower's own aging. Juliana is July, the hottest month of the dogstar's raging, the fever in the blood of life's summer season. Though he blames his hurt on her, Damon inflicts his wound and his fall upon himself:

The edged steel by careless chance
Did into his own ankle glance;
And there among the grass fell down,
By his own scythe, the mower mown.
(77-80)

Like Spenser's in "March," Marvell's satirical tone here underscores both comic and tragic implications of the theme: the adolescent male's helpless confusion in the face of his extreme and oscillating feelings toward women who appear threatening and desireable at the same time.

The erotic ideals of free love and chastity projected in pastoral provide escape from two evils attendant upon sexual pleasure: frustration and guilt. But there is another variety of the pastoral ideal of innocence which provides an alternative for the limitation and inadequacy of sexual intercourse itself. From the adult point of view—that is, one integrating the erotic into a larger texture of human relationships—the notion of an insufficiency in sexual intercourse itself may seem odd. But for the youth, whose bodily desire promises entry into a different world, the act of *coitus* often terminates in cosmic disappointment. As Renaissance poets never tire of warning:

Desire himself runs out of breath
And getting, doth but gaine his death
Desire attained is not desire
But as the sinders of the fire.[81]

Some pastoralists think of "young love" as a release from this trap in the human condition. They envision practises which can combine the carnal joys of liberty with the protective shield of chastity, and which thereby can triumph over the defect in desire itself—its enslavement to time. Though this particular ideal finds explicit articulation less frequently than either free love or chastity, it is latent in much pastoral imagery, tone and allusion.

A suggestion of the contrast between innocent and fallen sexuality occurs in one of the Blake poems considered earlier,

"The Little Girl Lost." Suspending the standard interpretation of its theme as the conflict between youth and age, a second reading reveals that the children's free pleasure is spoiled not by the aged priests of civilization, but by the dynamic of desire itself. Before the girl encounters her father and her chilling guilt, she and her companion become "tired" of their daytime play in the grass and agree to a secret rendezvous under the cover of darkness. The father, in fact, tries to comfort rather than reprimand his daughter, for he recognizes the pain of her loss in the memory of his own. What "moral on the representation of Innocence" is Blake thus setting forth? I believe he is drawing the same distinction between the innocent love of sexual play and the guilty, time-bound quality of orgasmic sex that Ben Johnson elaborates in this unfamiliar version of the invitation to love:

> Doing a filthy pleasure is and short
> And done, we straight repent us of the sport.
> Let us not then rush blindly on unto it
> Like lustful beasts, that onely know to doe it
> For lust will languish, and that heat decay.
> But thus, thus, keeping endless Holy-day
> Let us together closely lie and kisse,
> There is no labour, nor no shame in this;
> This hath pleas'd, doth please, and long will please; never
> Can this decay, but is beginning ever.[82]

In striking this contrast between the lustful sexuality of "Doing" and the innocent pleasure of lying and kissing, the narrator alludes to a number of pastoral motifs. He renounces the "labour" that makes the act as nasty, brutish and short as life in Hobbes' state of nature. In its stead he advocates the endless holiday *otium* of polymorphous petting. He emphasizes the difference with a carefully orchestrated shift in tone and rhythm. The anxious throbbing pulse of the first part gives way to a leisurely meandering flow, especially effective in the attenuated metrical pattern of the penultimate line. And he expands the meaning of the poem by suggesting that the "filthy pleasure" of orgasm is subject to time and decay, while the chaste touching of foreplay can lead to the experience of eternity.

Andrew Marvell develops the same "metaphysical" conceit through another pastoral invitation. In "Young Love," he connects the prospect of unconsummated sexual pleasure to the ideals of childhood and the evasion of mutability:

Come little infant, love me now,
  While thine unsuspected years
Clear thine aged father's brow
  From cold jealousy and fears.

Pretty surely 'twere to see
  By young love old time beguiled:
While our sportings are as free
  As the nurse's with the child.

Common beauties stay fifteen;
  Such as yours should swifter move;
Whose fair blossoms are too green
  Yet for lust, but not for love.

Love as much the snowy lamb
  Or the wanton kid does prize,
As the lusty bull or ram,
  For his morning sacrifice.

Now then love me: time may take
  Thee before thy time away:
Of this need we'll virtue make,
  And learn love before we may.

So we win or doubtful fate;
  And, if good she to us meant,
We that good shall antedate;
  Or, if ill, that ill prevent.

Thus as kingdoms frustrating
  Other titles to their crown,
In the cradle crown their king,
  So all foreign claims to drown;

So, to make all rivals vain,
  Now I crown thee with my love:
Crown me with thy love again,
  And we both shall monarchs prove.

Critics have been reluctant to discuss this poem because of its ambiguous suggestions of radical sexual perversion.[84] However, the children's play that the narrator proposes reflects a common Renaissance enjoyment of infantile sexuality:

> The practise of playing with children's privy parts formed part of a widespread tradition, which is still operative in Moslem circles. These have remained aloof not only from scientific progress but also from the great moral reformation at first Christian, later secular, which disciplined 18th and 19th century society in England and France.[85]

The nurse's "sportings" with the child that Marvell alludes to are reported by Heroard, the court physician to Louis XIII of France, in a journal widely quoted by historians of childhood:

> "He laughed uproariously when his nanny waggled his cock with her fingers," an amusing trick which the child soon copied. Calling a page, "he shouted, 'Hey there!' and pulled up his robe, showing him his cock.". . .The Marquise often put her hand under his coat; he got his nanny to lay him on her bed where she played with him, putting her hand under his coat. . .[86]

Marvell is not as explicit as Heroard, but like Ben Jonson he states his preference by invidious comparisons with "Common" sexuality. Better than the lust of the bull or the ram, which engenders babies and diseases as well as "cold jealousies and fears," is the "wantonness" of kid or lamb. Such ideal love will antedate time by combining the erotic potentialities of young and old and by avoiding the temporal fall of orgasm.

The ambivalence about orgasm which fuels the longing for an innocent kind of sex permeates Renaissance psychology. Not only does "to die" have the secondary meaning of "come to orgasm" during the Elizabethan period, but popular physiology also held that each ejaculation was an "expense of spirit" that literally brought a man close to death during the experience, and shortened his life as well. Marvell alludes to the associations among orgasm, violent death and the constriction of time in the last section of "To His Coy Mistress," when he urges the lady to grow up and abandon her childish restraint:

> Now let us sport us while we may;
> And now, like am'rous birds of prey,
> Rather at once our time devour,
> Than languish in his slow-chapt power.
> Let us roll all our strength, and all
> Our sweetness, up into one ball:
> And tear our pleasures with rough strife,
> Thorough the iron gates of life.[87]
>
> (38-44)

This call to experience functions as a 'Reply'' to the pastoral Invitation of the poem's opening. There the speaker spins out a nostalgic vision of the ideal of polymorphous play:

Had we but world enough and time
This coyness, Lady, were no crime.
We would sit down, and think which way
To walk, and pass our long love's day.
Thou by the Indian Ganges side
Shoulds't rubies find: I by the tide
Of Humber would complain. I would
Love you ten years before the Flood
And you should, if you please, refuse
Till the Conversion of the Jews.
My vegetable love should grow
Vaster then Empires and more slow.
An hundred years should go to praise
Thine eyes, and on thy forehead gaze:
Two hundred to adore each breast:
But thirty thousand to the rest
An age at least to every part
And the last age should show your heart
For, Lady, you deserve this state
Nor would I love at lower rate.
(1-20)

The hypothetical ''vegetable love'' native to the green world conflates landscape with the erogenous zones of the beloved's body. By a kind of universal tumescence, both body and pleasure gradually enlarge to encompass all space and time. This is the final projection of the pleasure principle: the same infantile paradise of floating in the purely sensuous described by the Freudian psychologist as fundamental to all sexuality.

Several cults of carnal perfection have emphasized this ideal and have pursued the millenium in the form of an unending extension of sexual foreplay. Their practises are intended to provide escape from the temporal processes of individual aging and of human history and to be steps on the path back to the Garden of Eden. Known as ''Karezza'' in the love courts of Provence, *Maithuna* among adepts of Tantric Yoga, and *Coitus reservatus* to the followers of J.H. Noyes in the 19th century utopian community at Oneida, all these disciplines have in common with pastoral's celebration of innocence a zeal to sublimate sex from its involvement with the cycle of copulation, birth and death. In doing so they neutralize its functions as the chief bonding force of worldly social relationships: marriage and the family.

The preference of premarital juvenile petting over adult consummated and procreative sex emerges clearly in one of the most popular of pastoral works, Longus' *Daphnis and Chloe.* Widely translated and imitated during the Renaissance, this late Greek romance chronicles the flowering of love between two foundling children of noble birth raised by Arcadian herdsmen. The story begins with descriptions of the infants suckling goats and sheep:

> He saw the ewe behaving just like a human being–offering her teats to the baby so that it could drink all the milk it wanted, while the baby, which was not even crying, greedily applied first to one teat and then to another a mouth shining with cleanliness, for the ewe was in the habit of licking its face with her tongue when it had had enough.[89]

It ends with consummation of the wedding night:

> Now, when night fell, all the guests escorted them to the bridal chamber, some playing Pan-pipes and some playing flutes, and some holding up great torches. When they were near the door, the peasants began to sing in harsh grating voices as if they were breaking the soil with hoes instead of singing a wedding song. But Daphnis and Chloe lay down naked together, and began to embrace and kiss one another; and for all the sleep they got that night they might as well have been owls. . .then for the first time Chloe realized what had taken place on the edge of the wood had been nothing but childish play. (p. 121)

The beauty of this "childish play" is the subject of lengthy pictorial descriptions which fill the book:

> So he went off with Chloe to the sanctuary of the Nymphs, where he gave her his shirt and knapsack to look after, while he stood in front of

> the spring and started washing his hair and his whole body. His hair was black and thick, and his body was slightly sunburnt—it looked as though it was darkened by the shadow of his hair. It seemed to Chloe, as she watched him, that Daphnis was beautiful; and as he had never seemed beautiful to her before, she thought that this beauty must be the result of washing. Moreover, when she washed his back, she found that the flesh was soft and yielding; so she secretly touched her own body several times to see if it was any softer. . .
>
> When they got to the pasture next day, Daphnis sat down under the usual oak and began to play his pipe. At the same time he kept an eye on the goats, which were lying down and apparently listening to the music. Chloe sat beside his and kept watch over her flock of sheep; but most of the time she was looking at Daphnis. While he was piping he again seemed to her beautiful, and this time she thought that the beauty was caused by the music; so when he had finished she picked up the pipe herself, in the hope that she too might become beautiful. She also persuaded him to have another wash; and while he was washing she looked at him and after looking at him she touched him. And again she went away full of admiration, and this admiration was the beginning of love. (pp. 26-7).

The children's continuously heightening arousal is intensified by their ignorance. Their feelings have no foreseeable limits; their momentary sensations remains unencoded into words, unmediated by patterns.

Such innocent ignorance disappears with the advent of carnal knowledge. After the wedding night has passed, Chloe's fascination with Daphnis' body and her delight in nature give way to the concern of the prospective mother. Daphnis' change occurs earlier, when the older woman, Lycaenion, shows him how to make love "like a man." From that moment on, he will no longer pet with Chloe for fear of getting carried away and "wounding" her. At the loss of virginity, he changes role from lover to suitor, and even before being accepted as the groom, he busies himself with activity relating to offspring and lineage. Though the two principals may not recognize their loss as they pass out of youth, an intense sense of mutability tempers the reader's response to the idyllic sweetness of the tale. But in typical pastoral fashion, the author's sophisticated tone of voice also mocks the naivete of the lovers and mixes longing with laughter.[90]

Whether it represents promiscuity, highly charged chastity or unconsummated petting, pastoral's central theme of childish Eros is not only stated in what herdsmen do or say; young love is also projected in the description of their surroundings. In bucolic poetry, setting does not merely furnish a backdrop; it functions as an essential foreground element. Indeed a good portion of pastoral consists of pure landscape, free of people but nevertheless redolent with meaning and feeling. The typical pastoral scene has been equated by E.R. Curtius with the rhetorical topos of the *locus amoenus*—the pleasureable spot—which he describes as follows: "The place of heart's desire, beautiful with perpetual spring. . .the lovely miniature landscape which combines tree, spring, and grass; the wood with various species of trees; the carpet of flowers. . .". He states that "from the Roman Empire to the sixteenth century" evocations of this setting "constituted the principal motif of all nature description," and he reads the whole bucolic tradition as an embellishment of this one device.[91] Though not relevant to the rough and rugged landscape of the pastoral of old age, Curtius' description evokes the world of innocence, where, in the words of Claudianus, surrounded by flowers, trees, nymphs and cupids, ". . .wanton Youth with haughty neck shuts out Age from the grove."[92]

So strong was the association of the natural pleasance with the pleasures of making love that medieval rhetoricians uncovered a false etymological similarity between *locus amoenus* and *locus amor*.[93] The pretty landscape is aphrodisiac for many reasons. Nature arouses the senses directly and also inspires by example:

> If the young and amorous are placed in a delightful grove, reeling on beds of flowers, in the midst of a happy country and under a bright and serene sky, these beauties of nature will increase the pleasing sensations that arise from representations of love.[94]

Thus writes an eighteenth century theorist of pastoral in the Edinburgh *Monthly Review.* The same agency operates in *Daphnis and Chloe*:

> What enflamed them even more was the time of year. It was now the end of spring and the beginning of summer and everything was at its best. There was fruit on the trees and corn in the fields; there was. . .a pleasant sound of grasshopper, a sweet smell of fruit, and a cheerful bleating of sheep. You would have thought that the very streams were singing as they gently flowed along, that the winds were making music as they breathed among the pines, that the apples were dropping on to the ground because they were in love, and that the sun was making everybody undress because he loved to see beauty.[95]

To complement such coltish exuberance, the landscape also offers a warm, moist, sweet and nourishing embrace. The *locus amoenus* provides a haven not only from spying eyes of the righteous but also from the demands of adult selfhood—*negotium.* Within its enfolding security a man can let down his guard, allow himself to be tender, passive and infantile:

> Cheerfully we stretched out on beddings of sweet
> Rushes and of the freshly cut vine leaves.
> Poplars and elms, tree upon tree, murmured
> Above our heads; the sacred water of the Nymphs
> Was splashing downward from a cave nearby.
> Tawny cicadas, on their shaded branches,
> Were busy with their chirping; the tree frog
> Was croaking on his distant perch in the thorns:
> The larks and finches sang, the dove was sighing
> They yellow bees circled the springs in flight
> There was a smell of harvest, of ripe fruits picking;
> Pears in profusion rolled at our feet
> And apples at our sides: branches hung down
> Heavy, dark plums touching the ground.[96]

The Keatsian sumptuousness of image and sound in the language of this passage from Theocritus engulfs and overwhelms the reader, so that he experiences directly a sense of passive release. One critic has named this lavish expansion of the *locus amoenus* the *locus uberrimus,* alluding to the double meaning of *uber* as copiousness and breast.[97] Similar passages appearing at the opening of Sannazaro's *Arcadia,* in Book IV of *Paradise Lost,* in Marvell's "The Garden," and in Spenser's description of the Bower of Bliss evoke the luxury of a specifically oral form of infantile sensual gratification:

> Thus being entred they behold around
> A large and spacious plaine, on euery side
> Strowed with pleasauns, whose faire grassy ground
> Mantled with greene, and goodly beautifide
> With all the ornaments of Floraes pride. . .
>
> So fashioned a porch with rare deuice,
> Archt ouer head with an embracing wine,
> Whose bounches hanging downe, seemed to entice
> All passers-by, to tast their luschious wine,
> And did themselues into their hands incline,
> As freely offering to be gathered:
> Some deepe empurpled as the *Hyacint,*
> Some as the Rubine, laughing sweetly red,
> Some like faire Emeraudes, not yet well ripened.[98]

The pleasure of this state has in some ways an even more elemental, primitivistic and unconscious quality than that of infantile oral passivity. It is literally a vegetative mode of being—one that Herrick summoned up in his dream of "The Vine:"

> I Dream'd this mortal part of mine
> Was metamorphse'd to a Vine;
> Which crawling one and every way,
> Enthrall'd my dainty *Lucia.*
> Me thought, her long small legs and thighs
> I with my *Tendrils* did surpirze
> Her Belly, Buttocks, and her Waste
> By my short Nerv'lits were embrac'd
> About her head I writhing hung,
> And with rich clusters (hid among
> The leaves) her temples I behung:[99]
>
> (1-11)

Another fantasy of "vegetable love" appears as a prevalent motif in Bosch's "Garden of Delights." Flowering vines entangle the bodies of lovers and emerge from every conceivable orifice. Nude revellers dine on gigantic strawberries; couples sit petting inside crystalline flowers; the topography itself takes shapes of plantlike sexual organs. In this vision of the resurrection of the body, as Fraenger observes, Bosch pictures an ideal of tenderness stipulated in the Adamite doctrine of sexuality: "A striving to regain a plantlike innocence in sexuality. . .expression is confined to a silent dreaminess and mute gazing. There is a stillness as of vegetation, so that the fine drawn groping hands appear like tendrils. . ."[100] Any reference to the green world of pastoral innocence at least hints at this vegetal eroticism.

One of the most striking features of Bosch's painting is the number of its plantlike people whose heads are lowered or buried and whose feet and buttocks are elevated skyward. This anatomical reversal of top and bottom mirrors the familiar *in*version of pastoral, which raises the peasant over king, child over adult and vegetative over animal and rational souls. The pastoralist descends even lower on the great chain of being when he projects the ideal of unfallen pleasure, "the place of heart's desire," onto the world of minerals. Leonardo da Vinci wrote of the body's intrinsic desire to return to the first state of chaos, to the elements of matter imprisoned by the soul.[101] Marvell dramatized that longing in "Dialogue Between the Soul and Body":

> Oh who shall deliver me whole
> From the bonds of this tyrannic soul. . .
> A body that could never rest
> Since this ill spirit it possesst.[102]

Purified of spirit, the body itself yearns to realize its essence—"to find its resting place"—in the repose of a stone. Marvell color-codes this yearning for stasis as another extension of pastoral's search for innocence:

What but a soul could have the wit
To build me up for sin so fit?
So architects do square and hew
Green trees that in the forest grew.[103]

Mineral lethargy is natural, sylvan, green, while the activity of thought and emotion is an artificial, courtly imposition.

This rejection of soul and affirmation of the mineral character of body verges closely on the perception of the earth itself as a beautiful human body and on the sensual enjoyment of its contour, texture and shape. With its mounds of Venus and grassy banks, its rifts and caves, its fountains and waterfalls, the *locus amoenus* contains "Lineaments of Gratified Desire" that are simultaneously topographical and anatomical. In a sonnet from *Amoretti,* Spenser, for example, refers to The Bower of Bliss as a garden within his beloved's body:

Fayre bosome, fraught with vertues richest treasure
The nest of love, the lodging of delight:
The bower of blisse, the paradice of pleasure,
The sacred harbour of that heuenly spright.
How was I rauisht with your louely sight,
And my frayle thoughts too rashly led astray.[104]

An analogous motif depicts the whole of the beloved's body as a park through whose flowering banks and meandering paths the lover is free to wander:

But who those ruddie lippes can misse?
Which blessed still themselves do kisse.
Rubies, Cherries, and Roses new,
In worth in taste, in perfitte hewe:. . .
So good a say invites the eye,
A little downward to espie,
The lovely clusters of her breasts,
Of *Venus'* babe the wanton nests:
Like pomels round of Marble cleere:
Where azurde veines will mixt appeere.
With dearest tops of porphyrie.
Betwixt these two a way doth lie,

A way more worthie beautie's fame,
Then that which beares the mylken name.
This leades unto the joyous field,
Which only still doth Lillies yeeld:
But Lillies such whose native smell
The Indian odours doth excell. . .[105]

Sidney's Philisides tours the Arcadian countryside for 150 lines. His mode of apprehension, which thus dilates the beloved's body to a Brobdignagian scale, implicitly shrinks the beholder to the size of a baby, thereby emphasizing once more the regressive, infantile quality of the desire he expresses with such witty elegance.[106] Just as Marvell's vegetable love englarged the domain of the Pleasure Principle "vaster than Empires and more slow," so the pastoral landscape expands from the enclosed garden to global proportions in other "enflamed" Renaissance imaginations. In "Elegy XIX," after undressing her verse by verse, John Donne exclaims at the sight of his naked mistress: "O my America, my new-found-land.[107]

It may be objected that this is all mere conceit. The *locus amoenus,* is after all, more a "place" of rhetoric—a *topos*—than an actual geographical location or an erogenous zone. These visions of vegetables and parks are flights of fancy, displays of intellectual virtuosity, hyperbolical compliments, instruments of seduction, expressed in a light, ironic tone. This perception, however, does not negate the intensity of longing that energizes the fantasies. The motive of seductive rhetoric, no matter how artful or self-conscious, is real desire. The *locus amoenus* is a mythic rather than a merely rhetorical place. Like all myths, it means more than any interpretation can articulate, and whether consciously believed in or not, it shapes people's sense of the world and it motivates their behavior. Even in its ultimate forms of exaggeration, the vision of the place of heart's delight was taken as a physical as well as imaginary reality. Men of the Age of Exploration thought of the Brave New Worlds of the Western Hemisphere not only as Edenic gardens but as pastoral landscapes of the body. In 1498, following the directions of the geographer Pierre D'Ailly, Christopher Columbus himself went looking for the *locus amoenissimus* at the mouth of the Orinoco river:

> Believing that fateful tract could not be entered without God's permission, he did not investigate further; but in an eloquent letter to his royal patrons, Ferdinand and Isabella, he. . .(stated). . .that the earth was pear-shaped rather that round, that the newly discovered hemisphere was shaped like a woman's breast, and that the Earthly Paradise was located at a high point corresponding to the nipple.[108]

From this explorer's literal search for a landscape of the body to the cavalier's disingenuous invitation to country pleasures; from simple evocations of Maying festivals to surreal fantasies of vegetable love, pastoral's "representation of innocence" issues in a rich variety of Utopian projections. What they share in common is an appeal to the memory of an ideal once possessed and then lost—a kind of Platonic *anamnesis*. All these visions of paradise tap the psychic energy of nostalgia—the motive force of the *Recherche de temps perdu*. Whether manifested as the *locus amoenus*, the Garden of Eden, the Golden Age, or the land of Arcadia, the ideal of innocence is itself a metaphor for another world in the past that all people have inhabited: the world of adolescence, childhood and infancy—the world of their own youth recollected as different and dislocated from their present selves.

The poets observing pastoral conventions have, as I have shown, repeatedly made explicit the connection between the ideals of rusticity and youth. Many, in fact, have gone one step further, and drawn upon bucolic motifs not only to indulge and express the sentiments of nostalgia, but to test, judge and even purge those sentiments in the light of changing perceptions of their own pasts. Once they have advanced to the major genre of epic, mature writers often return to the setting and literary mode of their youth by interrupting their hero's quest with bucolic interludes—episodes that one critic has referred to as "pastoral oases."[109] In these interludes, the poet employs the conventions of the pastoral of youth with a kind of retrospective cast which often includes an encounter with the *puer* figure of his previous self. Spenser, for example, in Book VI of *The Faerie Queene,* has the knight, Sir Calidore, discover Colin Clout in the *locus amoenus* at the top of Mount Acidale. Though the adult has passed out of youth, a portion of the child remains within his personality. The epic hero's entry into the oasis represents the resurgence of that residual child.

The pastoral interludes follow a similar pattern in many epics, *Odyssey, Aeneid, Divine Comedy, Orlando Furioso, Gerusalemma Liberata,* to name a few. In the midst of his strenuous ordeal, the hero's attention is diverted by the allure of a green world. His infantile longings are stirred by its promise of security and pleasure. He wishes to remain there, free of tension and responsibility, in a timeless, nameless state. But the dangers of such retreat soon become apparent: it dissolves personal identity, blurs purpose and direction, and leads ultimately to listlessness and despair. A.B. Giamatti has shown that the recognition of this danger typifies epic's ambivalent attitudes toward pastoral ideals:

> Exercising great attraction, those paradises offer satisfaction for deep almost buried needs. The gardens are therefore most dangerous precisely in the area they are most appealing. . .a man is tempted. . .to succumb to the desire for security and female domination which the garden promises.[110]

Seen from this perspective, the figure of the *puer eternus* no longer represents an ideal toward which to aspire, but rather a figure of maladjustment and sickness. Indeed, some psychologists use the term to diagnose a specific nuerotic syndrome, applying it to the young man who "won't grow up," who scorns the reality of adult society, shelters himself with escapist fantasies, and who ultimately suffers from a "provisional life," troubled, according to Marie-Louis von Franz, by Don Juanism and homosexuality.[111] Like the domineering parent of the "mother-complex" associated with this malady, the hostess of the garden of delight—whether Circe, Alcina or Acrasia—entraps her visitors and drains the virile life force from them.[112]

The remedies for the black magic of the oasis require rejection of bucolic ideals and of residual childishness. The hero may assert a violent masculine force over the sinister female and her seductive lodgings. Odysseus holds a sword to Circe's throat and brings her to his knees with the scornful question: ". . .am I a boy, that you should make me soft and doting now?"[113] And Spenser's Guyon, after being captivated by its delights, fells the grove and defaces the gardens of Acrasia's Bower of Bliss.[114] On the other hand, the hero may simple take a strong-willed leave from the remote, innocent life of the natural retreat and return to the complex "worldly" reality of the center, accepting, supporting and defending the hierarchy of legal authority and traditional institutions that the adult by nature inherits and transmits.

Such a departure from the pastoral oasis—a *second* passage from childhood to maturity—often involves the choice of adult marriage over adolescent eroticism. From the perspective of epic, the social regulation of matrimony is positive rather than repressive; it takes sexuality out of the wilderness and includes it within an officially sanctified system of human control and order. Odysseus cruises the Mediterranean from one oasis of young love to another under the pseudonym of "Nobody." But to achieve his life's purpose, he must come home, regain his name and title, and sleep with his wife after the work is done, in a bed of olive wood and not of roses.

The same passage from pastoral's young love to adult marriage takes place in the grandest of Western epics, the Bible. But in this case the protagonist is the reader guided by the interpretive tradition. The Bible's pastoral oasis is Solomon's *Song of Songs.* In the preface to his seventeeth century translation, Gervase Markham refers to its eight chapters as "eight eclogues."[115] Solomon's song includes a number of conventions of the pastoral of youth, among them the invitation to delight, with its invocation of holiday escape and *reverdie*:

> My beloved spake and said unto me, Rise up my love, my fair
> one, and come away.
> For lo, the winter is past, the rain is over and gone;
> The flowers appear on the earth; the time of the singing of
> birds is come, and the voice of the turtle is heard in
> the land:
> The fig tree putteth forth her green figs, and the vines
> with the tender grape give a good smell. Arise my love,
> my fair one, and come away. (Chapter 2, 10-13)

It also celebrates the landscape of the body:

> I am the Rose of Sharon, and the lily of the valleys.
> As the apple tree among the trees of the wood, so is my be-
> loved among the sons. I sat down under his shadow with
> great delight, and his fruit was sweet to my taste. . .
> (Chapter 2, 1-3)

> Awake, O north wind; and come, thou south; blow upon my garden,
> that the spices thereof may flow out, Let my beloved
> come into his garden, and eat his pleasant fruits
> (Chapter 4, 11-16)

And the blazons uttered by both lovers express the heightened intensity of innocent erotic perception:

> How beautiful are thy feet with shoes, O prince's daughter!
> the joints of thy thighs are like jewels, the work of
> the hands of a cunning workman.
> They navel is like a round goblet, which wanteth not liquor:
> thy belly is like an heap of wheat set about with lil-.
> lies.
> Thy two breasts are like two roes that are twins.
> Thy neck is as a tower of ivory. . . (Chapter 7, 1-4)

For milennia, adolescents delightedly pored over this book, while Jewish and Christian theologians were made uncomfortable by its sensuality. According to one Hebrew tradition, a man is not allowed to read *The Song of Songs* until he reaches the age of thirty and is presumably beyond temptation.[116] But resisting the wishes of their more puritannical colleagues, the elders of the church have never seen fit to expunge the book from the canon. Instead, as Renaissance Neoplatonists did with pastoral itself, they elevated Solomon's poem to the status of allegory and tried thereby to excise its literal meaning altogether. The commentators channelled the pastoral eroticism of the original into devotional and conjugal passion—"the spirit's lust for Union with its Spouse."[117] The Douay version of the Old Testament prefaces the *Song* with the following explanation:

> This Book is called the Canticle of Canticles, that is to say the most excellent of all canticles concerning the Union of God and his people, and particularly of Christ and his spouse. . .The spouse of Christ is the Church: more especially as to the happiest part of it, the perfect soul, of which every one is His Beloved, but above all other, the Immaculate and ever blessed Virgin Mother.[118]

By thus redefining the way the *Song of Songs* was read, the interpreters reversed the direction of its emotional pull, converting it from a pastoral of youth, an adoration of the body as landscape, to a hymn in celebration of the marriage of God and man. To prepare for such a marriage, the person must become a "perfect soul"—a completed and purified human being. This goal was to be achieved only through antiprimitivist struggle against the material body and through adult aspiration to transcend the natural world.

It was by way of St. Bernard's *Sermons on the Song of Songs* that Dante adapted the imagery and the ardor of *Canticles* to the metaphor of spiritual marriage in the *Paradiso* of the *Divine Comedy*.[119] This is not the place to expand that metaphor. But it is appropriate, I think, given the recurrence of the pastoral of youth in the major literary texts of the Western tradition, to conclude this study with a mention of the way Dante locates that ideal within his vision of the totality of existence.

Dante depicts the same Garden of Eden at the top of Mount Purgatory that Columbus sought in the Antipodes of the Carribean as a bucolic landscape to which the earthly body always seeks to return:

> Eager now to explore in and about
> the luxuriant holy forest evergreen
> that softened the new light, I started out
>
> without delaying longer, from the stair
> and took my lingering way into the plain
> on ground that breathed a fragrance to the air.
>
> With no least variation in itself
> and with no greater force than a mild wind,
> the sweet air stroked my face on that sweet shelf,
>
> * * * * *
>
> My feet stopped, but my eyes pursued their way
> across that stream, to wander in delight
> the variousness of everblooming May. . .
>
> . . .I saw come into view
>
> a lady all alone, who wandered there
> singing, and picking flowers from the profusion
> with which her path was painted everywhere.[120]

During what Vergil refers to as an interlude in the pilgrim's epic quest, Dante will rest in the oasis and prepare to reunite with Beatrice, the girl of his adolescent dreams. At the apex of the natural world—the green place where both time and space contract and converge—in a setting described as "the nest of human kind" and the scene of man's "innocent first laughter and sweet play," Dante's body is fulfilled and resurrected, so that the promptings of pleasure will conform perfectly with the dictates of reason and with the attraction of divine love.[121]

But though he yearns toward her like Leander toward Hero, the lady in the landscape of "love when love is free of pain," (XXIX, 3) is not the Beatrice whom Dante expects. She is a lovely Nymph named Mathilda, who represents his nostalgic memory of the Beatrice of his youth.[122] The distinction between the pastoral ideal of young love and the adult love that Beatrice now embodies is one that Dante has yet to grasp. Because, as the opening words of the *Divine Comedy* tell us, Dante lost his direction in the wilderness of middle age, he has, at age thirty five, gone through Hell to make his way back to the garden he left at age eighteen when Beatrice died. To gain his bearings on his life's path, he must be rejuvenated and cleansed by the apprehension of youth's pastoral innocence. But he is not meant to remain in Eden. At the moment Beatrice surprises him there with her entourage of twenty four elders, he recognizes the insufficiency of the *locus amoenus.* And at the same moment, it dawns upon him that he is no longer led by Vergil. With her appearance, the mentor of his youth whom Dante has known as "the singer of the *Eclogues*" and as the representative of the Golden Age of classical culture, has wordlessly withdrawn.[123] For a naturalist of the old dispensation like Vergil, the final destination lies in the green fields of Elyzium. But as Dante now discovers, for those of a higher faith, the pastoral landscape marks the end only of spiritual apprenticeship. He experiences the loss of Vergil as a second departure from childhood, a parting as painful as a boy's separation from his parents, as Eve's separation from the garden:

> I turned left with the same assured belief
> that makes a child run to its mother's arms
> when it is frightened or has come to grief,
>
> to say to Virgil: "There is not within me
> one drop of blood unstirred. I recognize
> the tokens of the ancient flame." But he
>
> he had taken his light from us. He had gone.
> Virgil had gone. Virgil, the gentle Father
> to whom I gave my soul for its salvation!

Not all the sight of Eden lost to view
  by our First Mother could hold back the tears
  that stained my cheeks so lately washed with dew.

Purgatory, XXX, 43-54

The Spouse herself appears, neither to charm nor to comfort, but instead to rebuke. The substance of Beatrice's accusation is that Dante has failed to grow up. Instead of learning the transience of youthful values from the experience of her early death, instead of gaining from it the awareness to escape the nets and arrows of folly, he remained the childish target of fleshly desire:

The fledgling waits a second shaft, a third:
But nets are spread and the arrow sped in vain
In sight or hearing of the full-grown bird. (XXXI, 61-63)

"Like a scolded child, tongue-tied for shame," he listens to her reprimand with bowed head, but she insists that he confront the full extent of his guilt: "If to hear me/Grieves you, now raise your beard and let your eyes/Show you a greater cause for misery." In the reference to his beard, Dante "sensed too well the venom of her phrase," for it is his childishness that constitutes his guilt, his callowness that the "thorn of repentance" must purge.

Indeed Purgatory itself is a kind of coming of age—all of Purgatory, including the Garden of Eden. For the fully conscious person, the oasis at the top presented as a pastoral of youth is neither a respite from striving nor "the place of heart's desire" that Vergil thinks it is. Instead it is the scene of testing and rigorous penance: for Dante the most difficult passage in the whole of his route. His penance is not complete until the pain of departure is transformed into the pain of understanding. Finally capable of lifting his beard and looking into Beatrice's eyes, he encounters the infinite love and wisdom that his immaturity has barred him from for the last seventeen years. At this point he swoons from an anguish that arises not from the loss of childhood innocence but from the awareness of what he has missed as an adult. Now he is ready to cross through the waters of Lethe and be washed of the nostalgic burden of the past.

Once he awakens on the other side and ventures from the shade of the *locus amoenus* into the blaze of the noonday sun, Dante leaves the landscape of the body and enters the orbit of the spheres. In transit from the Earthly to the Celestial paradise, he emerges from the protection of mother nature's bosom to the exposure of Beatrice's eyes, from pastoral courtship to spiritual marriage.

Dante gains an understanding of his past from a vantage point that has some similarities to Wordsworth's in "The Immortality Ode," similarities which locate the pastoral of youth in a system coordinating generic conventions, ethical ideals, and stages of the life cycle. At the confused midpoint in their journeys—Wordsworth was also about thirty five when he completed his poem—both men return briefly to the pastoral world of their departed youths and abandon themselves to flowered meadows, Maying festivity and songs of tabor and flute. Seen retrospectively, through the template of bucolic *topoi,* their early years appear to them as a utopian landscape, a condition out of time, free from its ravages and demands. But the fantasy is too fragile to last. Both writers come back to themselves in the discovery that the ideal of youth depends on adulthood, that the conception of childhood as a timeless state of innocence is a creation of time, which contains and elevates the past by putting distance between it and the present. The release and gratification they enjoy in the pastoral oasis blends with a typical Arcadian bereavement, for as Proust said, "les vraies paradies sont les paradis qu'on a perdus"—"the real paradise is paradise lost."[124]

Following both speakers' painful recognition that adulthood means departure from "the good place" of innocence comes the positive realization that such departure is not only necessary but desireable. Like many utopian visions, the pastoral of youth proceeds from praises of an ideal, to a dialectical perception of the ideal's limits. Making a garden of youth the first chapter of individual life history and of collective human history demonstrates the poverty of a world of perfect pleasure, security and stasis. For it renders that ideal *merely* childish in comparison to the larger world of choice, mystery and challenge that demands the fullest range of human response. For Dante and for Wordsworth, as well as for most other writers who follow "the Perfect Patterne of the Poete," epic and adulthood answer the pastoral of youth by justifying the ways of God to man with the moral of the fortunate fall.

There is within Arcadia itself, however, another vantage point from which to reply to youth's invitation to delight. This perspective forms the topic of the chapter that follows. Its response is uttered not by the active voice that leaves the grove to engage in an epic quest of larger scope within "the world" or beyond it, but rather by the passive voice that returns to the country at the end of life's journey. To the descant of innocence, "come hider love to me," the pastoral of old age bears the burden of experience.

NOTES

[1] (Both in the flower of youth, Arcadians both) Vergil, *Eclogue 7*, 1.4, translated by Paul Alpers, *The Singer of Eclogues: A Study in Virgilian Pastoral* (Berkeley: University of California Press, 1979), pp. 42-3. All later references to Vergil are to this edition and translation.

[2] *Guardian* #40, (1713).

[3] Raymond Williams, *The Country and the City* (New York: Oxford University Press, 1973), pp. 10-12.

[4] "December," lines 19-36 in *The Works of Edmund Spenser: A Variorum Edition: The Minor Poems*, eds. Charles Grosvenor Osgood and Henry Gibbons Lotspeich (Baltimore: Johns Hopkins Press, 1943), I, 114. All later references to this edition.

[5] Thomas Heywood, "An Apology for Actors," in *Early Treatises on the Stage* (London, 1853), pp. 52-3, cited in Harry Levin, *The Myth of the Golden Age in the Renaissance* (Bloomington: Indiana University Press, 1969), p. 117.

[6] (London, 1614), p. 183, cited by Harry Levin, p. 148.

[7] Peter Conveney, *The Image of Childhood: The Individual and Society: A Study of the Theme in English Literature* (Baltimore: Penguin Books, rev. ed. 1967), p. 29.

[8] Rainer Maria Rilke, *Ueber Kunst*, in *Verse und Prosa, aus dem Nachlass* (Lepizig, 1929) cited in George Boas, *The Cult of Childhood* (London: The Warburg Institute, 1966), pp. 77-8.

> Childhood is the realm of great fairness and deep love. . .Either the child's fullness of images remains undisturbed by new experiences, or the old love

sinks like a dying city under the rain of ash from this unexpected eruption. Either the new becomes the rampart that protects a portion of his child-being, or it becomes the flood that denies it without a backward glance; i.e. the child becomes either older and smarter in the bourgeois sense, as a seed of a serviceable citizen he takes his place and receives his initiation; or he simply ripens quietly from within, from his own child-being outward, which is to say, he becomes a person in the spirit of *all* times: an artist. (my translation)

[9] Thomas Rosenmeyer, *The Green Cabinet* (Berkeley: University of California Press, 1969), p. 57-8.

[10] Sir J.G. Frazer, *The New Golden Bough*, ed. Theordore Gaster (New York: Criterion Books, 1959), pp. 208-302; Marie-Louise von Franz, *The Probem of the Puer Eternus* (Zurich: Spring Publications, 1970), p. 1.

[11] Norman Cohn, *The Pursuit of the Milennium: Revolutionary Messianism in Medieval and Reformation Europe and its Bearing on Modern Totalitarian Movements*, (New York: Harper Torchbooks, 2nd ed., 1961), p. 99.

[12] *The Landscape of the Mind; Pastoralism and Platonic Theory in Tasso's* Aminta *and Shakespeare's Early Comedies* (Oxford: Clarendon Press, 1969), p. 58.

[13] *Blake's Night: William Blake and the Idea of Pastoral* (Cambridge: Harvard University Press, 1973), p. 7.

[14] C.G. Jung, "The Psychology of the Child Archetype," in *Archetypes and the Collective Unconscious* (New York: Pantheon, 1959), pp. 177-78.

[15] Wilfred P. Mustard, Introduction to *The Eclogues of Baptista Mantuanus* (Baltimore: Johns Hopkins Press, 1911), pp. 36-40.

[16] "To His Booke," *The Minor Poems*: I, 7.

[17] E.K., "Dedicatory Epistle" *The Minor Poems*, I, 7, 10.

[18] *The Minor Poems*, I, 10.

[19] Jacopo Sannazaro, *Arcadia and Piscatorial Eclogues*, trans. Ralph Nash (Detroit: Wayne State University Press, 1960), p. 74.

[20] Edwin Greenlaw, et. al. eds., *The Works of Edmund Spenser: A Variorum Edition* (Baltimore: Johns Hopkins Press, 1932), vol. I (I, i, 1-5).

[21] Richard Edwards, *A Paradise of Dainty Devices*, ed. H.E. Rollins, (Cambridge Press, 1927), p. 10.

[22] A round by David Melvill in W.H. Auden and Chester Kallman, *An Elizabethan Song Book* (London: Faber and Faber, 1957), p. 220.

[23] Words and music by John Dowland; W.H. Auden and Chester Kallman, p. 98.

[24] W.H. Auden and Chester Kallman, p. 72.

[25] C.L. Barber, *Shakespeare's Festive Comedy: A Study of Dramatic Form and its Relation to Social Custom* (1959); rpt. Cleveland: Meridan, 1966), pp. 10 ff.

[26] Andre Varagnac, *Civilisation Traditionelle et Genres de Vie* (Paris: Albin Michel, 1948), pp. 138-152.

[27] Edmund Spenser, "May," lines 1-10.

[28] N.Z. Davis, "Youth Groups and Charivaris in 16th Century France," *Past and Present*, 50 (1971), pp. 50-55.

[29] N.Z. Davis, p. 54. The anthropologist Victor Turner sees an analogy between these Saturnalian role reversals involved in seasonal festivals and the paradoxical role

alterations that take place in the rites of passage from childhood to maturity. Both exemplify what he calls "liminal" phenomena. "Variations on a Theme of Liminality," in *Secular Ritual*, ed. S. Moore and B. Meyerhoff, (Amsterdam, 1977), pp. 36-52.

[30] Phillip Stubbes, *The Anatomie of Abuses*, cited by C.L. Barber, pp. 21-2.

[31] Leah Sinanoglou Marcus, *Childhood and Cultural Despair; A Theme and Variations in Seventeenth Century Literature* (Pittsburgh: U. Pittsburgh Press, 1978), p. 79. She quotes Luther: "If these things had been kept as play for youth and for young pupils so that they would have had a childish game of Christian doctrine and life. . .if it were left at that, the palm-ass, the ascension and many things of the kind could be tolerated. . .But for us old fools to go about in mitres and finery, and take it seriously,. . .that is the very devil."

[32] N.Z. Davis, p. 74.

[33] *Prose Works of Sir Phillip Sidney*, ed. Albert Feuillerat. 4 Vols. (Cambridge: Cambridge University Press, 1962), I, p. 13.

[34] Cited by William Berg, *Early Vergil* (London: The Athlone Press, 1974), p. 115.

[35] "Puer and Senex" in *Puer Papers*, ed. Cynthia Giles (Irving, Texas: Spring Publications, 1979), p. 23.

[36] p. 24.

[37] William Empson, *Some Versions of Pastoral* (London, 1935; rpt. Norfolk, Conn.: New Directions, 1960), p. 241-9.

[38] Robert Herrick, "To his Saviour, A Child; a Present, by a Child," in *The Complete Poems of Robert Herrick*, ed. J. Max Patrick (New York: Doubleday-Anchor, 1963), p. 469.

[39] L.S. Marcus, pp. 58 ff.

[40] Richard Cody, p. 59.

[41] James Hillman, p. 26.

[42] Stanzas I and III, "Ode on the Intimations of Immortality from Recollections of Early Childhood," *The Poetical Works of William Wordsworth*, ed. Thomas Hutchinson and Ernest de Selincourt (London: Oxford University Press, 1959), p. 460.

[43] Theocritus, "Idyll I," 11. 21-29 in *The Poems of Theocritus*, trans. Anna Rist (Chapel Hill, N.C., University of North Carolina Press, 1978), pp. 28-29.

[44] Thomas Rosenmeyer, *The Green Cabinet: Theocritus and the European Pastoral Lyric* (Berkeley: Univ. of Cal. Press, 1969), p. 57.

[45] Christopher Marlowe, "The Passionate Shepheard to His Love," *England's Helicon*, p. 186.

[46] Rosenmeyer, p. 57. Precise and detailed description of this sort has been regarded largely as a rhetorical formula rather than as an expression of freshened perception by most modern scholars. But the fact that certain kinds of observations of the physical world are conventional doesn't detract from their immediacy. The pastoral inventory often conveys the clear spareness of the Imagist poem and the nuance of oriental lyric. See: R.H. Blyth, *Zen in English Literature and Oriental Classics* (rpt; New York: Dutton, 1960; first ed. Tokyo, 1942).

[47] Hallett Smith, *Elizabethan Poetry* (Cambridge: Harvard University Press, 1952), pp. 4-5.

[48] Rosenmeyer, p. 201.

[49] W.W. Greg, *Pastoral Poetry and Pastoral Drama* (London: Sidgewick and Jackson, 1906), pp. 400-401.

[50] Renato Poggioli, *The Oaten Flute: Essays on Pastoral Poetry and the Pastoral Ideal* (Cambridge: Harvard University Press, 1975), pp. 13-14; W.H. Auden, *The Age of Anxiety* (New York, 1947), p. 85.

[51] Theodore Lidz, *The Person: His or Her Development Throughout the Life Cycle* (rev. ed. New York: Basic Books, 1976), p. 450.

[52] Morton Bloomfield, *The Seven Deadly Sins* (East Lansing: Michigan State University Press, 1952), p. 76.

[53] *Elizabethan Lyrics* edited by Norman Ault (New York: Sloane Associates, 1949), p. 25.

[54] One disclaimer before I proceed. The concept of youth in this chapter relates largely to the male of the species and often excludes the experience of the female. The *puer* is a boy child; the ideal pattern of career is the man's; the basic pastoral dichotomy of nature vs. civilization is a particularly male outlook. This limitation of perspective to that of half the human race is primarily due to the male authorship of all our texts, but it is exaggerated in this case because of the emphasis that pastoral places on male sexual attitudes.

[55] *The Faerie Queene,* II, xii, 74.

[56] C.G. Jung, *Symbols of Transformation,* trans. R.F.C. Hull, *Collected Works* Vol. 5. Bollingen Series XX (Princeton: Princeton University Press, 2nd ed. 1967), p. 249.

[57] Aby Warburg, "Sandro Botticellis 'Geburt der Venus' and 'Frueling,' " *Gesammelte Schriften* (Leipzig, 1923), I, 1-45.

[58] Sannazaro, p. 43.

[59] "Pastoral poetry was often erotic, and the distinction between goddesses, nymphs and shepherdesses, or between beautiful young men of myth and the feigned shepherds of pastoral was often not clear." p. 93.

[60] *The Complete Works of Christopher Marlowe,* ed. Fredson Bowers (Cambridge: Cambridge University Press, 1973), II, 432.

[61] Sannazaro, p. 50-51.

[62] *Aminta,* I, ii, 343, cited by Poggioli, p. 13.

[63] William Paden, "The Medieval Pastourelle," Diss. Yale, 1971.

[64] *Elizabethan Lyrics,* p. 405.

[65] Charles L. Sanford, *The Quest for Paradise: Europe and the American Moral Imagination* (Urbana, Illinois: University of Illinois Press, 1961).

[66] Denis Diderot, *Supplement au Voyage de Bougainville,* ed. Gilbert Chinard (Baltimore: Johns Hopkins Press, 1935), pp. 151-2.

> At the moment that the male reaches full strength, that his sexual development reaches full maturity. . .at the moment that the young girl is tired of the fading stage of childhood and reaches the ripeness to conceive desire, to inspire it and to satisfy it fruitfully. . .he is permitted to approach a woman and be approached; she displays herself publicly, face uncovered and bare-breasted, either to accept or refuse the caresses of a man. . .it is a great festival. . .If it is a girl, in the evening the boys assemble in a great crowd around the hut and the air resounds all night with the sound of voices and instruments. . .the man is exhibited before her naked from all angles, in all postures. If it is a boy, it is the young girls who set out to please him with all the honors of the festival and expose to his gaze the naked woman without reserve and without secrets. The remainder of the ceremony takes place on a bed of leaves. . . (translation mine)

[67] Norman Cohn, pp. 149-191.

[68] *The Milennium of Hieronymus Bosch: Outlines of a New Interpretation,* translated by Esther Wilkins and Ernst Kaiser (Chicago: University of Chicago Press, 1951). This painting has generated controversy among interpreters at least since 1599 when the Spanish inquisitor, Siguenca saw in it the "apotheosis of sin" and the "flourishing of lust." Fraenger is one of the only writers willing to regard it as a celebration rather than a condemnation of the pleasures of the flesh. Despite the dubiousness of his more extreme claims—that Bosch was illustrating an esoteric program dictated to him by one Johannes Aegidius, the leader of an Adamite congregation—Fraenger's description of the overall atmosphere of the scene, as well as his explication of many specific details is far more persuasive to me than the orthodox explanations of the work. E.H. Gombrich's conjecture that the picture portrays the condition of the earth before the flood has been much more widely accepted, *The Heritage of Apelles, Studies in the Art of the Renaissance* (Ithaca: Cornell University Press, 1976). This acceptance probably rests on his previous reputation. His argument here depends largely on the presence of the Ark on Mt. Ararat, which in fact does not appear where it belongs on the enclosing panels of the tryptich, and which Gombrich argues most probably was covered by the panel's frame. Although Gombrich dismisses Fraenger's work as a "fantastic reading," the latter's interpretation does not depend on absent elements of the work and gives a better account of what is present in it. Gombrich (p. 87) admits that Fraenger's "wild hypothesis" does "discern something essential: the sense of joy rather than revulsion that pervades the painting." Gombrich explains this sense of joy by asserting, "the real sin of man before the flood was the absence of sin." Whatever the doctrinal intentions behind the painting, there is agreement that it sets forth a vision of ecstatic prelapsarian sexuality.

[69] "The Argument of Marvell's Garden," in William Keast, editor, *Seventeenth Century English Poetry* (New York: Oxford University Press, 1962), pp. 292-296.

[70] Richard Lovelace, *Poems,* ed. C.H. Wilkinson (Oxford: Clarendon Press, 1925), p. 146.

[71] Translated by Henry Reynolds, 1628. Cited in Frank Kermode, *English Pastoral Poetry: From the Beginnings to Marvell* (New York: Barnes and Noble, 1952), pp. 82-3.

[72] William Blake, *Songs of Innocence and Experience: Showing the Two Contrary States of the Soul,* facsimile edition by Geoffrey Keynes (New York: Orion Press, 1925), plate 51.

[73] Blake, plate 44.

[74] On Blake's debt to Spenser, see David Wagenknecht, *Blake's Night: William Blake and The Ideal of Pastoral,* pp. 1-8. On the genre of pastoral debate, see chapter four, below.

[75] Hallett Smith, pp. 89-90.

[76] Henry Hawkins, *Parthenia Sacra* (Rouen, 1633), p. 11, cited in Stanley Stewart, *The Enclosed Garden* (Madison: University of Wisconsin Press, 1966), p. 44.

[77] Muriel Segal, *Virgins, Reluctant, Dubious and Avowed* (New York: Macmillan, 1977), also John Layard, *The Virgin Archetype* (New York and Zurich: Spring Publications, 1972).

[78] Tom Moore, "Artemis and the Puer," *Puer Papers* (Irving Texas: Spring Publications, 1979), p. 190.

[79] Richard Barnefield, "The Shepheardes Content," in Kermode, *English Pastoral Poetry,* p. 179.

[80] Andrew Marvell, *Poems and Letters,* ed. H.M. Margoliouth, revised by Pierre Legouis, 2 Vols. (Oxford: Clarendon Press, 1971), I, 41-44, 11. 41-8.

[81] Sir Walter Ralegh, "A Poesie to prove Affection is not Love," in *The Poems of Sir Walter Ralegh,* ed. Agnes Latham (Cambridge: Harvard University Press, 1962), p. 17. Perhaps the strongest expression of these sentiments is found in Shakespeare's sonnet 129, beginning: "Th'expense of spirit in a waste of shame/Is lust in action. . ."

[82] *The Complete Poetry of Ben Johnson,* edited by William B. Hunter Jr. (New York: Anchor Seventeenth century series, 1963), p. 260.

[83] Marvell, I, p. 25.

[84] An exception to this reticence is Leah Singangoulou Marcus' chapter on Marvell, "Beyond Child's Play," in her recent *Childhood and Cultural Despair,* pp. 201-232. Her interpretation of Marbvell's concern with sexual innocence runs parallel to mine, but she makes no reference to either pastoral or to seventeenth century sexual attitudes to supply a context for his stance.

[85] Phillipe Aries, *Centuries of Childhood: A Social History of Family Life,* trans. Robert Baldick (New York: Alfred A. Knopf, 1962), p. 102.

[86] p. 100.

[87] Marvell, I, 26.

[88] See: Mircea Eliade, *Yoga: Immortality and Freedom,* trans. Willard R. Trask (Princeton: Bollingen Series LVI, Princeton University Press, 2nd ed., 1969), pp. 249-267 and Maren Lockwood, "Experimental Utopia in America," in *Utopias and Utopian Thought,* ed. Frank E. Manuel (Cambridge: Houghton Mifflin, 1966) pp. 183-200. Also N. Bishop, "The Great Oneida Love-In," in *American Heritage,* 20, 1969, pp. 14-17, 86-92. In *Life Against Death: The Psychoanalytical Meaning of History* (New York: Modern Library Paperback, 1959), Norman O. Brown's interpretation of Freud's discussion of the organization of the sexual drive parallels the pastoral motif discussed here. Brown states that the sexual and social organization of adulthood are interconnected: the pattern of "normal" adult sexuality or "genital organization is a tyranny which supresses some of the other components of sex altogether and subordinates the rest to itself. On the other hand, ". . .children explore in indiscriminate and anarchistic fashion all the erotic possibilities of the human body. . .From the Freudian point of view, the subordination of forepleasure to endpleasure in sexual intercourse is a compromise concealing a conflict between the desire of the immortal child in us for pure polymorphous play and the reality principle which imposes genital organization on us. . .the immortal child in us is frustrated even in the sexual act, by the tyranny of genital organization. Hence the attempt to overthrow genital organization in certain practises of mysticism. . .The heretical Christian sect of Adamites, who sought to recapture in this life the innocent eroticism of Adam before the Fall, practised *coitus reservatus*. . .Freud's doctrine of infantile sex. . .is a scientific reformulation of the theme of the innocence of chilhood. . .childhood remains man's indestructible goal. . ." pp. 28-30. Though Brown doesn't discuss pastoral ideals, their overlap with his theme is apparent. Indeed, *Life Against Death,* though it made no mention of goats or gardens, was an important intellectual inspiration for the "back to the land" movement of young people in the 1960' and '70's. See Theodore Roszak, *The Making of a Counter Culture: Reflections on the Technocratic Society and its Youthful Opposition* (Garden City: Doubleday, 1969).

[89] Longus *Daphnis and Chloe,* translated by Paul Turner (Harmondsworth: Penguin Books, 1968), pp. 12-13. All references to this edition.

[90] Free Love, virginity and sexual play, the three varieties of innocent love idealized in pastoral, correspond closely to the normal forms of adolescent sexual behavior categorized by Erik Erikson: "sex without commitment," "disciplined and devoted delay," and "erotic states without consummation." (*Youth: Change and Challenge* [New York: W.W. Norton, 1963], p. 9.) The contradictory appeals, demands and justifications of all three are likely to swirl in the young person's mind. The dominant culture providing the adolescent's models tends to reinforce either one or both extreme alternatives, extolling virginal chastity and promiscuous free love. It rarely advocates or even recognizes the important advantages of the middle way of "erotic states without consummation." This is unfortunate, for as Theodore Lidz has observed, "childish play" has an important developmental role in providing a young person shelter against the frightening urgency of awakening desire:

> Most adolescents, before they can feel free to enjoy sexual intercourse must slowly build up their security and confidence in their abilities to cope with the sexual drives, gain standards to protect themselves realistically, test their own limits of tolerating anxiety and guilt,. . .and learn in actuality that sexual expression will not lead to dissolution of the self. (p. 355)

Robert Sorenson, the author of *Adolescent Sexuality in Contemporary America* (New York: World, 1973) concludes his work with an exhortation that such "free sportings" be given their due by those whose salad days have passed:

> Our study has shown what we consider an unfortunate tendency toward premature intercourse among adolescents. (About 50% in 1973.) Most adolescents are giving themselves little time for beginning sexual activites and move directly to sexual intercourse. One reason for this may be that in our society sexual intercourse is widely considered the only valid expression of sexual love. Another reason may be the unwillingness of many parents to consider advanced sexual beginning activities as morally different from sexual intercourse.
>
> We feel strongly that beginning sexual activities should be encouraged. These activities enable a person to learn much about his and her values in sexual matters. . .In the petting process, all manner of experimentation is both permitted and possible in contrast to early adolescent sexual intercourse, when momentum, thrust and male orgasm seem to be the dominant elements of the process. . . (p. 355)

[91] Ernst Robert Curtius, *European Literature and the Latin Middle Ages,* trans. W.R. Trask (New York: Pantheon Books, Bollingen Series, XXXVI, 1953), p. 192.

[92] Claudian, "Epithalamium de Nuptiis Honorii Augustin," 11. 94-96. Cited by A.B. Giamatti, *The Earthly Paradise and the Renaissance Epic* (Princeton: Princeton University Press, 1966), p. 51.

[93] Curtius, p. 192.

[94] J.F. de St. Lambert, "Discours Preliminaire" to his *Saisons,* trans. in *The Monthly Review,* 41 (1769), 496; cf. J.E. Congleton, *Theories of Pastoral Poetry in England, 1684-1798* (Gainesville, Fla.: U. of Florida Press, 1952), p. 191.

[95] *Daphnis and Chloe,* pp. 34-5.

[96] Theocritus, "Idyll VII," translated by Thomas Rosenmeyer in *The Green Cabinet,* pp. 190-1.

[97] Rosenmeyer, p. 190.

[98] *FQ*, II, xii, 50, 51.

[99] *The Complete Poetry of Robert Herrick*, p. 26.

[100] Wilhelm Fraenger, p. 127. The Adamites claimed to have a special mode of sexuality: "modum specialem coendi, non tamen contra naturam quali decit Adam in paradiso fuisse usum." (p. 129).

[101] Leonard Barkan, *Nature's Work of Art: The Human Body as an Image of the World* (New Haven and London: Yale University Press, 1975), p. 43.

[102] Marvell, p. 48.

[103] Marvell, p. 21.

[104] *Amoretti*, LXXXVI, *The Minor Poems*, II, 137.

[105] *The Poems of Sir Phillip Sidney*, ed. Wm. Ringler (Oxford: Clarendon Press, 1962), p. 87.

[106] See also: Carew's "A Rapture," *The Poems of Thomas Carew*, ed. ed. Rhodes Dunlap (Oxford: Clarendon Press, 1949), pp. 49-53.

[107] *The Selected Poetry of John Donne*, ed. Marius Bewley (New York: Signet, 196), p. 145, 1. 27.

[108] Harry Levin, pp. 183-184.

[109] Poggioli, p. 10.

[110] A. Bartlett Giamatti, *The Earthly Paradise and the Renaissance Epic* (Princeton: Princeton University Press, 1966), p. 126.

[111] Marie-Louise von Franz, p. 2.

[112] Marie-Louise von Franz, p. III, 10 ff.

[113] Homer, *The Odyssey*, trans. Robert Fitzgerald (New York: Anchor-Doubleday, 1963), X, 336-7, p. 175. The restoration of adult identity after such regression is invariably painful. Odysseus' companions make a great moan when they are transformed back from animals into men.

[114] *Faerie Queene*, II, xii, 83.

[115] Stanley Stewart, p. 122.

[116] Janet Howell Marx, "The Marriage of Man and God: Solomon's *Song of Songs* and Resurrection in *The Divine Comedy*," Thesis, Columbia University, 1969, p. 12.

[117] Stanley Stewart, p. 26.

[118] Holy Bible, Douay Version (Maryland, 1914), p. 691.

[119] E.G. Gardner, *Dante and the Mystics* (London, 1913), p. 112, and J.H. Marx, pp. 5, 13, 15, 49-50, 55.

[120] *The Purgatorio*, trans. John Ciardi (New York: New American Library, 1961), pp. 283-4, Canto XXVIII, 11. 1-18; 34-42.

[121] A.B. Giamatti, p. 105.

[122] A.B. Giamatti, p. 109.

[123] In the title and introductory chapter of his book on Vergillian pastoral, Paul Alpers observes that Dante thinks of him as a bucolic poet. *The Singer of* the Eclogues (Berkeley: University of California Press, 1979).

[124] Cited by Levin, p. 186.

2

Fortunate Senex: The Pastoral of Old Age

The other world of pastoral, for all its emphasis on spiritual and physical innocence, has never been the exclusive province of the young. Though one rarely encounters an Arcadian of middle age, the swain and the nymph have always shared their domain with a vocal populations of elders. Some are gentle seniors, like Vergil's Tityrus and Meliboeus, Sannazaro's Opico, Spenser's Melibee, and Lodge's Old Damon. Others, like Piers and Thenot in *The Shepheardes Calender,* Googe's Amyntas, Wordsworth's Michael and Frost's yankee farmers, are hardnosed, leatherskinned old countrymen. These characters are no trespassers in the rural landscape; their old age reflects their rugged settings and generates an essential bucolic vision of the good life.

Like youth, old age marks a pastoral stage of life because its world is situated on the peripheries of socially defined reality, remote from the center of court or city. In Victor Turner's term, it is "liminal" to the worldly world possessed and created by those in their prime—mature adults who have completed the process of growing and who have not yet begun to shrink or walk on three legs.[1]

The shared exclusion of and by "the world" that attracts both young and old to the landscape of pastoral often brings them together into a tender relationship of mutual guardianship—a relationship that appears as a distinct bucolic motif from Vergil's *Eclogues* to Blakes *Songs of Innocence.* But just as often, when young and old meet in bucolic poetry, they find themselves in conflict rather than harmony. The debates of youth and age scattered throughout medieval and Renaissance eclogues provide an occasion for writers to articulate the attitudes and ideals of old age by contrast to those of youth and serve as exploratory essays on the meaning of life outside the limits of conventional society. But whether or not they appear in actual debates, all pastoral figures tend to feel emotions, espouse ideals, adopt styles and praise weather appropriate to one or the other—either youth or age.

Literary critics have been reluctant to recognize the pastoral of age.[2] Such oversight may arise from the same general societal preference that since the Renaissance has focussed more attention on youth than on age—witness the weight of psychological studies of early rather than late stages of human development. Neglect of the pastoral of age may also be due to the sentimental conception of the bucolic mode formulated by eighteenth-century theoreticians of pastoral like Rapin, Fontenelle and Thomas Purney.[3] These writers insisted that the point of all pastoral was to project a vision of a simple, lazy and pleasurable life.

This theoretical approach is perpetuated in the work of many modern scholars as well. Thomas Rosenmeyer, for example, seeks to achieve thrift in the definition of the pastoral mode by banishing the old herdsman altogether. According to Rosenmeyer, the aged shepherd is never "central to pastoral," but belongs to the scheme of Georgic, a world "rustic, agrarian, Boeotian. . . [which] is what pastoral is not."[4] The distinction upon which the expulsion is based—a distinction between idyllic Theocritean and realistic Hesiodic rusticity—is useful to delineate the antithetical primitivisms within the pastoral mode. But although they do signify distinct genres, "georgic" and "pastoral" cannot function as mutually exclusive categories. Looking back at his previous writings, Vergil himself conflated *Eclogues* and *Georgics* by referring to both at once as the rustic songs of aged Titryrus sung "with youthful daring beneath the spreading beech," and by grouping them as distinct from epic, which portrays active deeds of people in the middle of life.[5] Youth, innocence and soft rural landscape may more readily suggest a utopian world, but old age, experience and the hard rustic setting also embody a vision of the good life, that is, "a pastoral."

As early as Vergil's first eclogue, the bucolic world is identified as the ideal home of the old age. "Fortunate senex," declares the unhappy old man who is forced to leave Arcadia to the one who is permitted to stay:

> Lucky old man! And so the land will remain your land
> And for you it is enough. . .

Lucky old man! So here, among the streams you know,
Among the holy springs, you'll seek the shaded cool.

(I. 46-52)[6]

It is an old man, "reclining at ease beneath the cover of the shading beech," who first enjoys the "god-ordained" *otium* or peaceful leisure that Hallett Smith has shown to be an essential pastoral ideal.[7]

In English Renaissance pastoral old men are usually the ones who extoll the virtues of the rural mean estate and reject the aspiring mind of the court and city:

Carelesse worldings, outrage quelleth
  all the pride and pompe of Cittie:
But true peace with Sheepheards dwelleth,
  (Sheepheards who delight in pittie.)
Perfect peace with Swaines abideth,
  loue and faith is Sheepheards treasure.
. . .
What to other seemeth sorrie,
  abiect state and humble biding:
Is our joy and Country glorie,
  highest states have worse betiding.
Golden cups doo harbour poyson,
  and the greatest pomps, dissembling:
Court of seasoned words hath foyson,
  treason haunts in most assembling.[8]

These moral perceptions of Thomas Lodge's "Old Damon" justify his withdrawal from the court, but a force over which he has no control causes it. The rhythm of the life cycle demands his return to the natural setting from the artificial environment of the city. Gerontologists report that disengagement from the active and productive functions of a society defines the role of elder in almost every human culture.[9] Such disengagement and the corresponding shift of behavior from a mode of "active mastery" to one of "passive mastery" serves the welfare of old people by removing them from stress, and serves the welfare of the whole system by liberating positions of authority for young adults to move into.

Youth and old age, grandson and grandfather, share the vantage of the peripheries, share distance from the center of social control and from the height of ambition. Traditional schemata of the Ages of Man picture old age as second childhood; the opening and closing acts of "this strange eventful history" of the life cycle form the lower steps of a pyramid, while adulthood stands at the peak.[10] The old man plays out his "golden years" in the green setting of the "golden age" of youth. Indeed, the pastoral of age often depicts the retirement of the soldier and the rustication of the courtier as a return to the haunts of his own childhood. Toward the end of his life, Don Quixote plans to unbuckle his sword and once again take up the oaten flute in the landscape from which he first set out; and Colin Clout "Comes Home Againe" after finding that ten years in the court have aged him prematurely. Shakespeare, as he approached the end of his active career in London and prepared to retire in rural Stratford, turned to pastoral convention in his last plays, focussing on the conflicts and harmony of youth and age in the bucolic retreats of Bohemia and Prospero's island.[11]

As You Like It, the purest of Shakespeare's pastorals, stresses the partnership of old age and youth in the bucolic world, remote from the center. "Youth," "Young," "Old" and "Age" are among the words the dramatist uses most frequently throughout his career, but in no other play does any of them occur as often.[12] The propelling force of the play's plot is the expulsion from the court of the young and the old by the aspiring minds of those who are middle-aged. Like most situations in the play, this expulsion occurs twice. Duke Frederick, the middle-aged brother, usurps the throne of his older brother, Duke Senior, and forces him into early retirement, along with a band of merry young retainers. Then Oliver, the fully adult older brother, deprives his younger sibling, Orlando, of education and patrimony and forces him into the wilderness, accompanied by the ancient servant, Adam. Oliver's contemptuous epithets—"What, boy!. . .Get you with him you old dog" (I,i, 49,75)—convey the adult attitude of the court toward both youth and old age. Upon reaching the forest of Arden, the young and the old find two different states of nature—one "soft," the other "hard"—but both discover in common the virtues of necessity. In the words of Le Beau, youth and age arrive in "a better world" than the one from which they have been ejected.

Orlando and Adam give up what little they are left with to help one another in time of need. Their common alienation from "new news at the new court" explains why pastoral so frequently depicts youth and age in the relationship of mutual guardianship. From *Daphnis and Chloe* to *The Winter's Tale,* aged peasants kindly rescue and raise foundlings abandoned by their royal parents, and are in turn protected and delighted by their charges. The guardianship motif, which also pervades folk-tale and fairy story, elevates the pastoral values of humility, naivete and tenderness, while denigrating the worldly virtues of fortune, wealth and power. In the Pastorella episode in Book VI of *The Faerie Queene,* the guardianship of the generations plays a minor but exemplary role. Spenser's silver-haired Melibee enters the scene to protect his foundling daughter from the evening chill:

> Then came to them a good old aged syre,
> Whose siluer lockes bedeckt his beard and hed,
> With shepheards hooke in hand, and fit attyre,
> That wild the damzell rise; the day did now expyre. . . .
>
> * * * *
>
> She at his bidding meekely did arise,
> And streight unto her little flocke did fare:
> Then all the rest about her rose likewise,
> And each of his sundrie sheepe with seuerall care
> Gathered together, and them homeward bare.
>
> (VI, ix, 13, 15)

In his version of the familiar pastoral dispraise of courtly life, Melibee equates the superior condition of his present rustication with his age and experience, but also with his childhood days, the days before he was pricked with the vanities of aspiration:

> The time was once, in my first prime of yeares
> When pride of youth forth pricked my desire,
> That I disdain'd amongst mine equall peares
> To follow sheepe, and shepheardes base attire:
> For further fortune then I would enquire.
> And leuing home, to roiall court I sought . . .
>
> * * * *
>
> With sight whereof soone cloyd, and long deluded
> With idle hopes, which them doe entertaine,
> After I had ten yeares my selfe excluded
> From native, and spent my youth in vaine,
> I gan my follies to my selfe to plaine,
> And this sweet peace, hose lacke did then appeare.
> Tho back returning to my sheepe again,
> I from thence forth haue learn'd to loue more deare
> This lowly quiet life, which I enherite here.
>
> (VI,ix,24-5)

But Spenser qualifies the cliche when he puts it in dramatic context. Melibee addresses his praise of the mean estate which harmonizes youth and age to the middle aged battle-weary knight, Sir Calidore. Calidore's longing is kindled by the old man's idea of the simple life of retirement, but it bubbles and boils as it mixes with the erotic pastoral of youth embodied in the shepherd's daughter:

> Whylest thus he talkt, the knight with greedy eare
> Hong still vpon his melting mouth attent;
> Whose sensefull words empierst his hart so neare,
> That he was rapt with double rauishment,
> Both of his speach that wrought him great content,
> And also of the obiect of his vew,
> On which his hungry eye was alwayes bent;

That twixt his pleasing tongue, and her faire hew,
He lost himselfe, and like one halfe entraunced grew.
(VI, ix, 26)

The two-fold nostalgia for youth and for age immediately turns to disingenuousness in the mind of the sophisticated and aggressive courtier. Calidore attempts to manipulate the old man and seduce his daughter by reciting a rhetorical version of the primitivistic sentiments that are fully genuine only when uttered by Melibee. This is not deliberate deception, just a sample of the courtly manner by which a momentary sentimental flash issues in a fatuous pledge of lifelong commitment:

Yet to occasion meanes, to worke his mind,
And to insinuate his harts desire,
He thus replyde; Now surely syre, I find,
That all this worlds gay showes, which we admire
Be but vaine shadowes to this safe retyre
Of life, which here in lowlinesse ye lead. . .
. . . . .
Than even I. . .
. . . . .
Now loath great Lordship and ambition
And wish the heavens so much had graced mee,
As graunt me liue in like condition;
Or that my fortunes might transposed bee
From pitch of higher place, unto this low degree.
(VI, ix, 27-28)

The old man doesn't bite this lure any more than the offer of gold which follows. He knows that the pastoral cliches which are true for him are false when repeated by those who have not yet achieved the genuine disillusionment of age. In the first flush of enthusiasm Calidore experiences the pastoral world as "the happie life,/Which shepheards leade, without debate or bitter strife." (VI, ix, 18) But just as he himself envies the world which is supposedly free of envy, and just as the supposedly invulnerable condition of the mean estate is destroyed by the true meanness of the brigands, so the harmonious convergence of the pastoral ideals of youth and age is unmasked in the framework of most pastoral poetry as the dialectical opposition of generational conflict.

The contrast between aged and youthful shepherds centers, predictably, on their differing perceptions of time. First of all, they regard history in opposite ways. The old herdsman thinks of the pristine prehistorical condition that all pastoral celebrates not as "the childhood of the race," but as the "good old days." For him, *illud tempus* becomes the Silver Age instead of the Age of Gold with its free love and eternal springtime; his version of cosmogony follows Hesiod and Ovid, who relate that the human race stagnated under the benign Saturnian reign. The Silver Age ushers in the order of time and the natural cycles of growth, maturation and decay, including the alternation of summer and winter.[13] In the Judaeo-Christian tradition, the same change is marked by the fall, which brought about "the penalty of Adam/ The seasons' difference." (*AYLI*, II, i, 5-6) While the pastoral of youth paints this fall into time and mutability as a disaster which destroyed the *otium* of perfected human existence, old shepherds think of it as a *felix culpa* into a salubrious educational regimen:

> The father of mankind himself has willed
> The path of husbandry should not be smooth
> He first disturbed the fields with human skill
> Sharpening the wits of mortal man with care
> Unwilling that his realm should sleep in sloth. . .
> So that experience by taking thought
> Might gradually hammer out the arts. . .
>
> (*Georgics*, I, p. 17)

When the old herdsman invokes past greatness, it is a time of austerity rather than ease:

> The time was once, and may againe retourne. . .
> When shepherds had non inheritaunce
> Ne of land nor fee in sufferaunce
> But what might arise of the bare sheepe. . .
> And little them served for their maintenaunce. . .

But tract of time and long prosperitee
Lulled the shepheards in such securitee. . .
Tho gain shepheards swains to look a loft
And leave to live hard and learne to ligge soft. . .
(''Maye: 104-115)

To ''moral on the time'' is an appropriate occupation for the old shepherd. The temporal process in general and the winter wind in particular perform the invaluable service of teaching ''who he is''—a phrase used both by Duke Senior and the newly converted Oliver to describe the instruction in self-knowledge offered by the forest. And old Opico repeats the lesson that his aged father taught him as a boy: though the world is sinking into worsening corruption, true virtue shines the brighter by contrast. Its very cost testifies to the value of the wisdom of experience:

And I. . .
Who am old indeed have bowed my shoulders
In purchasing wisdom, and even yet am not selling it.[14]

Old Thenot offers Cuddie a similar homily in Spenser's ''February'':

Who will not suffer the stormy time
Where will he live till the lvsty prime?
Selfe haue I worne out thrise threttie yeares,
Some in much joy, many in many teares:
Yet neuer complained of cold nor heate,
Of sommers flame nor of Winteres threat:
Ne ever was to Fortune foeman,
But gently took that ungently came
And ever my flocke was my chiefe care,
Winter or Sommer they mought well fare.
(15-24)

Such teaching is antidote to the folly of youthful Epicurism—a source of Stoic fortitude.

Thenot's concern for the welfare of his flock and his sense of responsibility in the face of hardship exemplify another aspect of the pastoral of age. *Otium*, pleasure and play accompany the holiday pastoral of youth, but most old shepherds and farmers are more interested in an honest day's work. "My serious business gave way to their playing" says Vergil's old Meliboeus, referring to Corin and Thyrsis, "both in the flower of youth, both Arcadian, equal in song."[15] Pastoral's work ethos praises the down-to-earth labors that sustain the high and mighty of the world. This georgic aspect of the mode is what Empson designated as "proletarian literature."[16] Such literature describes the worker's tasks with an attention to detail that magnifies their dignity and charm. The pastoral of age also stresses that labor demands sweat—what Hesiod calls *ponos* or pain—and that painful effort has moral value. While youth invites the reader to "go with the flow" uniting nature and human nature, age teaches the discrepancy between desire and reality, and exhorts the reader to work against the entropic drive in the universe and himself:

> . . .it is a law of fate
> That all things tend to slip back and grow worse
> As when a man, who hardly rows his skiff
> Against the current, if he once relax
> Is carried headlong down the stream again.
>
> (*Georgics*, p. 19)

The universe ruled by this law requires not only sweat to resist the current, but also the canniness, the discrimination and the technique that only experience can provide. Vergil explains that though survival in a fallen nature demands unrelenting effort, the seasonal cycle also provides the clues and the tools that enable human beings to thrive—if they observe and learn. The paths of the constellations and the phases of the moon remind men of the correct days and times to sow, cultivate and reap, to plant vines, break oxen, warp looms.[17] Time creates not only the necessity for work, but the possibility for success.

The stated purpose of Vergil's georgic is to draw attention to the appropriate connections of "Works and Days" and to disseminate the basic practical knowledge of a peasant culture. In preliterate societies such knowledge is lodged in the elders of the tribe and passed down from generation to generation. In postliterate agricultural and herding communities, the folk wisdom is often codified in farmers' almanacs, like the *Kalendar of Shepherds* that Spenser chose as one structural model of *The Shepheardes Calender*.[18]

The centrality of these georgic themes to the pastoral of age is brought to light in the tenth chapter of Sannazaro's *Arcadia*. Led by the ancient magus Enareto, old Opico conducts the uninitiated young shepherds to the sanctuary of Pan hidden in a cave. In front of the statue of the pastoral god stands an altar:

> Down from either side of the ancient altar hung two long beechen scrolls, written over with rustic lettering; these were preserved by shepherds from one age to another in succession over many years and contained within them the antique laws and rules for the conduct of pastoral life, from which all that is done in the woods today had its first origin. On the one were recorded all the days of the year and the various changes of the seasons, and the inequalities of night and day, together with the observation of the hours (of no little utility to human beings), and unerring forecasts of stormy weather;. . .and which days of the moon are favorable and which infelicitous for mankind's tasks; and what each man at every time ought to shun or pursue, in order not to transgress the manifest will of the gods. . . and how if one binds up the right testicle rams produce females and if the left males. . .[19]

The wisdom of experience contains disparate precepts, but all in some way have to do with the proper use of time. The material question of the right time of day to cut the corn is related to the religious question of the appropriate time for prayer and sacrifice, to the moral question of when to trust and when to suspect, and to the political question of when to support and when to oppose the church or the government. In his "moral eclogues," dominated by aged shepherds, Spenser adheres to this tradition. In the *envoi* which sends his book from author to reader, he makes that adherence explicit: "Loe

I have made a Calender for everie yeere/. . .To teach the ruder shepherede how to feed his sheepe/And from the falsers fraud his folded flocke to keepe."[20]

As Spenser suggests, the work ethos of the pastoral of age demands a particular kind of intellectual and moral labor: the winnowing of grains of truth from the chaff of sentimental illusion. That winnowing gives sharp definition to the contrast between innocence and experience, and it gives shape to the most famous of all pastorals of age, "The Nymph's Reply to the Sheepheard":

> If all the world and loue were young,
> And truth in euery Sheepheards tongue,
> These pretty pleasures might me moue,
> To liue with thee, and be thy loue.
>
> Time driues the flocks from field to fold,
> When Riuers rage, and Rocks grow cold,
> And Philomell becommeth dombe,
> The rest complaines of cares to come.[21]

Of course Ralegh's speaker is no old woman. But she repeatedly invokes the perspective of age while rejecting the childish appeal of the passionate shepherd's "Come live with me and be my love." Modulating from a caustic to a wistful tone, she lays bare the distortions of wishful thinking in the pastoral ideal of innocence by confronting that ideal with the practical wisdom of maturity. The age-linked nature of such ethical sifting was observed by Izaak Walton, who made the milkmaid's mother in *The Compleat Angler* append her recitation of both invitation and reply with this gloss:

> I learned the first part in my golden age, when I was the age of my poor daughter; and the latter part, which indeed fits me best now but two or three years ago, when the cares of the world began to take hold of me.[22]

The honest labor of differentiating sober verities from gay fantasy is the traditional function of moral satire, another mode which plays an important role in the pastoral of age. The old shepherds in the eclogues of Barclay, Turberville and Googe—the only pre-Spenserian English pastoralists—attack youthful recreation and erotic preoccupation in the accents of medieval moralists and old testament prophets:

And now to talke of spring time tales
My heares to hoare do growe,
Such tales as these I tolde in tyme,
When youthfull yeares dyd flowe.
. . .
Now Loue therefore I will define
And what it is declare,
Which way poor souls it doth entrap
And how it them doth snare.[23]

According to old Amyntas in Googe's first eclogue, a clear understanding of what passion really is can alleviate youth's folly in love. He goes on to provide just that: a detailed physiological explanation of how kindled humors and poisoned blood break down the rational faculties.

In addition to pleasure, youth and love, the other chief target of the pastoral satire of age is the vice of those in high places—urban types in general and the hierarchy of court and church in particular. The winnowing of reality from illusion here involves unmasking the corruption beneath the veneer of glamour. Petrarch was the first to adapt the Old Testament figure of the ancient prophet crying out in the wilderness against the hypocrisy of the priests, and it continues to rail in the pastorals of Boccaccio, Sannazaro, Mantuan, Spenser, Milton and Blake.[24] In "Lycidas," venerable St. Peter's invective interrupts the youthful narrator's elegaic mourning:

He shook his mitr'd locks, and stern bespake,
How well could I have spar'd for thee, young swain,
Anow of such as for their bellies' sake
Creep and intrude, and climb into the fold?
Of other care they little reck'ning make,
Then how to scramble at the shearers feast,

And shove away the worthy bidden guest;
Blind mouthes: that scarce themselves know how to hold
A sheep-hook, or have learn'd aught els the least
That to the faithfull Herdsman's art belongs!
(108-121)[25]

And the limpid songs of Blake's child-inspired Piper in *Innocence* are succeeded by the strident homilies of the Ancient Bard of *Experience,* calling the lapsed soul to return and excoriating the abuses of king and clergy.[26]

Didactic satire traditionally demands the *stile humile*—the direct manner of speech and humble choice of words of the rustic. In contrast to the flowery, courtly language of the pastoral of youth, the aged pastor uses diction that is straightforward and often crude. This crabbed style has offended some readers of pastoral like Sidney and Dr. Johnson. Spenser's apologist, E.K., anticipated the criticism by pointing out the appropriateness of rough diction to old age and to the hard pastoral landscape:

> . . .Tullie. . .sayth that ofttimes an auncient worde maketh the style seem graue, and as it were reuerend: no otherwise then we honour and reuerence gray heares for a certein religious regard, which we haue of old age. . . . . .as in most exquisite pictures they use to blaze and portraict not onely the daintie lineaments of beauty but also rounde about it to shadow the rude thickets and craggy clifts, that by the basenesse of such parts, more excellency may accrew to the principall; for oftimes we fynde ourselves, I know not how, singularly delighted with the shewe of such naturall rudenesse, and take great pleasure in that disorderly order.[27]

Though the harshness of this prophetic voice clashes with the mellifluous strains of the pastoral of youth, it is appropriate to the embattled seriousness of the pastoral of age. Many literary theorists have expressed aversion for the satiric aspect of pastoral and have also attempted to exclude it from their definitions of the mode. Poggioli, for instance asserts that "the bucolic ideal stands as the opposite pole from the Christian one," and Rosemeyer claims that "this [satiric] element is most usefully employed to offset pastoral by way of contrast."[28] Once again, the polarity is real but the generic exclusion is misleading. The contrasting ideals and tonalities are best understood within the pastoral domain, where they correspond to the polarity of the seasons of the year and the seasons of human life. There pastoral satire finds its appropriate place in the natural scheme as what Northrop Frye calls "the mythos of winter."[29]

"Christian" and moralistic sentiments are almost invariably associated with pastors of advanced age. They are good rather than jolly shepherds, but they are shepherds nevertheless. Like youth's, their age's social position accounts largely for their expression of unconventional values. Like youth, they are outsiders, free from the pressures of sustaining families and institutions and from the entanglements of mutual support, threat and compromise that go with a place in society. Unlike youth, they have attained the wisdom of experience that enables them to transmit the non-secular values of that society. When Spenser draws on hard-working rustic heros of earlier British satire like Langland's Piers Plowman and Skelton's Colin Clout as tutelary presences of the *Shepheardes Calender*, he does not go outside the pastoral tradition but rather emphasizes the satiric strain of the pastoral of age.

That satiric and moral strain is also a response to the old person's treatment by a society that considers the aged as expendable. In *AYLI*, both old men, Corin and Adam, make mention of this abuse: "When service should in my old limbs lie lame/And unregarded age in corners thrown. . ." (II, iii, 41-2). Lawrence Stone reports that in the late sixteenth and early seventeenth centuries the aged were victims of a number of social changes: "Old age had previously been seen as a time when weakening physical powers were compensated by the accumulation of wisdom and dignity; it now came to be seen as a period of decay of all faculties, as the body approached death. . . .Folly and miserliness were now regarded as the predominant character of the old people."[30] As a protest against these abuses and on behalf of those "oppressed by two weak evils: age and hunger," (II, vii, 133) biting moral satire forms an essential component of the pastoral of age. When Orlando sets down his "venerable burden"—the starving, exhausted old servant—Amiens sings a bitter version of the bucolic "song of the good life" which echoes the Senior Duke's famous praise of the sweetness of adversity:

> Blow, blow thou winter wind
> Thou art not so unkind
> As man's ingratitude.
> Thy tooth is not so keen,
> Because thou are not seen
> Although thy breath be rude.
> Hey-ho, sing hey-ho, unto the green holly,
> Most friendship is feigning, most loving mere folly;
> Then hey-ho the holly
> This life is most jolly.
> (II, vii, 175)

Here, as in King Lear's ordeal on the heath, the metaphors and ideals of the pastoral of age are set forth in a tragic variation, whereby the wisdom of experience—"Ripeness is all"—can be won only at the cost of unbearable suffering.

This neglect and abuse of old age violates a number of traditional precepts. In rejecting its aged members, the society described by Stone denies not only its own past and future, but also its relation to any higher power. In almost all "primitive" cultures, the elderly are accorded positions of high respect because of their practical knowledge and their moral wisdom. But the central source of their veneration is old people's proximity to the realm of the sacred. Along with the poor and with children, those who have reached their later years supply a link to the Kingdom of Heaven. If infants trail clouds of glory from whence they came, "the elderly who are returning there already seem surrounded by the aura of its mystery."[31]

In traditional agricultural societies, special offices, like lighting the ritual fires of the winter solstice and Christmas, signal the noumenal quality of old age. They are also manifest in the old person's cultivation of occult powers: "In the countryside during former times there was hardly an old person who wasn't a bit (or a great deal) of a sorcerer, *breiche,* as they say in old Provencal. Old people are divine." As they retire from the life of active involvement in the conflicts of history and of love, and eventually from the struggles of georgic pursuits and moral reformation, old people's abilities and concerns become more and more focussed on what David Guttman has designated "magical mastery": ". . .a relatively seamless fit exists in traditional communities between particular social roles and psychic potentialities that are developmental in nature. . . . The religious role requires and gives definition to psychic potentials released by the older man's withdrawal from active tasks of parenthood and production."[32]

The learned tradition also identifies old age with the contemplative way of life. At the opening of *The Republic,* Socrates mentions his appreciation for age's wisdom, and Cephalus reports that "in proportion as bodily pleasures lose their savor, my appetite for the things of the mind grows keener."[33] A closely parallel passage of Cicero's *De Senectute* reaffirms that philosophical proclivity, as do medieval pictorial schemata of the ages and the virtues.[34] According to the symbolism of the *vita triplex,* the life of love and pleasure is appropriate to youth, the active life belongs to the middle years, whereas contemplation is the special province of old age. Thus, Basileus, the exiled king in *Arcadia*:

> Old age is wise and full of constant truth
> Old age well stayed from raunging humor lives:
> Old age hath knowne what ever was in youthe:
> Old age o'ercome, the greater honor gives.[35]

In the pastoral setting, contemplative and magical mastery often involves an eclectic mixture of pagan and Christian elements. The *topos* of the old gnarled oak renders that chthonic sense of age's sacredness. In his tale of age and youth in "February," Thenot designates it as a symbol of "holy eld":

For it had been an ancient tree,
Sacred with many a mysteree,
And often crost with the priestes crewe,
And often hallowed with holy water dewe.
(207-210)

The same oak magically appears in *As You Like It* to mark the power spot where Oliver is converted from a courtly hypocrite into a divine penitent:

He threw his eye aside
And mark what object did present itself
Under an oak, whose boughs were mossed with age
And high top bald with dry antiquity
A wretched ragged man, o'er grown with hair
Lay sleeping on his back. . .
(IV, iii 103-107)

At the end of the play Duke Frederick is also reported to have met "an old religious man" at "the skirts of the wild wood," and the recluse inexplicably awakened him from his erring ways. As a result, the Duke is said to have bequeathed his crown to his brother and to have remained permanently in the woods, taking up the calling of a holy hermit in a cave. And Enareto, the "holy shepherd" pagan priest of Sannazaro's *Arcadia,* is first discovered at the foot of a tree, his hair and beard long and "whiter than the flocks of Tarentina."[36] In Drayton's "Seventh Eclog" Old Borrill sits musing in his sheepcoate "like dreaming Merlin in the drowsie Cell" and counts his beads. When Batte the shepherd boy tries to induce him to join in springtime frolics, Borrill offers a counter-invitation that states the old man's ideals of religious contemplation:

Batte, my coate from tempest standeth free,
  when stately towers been often shakt with wind,
And wilt thou Batte, come and sit with me?
  contented life here shalt thou onely finde,
Here mai'st thou caroll Hymnes, and sacred Psalmes,
And hery Pan, with orizons and almes.[37]

Renaissance pastoral often portrays religious devotion as age's replacement for the erotic devotion of youth, for instance in this lyric by George Peele:

His golden locks time hath to silver turned;
  O time too swift, O swiftness never ceasing!
His youth 'gainst time and age hath ever spurned,
  But spurned in vain; youth waneth by increasing:
Beauty, strength, youth, are flowers but fading seen;
Duty, faith, love, are roots, and ever green.

His helmet now shall make a hive for bees;
  And, lovers' sonnets turned to holy psalms,
A man-at-arms must now serve on his knees,
  And feed on prayers, which are age his alms:
But though from court to cottage he depart,
His saint is sure of his unspotted heart.

And when he saddest sits in homely cell,
  He'll teach his swains this carol for a song,
"Blest be the hearts that wish my sovereign well,
  Curst be the souls that think her any wrong."
Goddess, allow this aged man his right,
To be your beadsman now that was your knight.[38]

Here the central pastoral ideals of contemplation, piety and the mean estate cluster around the reference point of old age. With a passing allusion to the change from gold to silver, the poem depicts the shepherd as an elder who has relinquished the *vita activa* of middle age proclaiming the primacy of the *vita contemplativa* over the *vita amoris* to a band of youthful swains sitting at his feet.

Competition between the claims of youthful love and aged contemplation generates the palinodal structure of much Renaissance poetry, whether or not it is explicitly pastoral in mode or debatelike in form. That contrast shapes paired and mutually contradictory collections of poems like Donne's *Songs and Sonnets* and his *Holy Sonnets*, or Herrick's *Hesperides* and his *Noble Numbers*. It also determines the design of Spenser's *Fowre Hymnes:*

> Having in the greener times of my youth, composed these former two Hymnes in the praise of Loue and beautie, and finding that the same too much pleased those of like age and disposition. . . .I was moved. . .to call in the same. But being unable so to doe. . .I resolved. . .by way of retractation to reforme them, making instead of those two Hymnes of earthly or naturall love and beautie, two others of heauenly and celestiall.[39]

And the reversal of outlook from youth to age that the self undergoes as it matures provides a frequent subject of lyric meditation:

> I have lovde her all my youth
> But now ould as you see
> Love lykes not the falling fruite
> From the withered tree.
>
> Know that love is a careless chylld
> And forgets promyse paste. . .
> He is won with a world of despayre
> And is lost with a toy. . .
>
> Butt true loue is a durable fyre
> In the mynde ever burnynge;
> Neuer sicke, neuer ould, neuer dead,
> From itself neuer turnynge.[40]

The dichotomy of youth and age is one of those conceptual polarities, like body and soul or nature and art, that Renaissance writers thought *with* as much as they thought *about*. It was linked with other polarities—like summer and winter, hot and cold, wet and dry, passion and reason—in astrological systems of correspondance that supplied a coherent, symmetrical picture of the cosmos. So familiar was that dichotomy as a way to organize ethical alternatives that the poet often mixed the extremes to suggest the unique, the paradoxical or the transcendant.

In *As You Like It*, Jaques tries to distinguish himself from the young men around him by adopting the old man's stance of satirical and contemplative wisdom. Despite others' recognition of his pose's youthful callowness, at the end of the play, when they return to court, Jaques remains in the forest as an acolyte to one of its mysterious old hermits. And the speaker of Milton's "Il Penseroso" idealizes his aged future rather than his childish past by envisioning his attainment of "old experience" as another such sylvan sage:

> And may at last my weary age
> Find out the peaceful hermitage
> The Hairy Gown and Mossy Cell
> Where I may sit and rightly spell
> Of every star that Heaven doth shew,
> And every Herb that sips the dew;
> Till old experience do attain
> To something like prophetic strain
> These pleasures melancholy give
> And I with thee will choose to live.[41]

Echoing Ralegh's "Reply" to the Passionate Shepherd, the sober satisfactions of "Il Penseroso" run counter to the youthful "vain deluding joys" praised in its companion poem, "L'Allegro." However, Milton locates the contemplative life not in a rough cave but in a place of comfortable repose, "a mossy cell." Here there is none of the harshness of landscape—or of native diction—that we expect of the pastoral of age. Instead of winter wind and rocky ground, there is an "Herb that sips the dew," and other delicate details that evoke the sensuous beauty of the *locus amoenus.* Milton's old man lives not in the woods but in a garden. Indeed, by the seventeenth century the word "hermitage" denoted an artificial grotto or deliberately fashioned ruin designed for sober meditation or relaxation. Found in most of the parks of great estates, it was as essential a feature as the erotic bower, and it was usually situated nearby.[42]

Milton's "Il Penseroso" exemplifies what has been called "the pastoral of solitude," a strain of the bucolic tradition reflecting the cultural influence of neoplatonism.[43] Much neoplatonic doctrine attempts to unify the divergent paths of the *vita amoris* and the *vita contemplativa* by reconciling the corresponding conflict between young and old. Thus, at the climax of Castiglione's *The Courtier*, Cardinal Bembo discourses on the ladder of love as a means to transcend and thereby eliminate the antinomy of youth and age, pleasure and wisdom:

> My Lordes, to shew that olde men may love not onely without slaunder, but otherwhile more happily than yong men I must be enforced to make a little discourse to declare what love is, and wherein consisteth the happiness that lovers may have.[44]

And Pico Della Mirandola, in his "Oration on the Dignity of Man," refuses to accept the time-honored limitations of youth, claiming the sage's mantle for himself:

> . . .and fathers, noone should wonder that in my early years, at a tender age at which it has been hardly permitted me (as some maintain) to read the meditations of others I should wish to bring forward a new philosophy.[45]

The neoplatonists symbolized their ideal of humanity in the ancient archetype of the *puer senex*, the youthful elder who combined vigor with sagacity.[46] Sidney himself was remembered by Ralegh as one who fulfilled that ideal before his early death:

> The fruits of age grew ripe in thy first prime,
> Thy will thy words: thy words the seales of truth. . .
> Such hope men had to lay the highest things
> On thy wise youth, to be transported hence.[47]

The neoplatonic "landscape of the mind," like the concept of the *puer senex*, unifies the contrary pastoral ideals of innocence and experience. In Marvell's "The Garden," for example, youth and age come together in the setting of the sensual hermitage. The scene is described as "two paradises in one."[48] It is both the green world of the body's infantile pleasure and the silver world of the soul's withdrawal into its own happiness. It preserves the past of prelapsarian enjoyment and provides a foretaste of future flights. Here the speaker finds his own childhood condition of innocence, but he arrives late in life, after running his passion's heat and after ending a long career among the busy companies of men. With its harmony of pleasure and wisdom, love and contemplation, the neoplatonic pastoral of solitude mirrors the ideal of the mean estate embodied by Pastorella and other figures of mutual guardianship: a vision of the good life for youth *and* old age, coexisting "without debate or strife."

Perhaps the most memorable image of that *concordia discors* appears close to the source of both pastoral and neoplatonic traditions:

> Here is the lofty, spreading plane tree and the agnus castus, high clustering with delightful shade. Now that it is in full bloom, the whole place will be wonderfully fragrant; and the stream that flows beneath the plane is delightfully cool to the feet. To judge from the figurines and images, this must be a spot sacred to Achelous and the Nymphs. And please note how welcome and sweet the fresh air is, resounding with the summer chirping of the cicada chorus. But the finest thing of all is the grass, thick enough on the gentle slope to rest one's head most comfortably.[49]

It is here, in this *locus amoenus,* this lovely spot outside the city walls, that we discover young Phaedrus talking love, rhetoric and philosophy with his master Socrates, the elderly sage.

NOTES

[1] Victor Turner, *Ritual Process: Structure and Anti-Structure* (Chicago: University of Chicago Press, 1969); also his "Variations on a Theme of Liminality," in *Secular Ritual,* ed. S. Moore and Barbara Meyerhoff (Amsterdam: 1977), 36-52.

[2] In the rare instances that the old shepherd is mentioned, the significance of his age is largely overlooked. Kronenfeld, ("The Treatment of Pastoral Ideals. . ." p. 19, 145), mentions in passing the stereotype of "the wise old shepherd" as an example of the pastoral of contemplation, and she touches on the debate of youth and age in her discussion of the Colin-Silvius episode in *AYLI,* calling it "a minor convention of pastoral literature." (p. 177) In her excellent concluding chapter, "Nature and Art and the Two Landscapes of Pastoral," she once again mentions the opposition of the stages as a typical pastoral dichotomy congruent with soft and hard landscapes. Patrick Cullen (*Spenser, Marvell & Renaissance Pastoral* [Cambridge, Harvard University Press, 1970]) discusses *SC* in terms of the Age-Youth debate, but sees that debate simply as a

corollary of his own idiosyncratic conception of the Arcadian-Mantuanesque dichotomy, not as an intrinsic pastoral convention. Renato Poggioli associates old age with what he calls "the pastoral of innocence"—i.e. the praise of humble felicity and the mean estate. But he supplies no explanation of why this bucolic ideal should be linked with elderly characters. He organizes his discussion of old shepherds around the archetypes of Baucis and Philemon, the aged domestic couple who appear in Ovid's *Metamorphoses* and Goethe's *Faust*. In my opinion, this "idyll of domestic happiness" is but one minor subdivision of the pastoral of age. (*The Oaten Flute,* p.12). Later Poggioli says "adolescence and early adulthood are the only important pastoral ages" (p. 57).

[3] See J. E. Congleton, *Theories of Pastoral Poetry in England, 1684-1798* (Gainesville, Florida, 1952).

[4] *The Green Cabinet: Theocritus and the European Pastoral Lyric* (Berkeley: University of California Press, 1969), p. 58.

[5] Vergil, *The Georgics,* trans. K. R. Mackenzie (London, Folio Society, 1969), p. 87. It may be objected that pastoral and georgic are distinct genres and traditions. However, their overlap has persistently confounded categorizers. See for example, John F. Lynen's book, *The Pastoral Art of Robert Frost* (New Haven: Yale University Press, 1960), Wordsworth's "Michael: A Pastoral," William Empson's discussion of "Proletarian Literature" as one "version of pastoral" and my arguments below. I believe the difficulty of separating georgic aspects of pastoral from pastoral aspects of georgic can be alleviated with the schema I propose.

[6] Translated by William Berg, *Early Vergil* (London: The Athlone Press, 1974).

[7] Hallett Smith, p. 2.

[8] *England's Helicon,* ed. Hyder Edward Rollins(Cambridge: Harvard U. Press, 1935) I, 24.

[9] Wilbur H. Watson and Robert J. Jaxwell, *Human Aging and Dying: A Study in Sociocultural Gerontology* (New York: St Martin's Press, 1977), p. 31. This book and other gerontological studies cited later expand and revise the classic "disengagement theory" of aging.

[10] Samuel C. Chew, *This Strange Eventful History* (New Haven and London, 1962), p. 162. Iconographical representations of the ages of man frequently include images of different animals for the different stages. Here again the life cycle subsumes human states into the order of nature.

[11] In the case of Edmund Spenser, two recent critical works make mention of the poet and his persona's return to the pastoral world of youth in the retirement of his old age. See Isabel McCaffrey *Spenser's Allegory: The Anatomy of Imagination* (Princeton: Princeton University Press, 1976), pp. 366-70 and Richard Helgerson, "The New Poet Presents Himself: Spenser and the Idea of a Literary Career," *PMLA* 93 (1978) 895-6.

[12] In *AYLI,* there are twenty-nine instances of the word "Young," twenty-nine instances of "Youth," fourteen instances of related words, like "Youthful." The nearest runner up is *Twelfth Night,* with twenty-two references to "youth." *AYLI* contains thirty-seven references to "old" and twenty references to "age." Marvin Spevak *Harvard Concordance to Shakespeare* (Cambridge: Belknap Press, 1973).

[13] A.O. Lovejoy and George Boas, *Primitivism and Related Ideas in Antiquity,* pp. 24-50.

[14] *Jacopo Sannazaro, Arcadia and Piscatorial Eclogues,* Edited and translated by Ralph Nash (Detroit: Wayne State University Press, 1966), p. 68.

[15] Vergil, *Eclog 7,* l. 4, 17.

[16] *Some Versions of Pastoral,* pp. 8 ff.

[17] *Georgics*, p. 24.

[18] *The Kalendar of Shepherdes*, vol. III, ed. H. Oskar Sommer (London, 1892). See also *The Kalender of Sheephardes: A Facsimile Reproduction*, Edited and with the introduction by S.K. Heninger Jr. (Scholars' Facsimiles and Reprints: Delmar, New York, 1979).

[19] *Arcadia*, pp. 102-3.

[20] *The Minor Poems*, vol. I, p. 120. Though it is often referred to as courtly pastoral, and though its characters are thinly disguised stand-ins for members of the aristocracy and the royal family, even Marot's "Eglogue sur le Trespas de ma Dame Loyse de Savoye. . ." (1531) contains some homely advice of this sort, in the style of *Poor Richard's Almanac*. Here the aged shepherdess Louise (actually the Queen Mother) sits under an elm tree and addresses the daughters of neighboring shepherds:

Aulcunesfois Loyse s'advisot
 Les faire seoir toutes soubz ung grand Orme,
 Et elle estant au millieu leur disoit:
 Filles, il fault de d'ung poinct vous informe;
Ce n'est pas tout qu'avoir plaisante forme,
 Bordes, trouppeaux, riche Pere et puissant;
 Il fault preveoir que Vice ne difforme
 Par long repos vostre aage florissant.
Oysiveté n'allez point nourrissant,
 Car elle est pire entre jeunes Bergeres
 Qu' entre Brebis ce grand Loup ravissant
 Qu vient au soir tousjours en ces Fourgeres!
A travailler soyes docques legeres!
 Que Dieu pardoint au bon homme Rober!
 Toujours disoit que chez les Mesnageres
 Oysiveté ne trouvoit à loger.

For Louise, "Oysiveté" or indolence—cognate with "otium," the pastoral ideal of leisure—represents a threat rather than a value. The elderly shepherdess warns her young charges that they should keep an eye to the future, that the wolf at the door cannot be kept away by riches or beauty or power, and that work, the virtue of the housewife, is the only way to prevent vice from deforming their tender ages. *Oeuvres Lyriques*, ed. C. A. Mayer (London, 1964), pp. 321-37. Translation: *The Pastoral Elegy: An Anthology* with Introduction, Commentary and Notes by Thomas Perrin Harrison, Jr., and English translation by Harry Joshua Leon (Austin, 1939), pp. 50-54.

> Sometimes Louise would see fit to have them all sit under a great elm and being in their midst, she would say to them: "Daughters, I must inform you on one point. It is not everything to have a charming figure, lands, flocks, a father rich and powerful; you must take care lest through long idleness vice disfigure the bloom of your life. Do not encourage indolence, for this is worse among young shepherdesses than among the sheep is that big ravening wolf which always comes at evening to these thickets. So then be alert to work; may God pardon good Roger: he always said among good housewives indolence found no place."

[21] *The Poems of Sir Walter Ralegh*, ed. Agnes Latham (Cambridge: Harvard U. Press, 1962) p. 17.

[22] *The Complete Angler or the Contemplative Man's Recreation of Izaak Walton and Charles Cotton*, ed. James Russell Lowell (Boston: Little Brown, 1891), p. 88.

[23] Barnabe Googe, *Eglogs, Epytaphes, and Sonettes*, ed. E. A. Arber (London, 1871) "Egloga prima," p. 32.

[24] Frank Kermode, *English Pastoral Poetry, From the Beginnings to Marvell* (N.Y.: Barnes and Noble, 1952), p. 14.

[25] John Milton, *The Complete Poems and Major Prose*, ed. Merritt Y. Hughes (N.Y.: The Odyssey Press, 1957), p. 122-3.

[26] "Introduction," in *Songs of Innocence and of Experience*, ed. Goeffrey Keynes, plate 30.

[27] Spenser, *Minor Poems*, p. 8. This contrast of diction reflects the distinction between what C.S. Lewis called the "aureate" or golden and the "drab" styles of sixteenth century poetry, a distinction that Yvor Winters reformulated as "petrarchan" vs. "native." Winters asserted that the former style was artificial and decadent, a meaningless display of verbal pyrotechnics, whereas the latter style was honest and rational, the speech of a man speaking to men about a subject of real import. But in fact, most English-speaking poets use both styles interchangeably when playing different roles. In presenting serious ideas involving social and moral criticism, Wyatt, Surrey, Vaux, Ralegh, Donne and Greville often adopted the narrative pose of the old man, whether or not it corresponded to their actual age, and they moved into character by expressing themselves in the native plain style.

[28] Poggioli, p. 1; Rosenmeyer, p. 26.

[29] *Anatomy of Criticism* (Princeton: Princeton U. Press, 1957) Frye calls Satire one of "the mythical patterns of experience, the attempts to give form to the shifting ambiguities and complexities of unidealized existence." Frye's scheme of literary structures and genres analogous to the cycle of the seasons and to the contrary states of innocence and experience has influenced the formulation of my thesis about genre and life cycle. The parodic nature of the pastoral of age's "Reply" to the idealism of the pastoral of youth fits Frye's description: "As structure the central principle of ironic myth is best approached as a parody of romance: the application of romantic mythical frames to the more realistic content which fits them in unexpected ways. . ." (p. 233).

[30] *The Family, Sex and Marriage in England, 1500-1800* (London: 1977), p. 403.

[31] Andre Varagnac: *Civilization Traditionelle et Genres de Vie* (Paris, 1948), p. 210 (author's translation).

[32] "Alternatives to Disengagement: The Old Men of the Highland Druze," in Jaber Gubrium, *Time, Roles and Self in Old Age* (New York, 1976), p. 103.

[33] *The Republic of Plato*, translated and with an introduction by F.M. Cornford (New York: Oxford University Press, 1945), p. 4 (I, 328); also see Adolf Dryer, *Der Peripatos ueber das Greisenalter* (Paderborn: 1939. N.Y. Johnson Reprint Corp. 1968); and Bessie Richardson, *Old Age among the Ancient Greeks: The Greek Portrayal of Old Age in Literature, Art and Inscriptions* (Baltimore: Johns Hopkins, 1933).

[34] Cicero's protagonist, the Stoic hero, Cato the Elder, defends the state of old age from attack by arguing that age's retirement from the active life means not disgrace and boredom, but freedom, time and energy for worthwhile private pursuits; that its decrease of animal spirits means not deprivation of enjoyment but release from desire, "the bait of ills"; that its closeness to death means not fear and trembling but the

broadening of perspective and the enrichment of contemplation. *Cicero on the Art of Growing Old* (*De Senectute*), trans. H. N. Couch, (Providence, R. I.: Brown University Press, 1959). In the course of this panegyric, Cicero reinforces the association between ideals of old age and rustic pursuits. In a long digression from the argument, his Cato enumerates the pleasures and satisfactions of farming which "approximate most closely the ideal life of the wise man." (xv, p. 51) Nature makes strong demands of self-discipline and effort but justly rewards those who have learned to benefit from experience. Contact with the soil, with the plants and with animals is also valuable for the old man, according to the speaker, because it provides intimate involvement with the workings of the life force in both its declining and regenerative aspects.

[35] *The Poems of Sir Phillip Sidney*, ed. Wm. Ringler (Oxford: Oxford University Press, 1962), p. 38.

[36] *Arcadia*, p. 95.

[37] 11. 19-24 in "The Seventh Eclog" in *Idea: The Shepherd's Garland* in *The Works of Michael Drayton*, ed. J. W. Hebel (Oxford: Oxford University Press: 1961) Vol. 5, p. 77.

[38] *Elizabethan Lyrics*, ed. Norman Ault (New York: Wm. Sloan, 1949), p. 145.

[39] *Minor Poems*, I, 193.

[40] *The Poems of Sir Walter Ralegh*, p. 23.

[41] *Complete Poems and Major Prose*, p. 76 (11. 167-176)

[42] See John Dixon Hunt, *The Figure in the Landscape: Poetry, Painting and Gardening during the Eighteenth Century* (Baltimore: Johns Hopkins Press, 1976), pp. 1-9.

[43] On neoplationism and pastoral, see Richard Cody, *The Landscape of the Mind* (Oxford, 1969) and *The Life of Solitude by Francis Petrarch*, Translated by Jacob Zeitlin (Urbana, 1924), p. 143, cited in Kronenfeld, p. 211.

[44] Baldassare Castiglione, *The Courtier*, trans. Sir Thomas Hoby (1561) in *Three Renaissance Classics*, ed. Burton A. Milligan (New York: Scribner's, 1963), p. 592.

[45] *On the Dignity of Man*, trans. Charles G. Wallis, ed. Paul J. W. Miller (New York: Library of Liberal Arts, 1965), p. 25.

[46] E. R. Curtius, *European Literature and the Latin Middle Ages*, pp. 98-105. After tracing the appearance of the ideal of the *puer senex* from Vergil throughout medieval literature, Curtis concludes with a more general observation about this *topos*:

> Digging somewhat more deeply, we find that in various religions saviors are characterized by the combination of childhood and age. The name Lao-tzu can be translated as "old child." . . .From the nature worship of the pre-Islamic Arabs the fabulous Chydhyr passed into Isalm. 'Chydhyr is represented as a youth of blooming and imperishable beauty who combines the ornament of old age, a white beard, with his other charms.'
>
> The coincidence of testimony of such various origins indicates that we have here an archetype, an image of the collective unconscious in the sense of C. G. Jung. (p. 101)

[47] *The Poems of Sir Walter Ralegh*, p. 6

[48] *Marvell*, ed. Joseph H. Summers (Dell: New York, 1961), p. 103, 11. p. 63-4.

[49] *Plato's Phaedrus*, ed. W. C. Helmhold and W. G. Rabinowitz (New York: Liberal Arts Press, 1956), p. 7 (230).

3

"The Sheepheard's Sorrow": Anti-pastorals of Youth and Age

The preceding chapters have explored the pastoral world as a vision of the good life, a utopia whose rustic features represent an array of ethical, aesthetic and psychological ideals appropriate to the stages of youth and old age. Though some of these ideals contradict others, all of them affirm an alternate existence peripheral to the dominant social order; and they envision non-urban, non-adult phases of life as a "golden world" or a "better world." In the form of invitations, exhortations and enticing descriptions, the pastorals thus far cited advertise the herdsman's life as happy—a life that feels joyful and content and at the same time fulfills an abstract ethical principle. They convey the message that simply to "come away" from *this* world, wherever it is, and to enter the other world is to attain some longed-for felicity. By relocating to the good place, they imply, one loses individuality and becomes identified with the ideal the environment embodies.

But evident and fruitful as this notion of pastoral may be, it is challenged by an abundance of counter-examples. A large body of bucolic poetry complains rather than celebrates, complains not only about the abandoned life of city and adulthood, but about the country and the conditions of youth and age as well. In collections by Vergil, Sannazaro, Garcilaso, Sidney and Spenser, what E. K. categorizes as "plaintive" eclogues alternate with those that are "recreative." Anthologies of lyrics with titles like *Bower of Delights* or *Pills to Purge Melancholy* contain more sad songs than happy ones. "The Second Dayes Lamentation of the Affectionate Shepheard" is as popular as "The Shepheardes Content."

This phenomenon of pastoral melancholy seems to contradict the assertion that the pastoral mode is based on the projection of ideals of happiness. The present chapter attempts to resolve that contradiction by showing how this large exception in fact proves the rule. In it I trace the psychological processes and the philosophical arguments by which negations of pastoral ideals are generated out of their affirmation. I show how the three elements by which I have defined the mode—motifs of rustic life and landscape, primitivistic values, and conceptions of youth and age as ideal states—are reversed and rejected within the mode itself. I demonstrate that the pastoral complaint is a species of "counter-genre," an "anti-pastoral" convention that transforms the landscape of innocence into a hostile desert, transforms young love into neurotic frustration and transforms the harvest of experience into the famine of despair. I show that by repudiating peripheral styles and stages of life, the sad shepherd asserts himself as an alienated, unlocated individual, and thereby violates the conventional expectations of his generic setting—but in a manner that is itself governed by convention. As Eleanor Winston Leach has noted, "the pastoral is the only mode that contains the image of its own dissolution."[1]

There are a number of ways that a theory of pastoral can account for this "self-consuming" dialectic. Bucolic poetry's oscillations of mood from gay to gloomy and back, at the most minute as well as at the largest levels of structure, are typical of the lyric in general, for the emotion it musically expresses is itself a form of motion, a wave-like progression between poles of dissonance and harmony. And this undulatory characteristic is especially typical of lyric associated with natural process. In the words of Wallace Stevens:

> Passions of rain, or moods in falling snow
> Grievings in loneliness, or unsubdued
> Elations when the forest blooms; gusty
> Emotions on wet roads on autumn nights;
> All pleasures and all pains remembering
> The bough of summer and the winter branch.[2]

Or as Theocritus' herdsman says to his grieving companion: "Zeus sends blue skies sometimes, and sometimes he sends rain."[3]

But the presence of anti-pastoral melancholy and counter-utopian attitudes in a world of projected ideals also has more specific explanations, explanations that follow from that world's claims to embody a happier, better life. First, there is a need to maintain interest. A fiction that portrayed only perfection would soon turn boring or run out of subject matter. Second, the idea of a land of heart's desire by definition invites argumentative challenge. Plato and More both realized that their utopian visions would inevitably attract objections, so they included attacks on the value and feasibility of their ideals within the works themselves. Indeed by anticipating and articulating sceptical responses, they could partially disarm criticism and gain more of their audience's sympathies. Likewise in Arcadia, anti-pastoral elements show the author's awareness of the limitations of wish fulfillment, but at the same time strengthen visions of a better life. Ralegh's nymph unveils the deceptions and fallacies of the world she has been invited to come away to:

> The flowers doe fade and wanton fieldes,
> To wayward winter reckoning yeeldes,
> A honny tongue, a hart of gall
> Is fancies spring, but sorrowes fall.
>
> Thy gownes, thy shooes, thy beds of Roses,
> Thy cap, thy kirtle, and thy poesies,
> Soone breake, soone wither, soone forgotten
> In follie ripe, in reason rotten.

But after such bitter rebuttal, the speaker—and the reader—can affirm the longings that the intellect rejects:

> But could youth last, and loue still breede
> Had ioyes no date, nor age no neede,
> Then these delights my minde might moue,
> To liue with thee, and be thy loue.

Having proven the illusory nature of pastoral ideals of both youth and age, she modulates her tone from sarcasm back to nostalgia.

A final explanation for the anti-pastoral reversal of mood and attitude lies in the psychological makeup of the person who has gone to live "under the green wood tree"—the fictional or real follower of the pastoralist impulse. Having committed himself to the notion that he has arrived in a better world, such a person is likely to find that any disappointment he encounters there causes him to question his own choice, and hence the value of the whole place. Thus melancholy Jaques adds a verse to Amiens' invitation:

> If it do come to pass
> That any man turn ass,
> Leaving his wealth and ease,
> A stubborn will to please:
> Ducdame, ducdame, ducdame.
> Here shall he see
> Gross fools as he,
> an if he will come to me.[5]

A large frustration of inflated utopian expectations may well grow into a violent reaction against the pastoral world as such:

> K: I that was once delighted every morning.
> Hunting the wilde inhabiters of forrests,
> I that was once the musique of these vallies,
> So darkened am, that all my day is evening,
> Hart-broken so, that molehilles seeme high mountaines,
> And fill the vales with cries in steed of musique.
> . . .
> I wish to fire the trees of all these forrests;
> I give the Sunne a last farewell each evening;
> I curse the fidling finders out of Musicke:
> With envie I doo hate the loftie mountaines;
> And with despite despise the humble vallies:
> I doo detest night, evening, day and morning.[6]

Such intemperate revolt against the other world resembles the kind of wholesale disillusionment with the status quo that motivated the escape to Arcadia in the first place.[7] People fed up with society often seek the good life by taking up residence in the outback, but after a brief sojourn, some of them discover that the same inner sources of discontent that drew them away are heightened in what had seemed from afar to be the ideal place. In such cases, the rural utopia becomes even more constricting than the world they originally fled.

These general principles of anti-pastoral reversal manifest themselves in the utterances of typical herdsmen. The young singers of love-laments and pastoral elegies correspond to what modern psychologists have called "negative puer" or "sick youth."[8] C. G. Jung has diagnosed their afflictions:

> If we try to extract this common and essential factor from the almost inexhaustible variety of individual problems found in the period of youth, we meet in all cases with one particular failure: a more or less patent clinging to the childhood level of consciousness, a resistance to the fateful forces in and around us which would involve us in the world. Something in us wishes to remain a child—to do nothing, or else indulge our own craving for pleasure or power. . .[9]

This diagnosis suggests that the melancholy youth feels the same yearning for childhood expressed in the pastoral of innocence, but at the same time knows that yearning's futility. That is to say, the vision of innocence is really only the wish fulfillment of the sad young man, whereas the sorrowful shepherd is the image of the actual youth who entertains those wishes.[9a]

The speaker of the largely ignored pastoral subgenre of old-age elegy portrays the archetype of "negative senex" as another diametric reversal of pastoral ideals: those of experience. His complaints about his bodily and mental degeneration violate the assumption of natural harmony and express the absence of those gifts reserved for the wise old shepherd: humble content, stoic fortitude, philosophic understanding and access to the divine.

The double aspect of the figure of old age as positive and negative senex accounts for some of the confusion that is likely to arise between the pastoral of age and the anti-pastoral of melancholy. Both contradict youthful ideals of innocence, but they do so from different points of view. The positive senex bases his opposition on the affirmation of old age and on the whole cycle of life that includes summer as well as winter; the negative senex rejects youth because the hopelessness of his own condition makes him reject the life cycle as a whole. Distinguishing among positive and negative senex and puer helps the reader track the variations, paradoxes and inversions of basic pastoral formulae that may not be obvious in the surface texture of a work.

The themes of youth and age often determine the resolution of anti-pastoral melancholy. Such resolution emerges at the end of many works, when negations of pastoral ideals give way to a more positive mood and a change of outlook. In some conclusions, the solace afforded by "placing sorrow" in the natural setting appears as a recognition and acceptance of one's fate—an acceptance commonly characterized as the wisdom of age. In other conclusions, departure from the pastoral world to yet another "better world" suggests forms of metamorphic passage from old age to rebirth and from youth to adulthood.

In addition to completing the case for the identification of pastoral ideals with the stages of youth and age by showing them all subject to the same negations, this chapter lays the groundwork for the formal study of the genre of the pastoral debate of youth and age that follows. The polarities it distinguishes—Innocence vs. Experience and positive vs. negative attitudes toward each—are articulated in the structure of poetic disputation. Puer and senex and their negative counterparts correspond to the four basic debate positions: proposal, counterproposal and the rebuttals to each. Seeing the correspondence clarifies the way writers like Henrysson, Sidney, Lodge, Shakespeare and Drayton apply the rhetorical principles of debate to dramatize the themes of generational conflict and of nature vs. art in the setting of Arcadia.

* * *

The better world of pastoral is not the best of all possible worlds. Its joys are always relative, validated by invidious comparisons. The most common of these praises the virtues of the countryside to the detriment of the town:

> I, synce I sawe suche synfull syghts, dyd never lyke the Towne,
> But thought it best to take my sheepe and dwell upon the downe.
> Whereas I lyve a plesaunt lyfe, and free from cruell handes;
> I wolde not leave the pleasaunt fyelde for all the Townysh
>   Landes.
>
> For syth that Pryde is placed thus, and Vice get us so hye,
> And Crueltie doth rage so sore, and men lyve all awrye.
> Thynkste thou that God will long forbere his scourge and
> plague to sende
>   To suche as hym do styll despyse, and never seke to mende?[10]

But sorrow also appears within the land of heart's desire as a foil to define and intensify the shepherd's happiness. Completely absorbed in their lovely springtime setting, the carefree innocent boys of Theocritus' first Idyll entertain themselves by singing songs of woe. The sweet music of their pipes, which mingles with the sweet music of the whispering pine, accompanies a recital of the passion, despair and death of the shepherd-singer, Daphnis. Their distance from his suffering heightens their own enjoyment of nature and their freedom from care.

The grand passion expressed in Daphnis' complaint is itself an emotion as alien to the idyllic rapport of boys, goats, wind and pine as the world of courtly intrigue and adult sophistication. As Paul Alpers observes, "Theocritus' Daphnis is heroic precisely to the extent of his defiant isolation from the pastoral world."[11] Though kindled by youthful erotic energy, Daphnis' anti-pastoral aspiration is frustrated rather than fulfilled by the rustic environment. The precise cause of his suffering is never specified; it has to do with young love, but it cannot be assuaged by the many nymphs who would pursue him. For the wound inflicted by beauty itself is one that beautiful landscapes and beautiful bodies cannot heal. In those who would strive for the highest, the loveliness of the pastoral world stimulates longings that it can never fulfill.

Anti-pastoral aspiration is the cause of the bucolic melancholy that plagues young Daphnis and his later progeny—Aminta, Sincero, Phillisides and Colin Clout—to name but a few of the romantic adolescents who roam the woods and fields, in the setting but not of it. For them, April is indeed "the cruelest month":

> Tho while his flocke went feeding on the greene
> And wantonly for joy of Summer plaid
> All in despight as if he n'ould be seene
> He cast himself to gound full ill appayed.
> Should seem their pleasance made him more complaine
> For joy in sight not felt, is double paine."[11a]

Such double pain transforms the shepherd's landscape of heart's desire into its own opposite, a remote world not better than the one of everyday but worse—a "desart place," a waste land.

The transformation of garden utopia to wilderness dystopia is a familiar pastoral motif, one whose sources can also be traced to Theocritus' first Idyll. As Daphnis sinks under the waters of morbid passion, he utters a final curse of the natural environment he once loved:

> Now briars bear violets! Violets spring on thorns!
> Junipers blossom with narcissus flowers,
> and all things be confounded: pines grow pears!
> Since Daphnis is dying, the hart may harry the hounds,
> And mountain owls find tongue of nightingale![12]

His prayer that the order of nature be so confounded employs a series of rhetorical formulae known as *adynata*—images of impossible couplings and reversals of normal processes.[13] Such *adynata,* which sprinkle the utterance of all later melancholy shepherds, supply a concentrated instance of the diametric negation of ideals signified by the term "anti-pastoral."

Vergil's tenth eclogue includes another example of this transformation. The urban poet Gallus enters the Arcadian landscape longing for the ideal of innocence and inviting his unfaithful mistress, Lycoris, to join him "here" in a world of love free from violence and political jealousy:

Had only I been one of you—the one
To tend your flocks or cultivate your vines!
Whether it's Phyllis or Amyntas by me. . .
We'd lie by willows, under pliant vines;
Phyllis would bind me wreathes, Amyntas sing.
Here are cool springs, Lycoris, meadows soft
And groves: here time alone would use us up.[14]

But Gallus finds that neither this ideal nor the consolation of sheep, herdsmen and rustic gods will suffice to calm the "passion that keeps him under arms of cruel Mars." Infuriated by the inability of the pastoral world to satisfy his needs, he rages incoherently:

I'll go, and all my witty compositions
Pipe as a shepherd to Sicilian measures.
In woods and lairs of beasts I choose to languish,
Carve my love sufferings on the tender trees.

His stormy passion drowns out the elegaic serenity of the bucolic singer, while the landscape itself changes from the enfolding *locus amoenus* to a hostile and dangerous forest.

These dialectical reversals also appear frequently in Sidney's pastorals. His melancholy shepherds "reply" to another herdsman's expression of bucolic ideals with a purely negating response, one that offers no counter-values but simply expresses a stubborn, despondent individualism and a refusal to enter the landscape. To Dorus' sonnet beginning,

Feede on my sheepe, my chardge my comforte feede,
With sonne's approache your pasture fertill growes,
O only sonne that suche a fruite can breede,

Phillisides answers,

Leave off my sheepe: it is not time to feede
My sonne is gonne, your pasture barrein growes
O cruell sonne thy hate this harme dothe breede.[15]

Nature cannot heal the troubled mind; instead the mind's affliction pollutes the pastoral world:

> The restfull Caves, now restlesse visions giue,
> In dales I see each way a hard assent:
> Like late mowne Meades, late cut from ioy I liue
> Alas sweet Brookes, doe in my teares augment.
> Rocks, woods, hills, caues, dales, meades, brookes aunswer mee:
> Infected mindes infect each things they see.[16]

In a later dialog, the old man, Geron, attributes such sufferings to the excessive passion of youth: "If that thy face were hid, or I were blinde,/ I yet would know a young man speaketh now, Such wandring reasons in thy speech I finde. . .Fondlings fonde, know not your owne desire. . ."[17] By the same process of reversal that transforms the landscape, the pastoral ideal of youth becomes an antitype. Daphnis' melancholy may be heroic, but it also fits a typical pattern of youthful neurosis.

In addition to youthful passion, another source of pastoral melancholy is the presence of death. "*Et in Arcadia Ego*" proclaims the inscription on the tomb in the famous paintings by Poussin, making the familiar bucolic admission that the golden world is not exempt from mortal reckoning.[18] Death's ironic triumph over youth's promise supplies the occasion for one of the most compelling of pastoral subgenres—the pastoral elegy. Like the love lament, this convention of complaint also hinges on a negation of the ideals of innocence. Caused by a specifically anti-pastoral emotion—the despair that accompanies bereavement—that negation likewise drains vitality from the idyllic landscape youth inhabits and turns it to a wilderness.

Theocritus' first Idyll again supplies the original model for this convention. In their imitations of his lament for Daphnis, many later writers—among them Vergil, Spenser, Sidney and Milton—exhibit the horror of death and meditate upon its meaning by focussing upon the destruction of youth, since all the living seem innocent in death's shadow and since all life appears like a green world before the final sunset.[19]

While the young swain complains about the destruction of the ideals of innocence, the old herdsman often sings sad songs mourning rather than celebrating the condition of experience. Vergil's first eclogue opens with another imitation of Theocritus—a landscape that contains, enfolds and absorbs its inhabitants: "You, Tityrus, under the spreading, sheltering beech,/ Tune woodland musings on a delicate reed."[20] But a sorrowful, antipastoral movement follows immediately, as old Meliboeus contrasts his friend's good fortune with his own impending exile. The beauty of home makes it all the more painful to take leave of. Meliboeus says farewell to the land with a Wordsworthian sadness "that lies too deep for tears":[21]

> Go now, my goats; once happy flock, move on.
> No more shall I, stretched out in a cavern green,
> Watch you, far off, on brambly hillsides hang.
> I'll sing no songs, nor shepherd you when you
> Browse on the flowering shrubs and bitter willows.[22]

This passage once again imitates Theocritus: the place in the first Idyll where Daphnis takes leave of his homeland:

> O wolves! O jackals! O bears that lie in the mountains!
> Farewell! No more will you see Daphnis the cowherd in the coppices,
> in the glades. . .no more. Farewell
> Arethusa, and streams that pour your waters clear down
> Thybris. . .This is I! This is Daphnis! Here I pastured
> my herds. Daphnis, who here watered my bulls and heifers!

The motifs and the sentence structure are similar, but the tone is very different. Instead of the boy's rebellious self-assertion in face of his fate, the old man's song of departure is passive and muted. The fault of Meliboeus' better world lies in its contingency, not its limits. The old man is alienated from the pastoral landscape not by restless inner aspirations to go beyond it, for his years have taught him to love life just as it is in Arcadia. The sources of chaos that create the gulf now come from without. Meliboeus is wrenched from the land by forces originating in the great world of Rome, influences of the *vita activa* over which as rustic and old man he has no control. In the aftermath of civil war his land has been appropriated and awarded to a veteran of the victorious army. His predicament resembles that of many an old dispossessed Renaissance rustic like Spenser's Melibee or Corin in *AYLI.* The mean estate's ideal of security is shattered. Politics rather than love is the anti-pastoral threat to the pastoral of age.

However, the old man's loss of pastoral felicity is caused not only by external civilization. It is also a function of nature itself. There is no mention of aging in Eclogue I, but Vergil introduces the melancholy motif of senescence in his portrait of another old man on the verge of exile, Moeris of Eclogue IX:

> Age steals all, even my wits. Oft I recall my
> boyish music set the lingering sun.
> Now all those songs forgotten! and my voice
> itself is gone—the wolves saw Moeris first.[24]

Political exile here is identified with the impending biological exile of death. The process of aging is symbolized by the traveller's approach to the tomb of Bianor. The road's bleakness, the gathering storm and the decay of memory intensify the beauty of half-forgotten snatches of youthful songs and of the landscape left behind.

Like the love complaint and the death elegy, the old man's complaint is also a distinct pastoral genre. The late latin poet Nemesianus expands Moeris' lament, and he in turn is imitated by Maximian and later by Sannazaro.[25] One scholar claims that Moeris' speech is the original inspiration of Colin Clout's lengthy elegy in the "December" eclogue of *The Shepheardes* Calender:[26]

So now my yeare drawes to his latter terme,
My spring is spent, my sommer burnt up quite:
My harueste hasts to stirre vp winter sterne,
And bids him clayme with rigorous rage hys right.
So nowe he stormes with many a sturdy stoure,
So nowe his blustring blast eche coste doth scoure.

The carefull cold hath nypt my rugged rynde,
And in my face deepe furrowes eld hath pight:
My head with hoary frost I fynd,
And by myne eie the Crow his clawe dooth wright.
Delight is layd abedde, and pleasure past,
No sunne now shines, cloudes han all ouercast.

Now leave ye shepheards boys your merry glee
My muse is hoarse and weary of thys stounde
Here will I hang my pipe upon this tree
Was never pype of reede did better sounde.
Winter is come that blowes the bitter blaste
And after Winter dreerie death does hast.

Adieu delights, that lulled me asleepe,
Adieu my deare, whose loue I bought so deare
Adieu my little Lambes and loued sheepe
Adieu ye Woodes that oft my witnesse were,
Adieu good Hobbinoll, that was so true,
Tell Rosalind her Colin bides her adieu.[27]

Spenser was indeed imitating Vergil in this passage—not only Moeris' speech but also the one of Moeliboeus cited earlier. But here, as well as in many other descriptions of old age in the *Calender,* he was combining traditional pastoral themes with the persistent English convention of old age elegy, a form equally popular among Renaissance and medieval poets. Thomas, Lord Vaux's "I Loathe that I did Love" is a typical example:

My lusts they do me leave,
My francies all be fled
And tract of time begins to weave
Grey hairs upon my head.

For age with stealing steps
Hath clawed me with his clutch,
And lusty life away she leaps,
As there had been none such.

My muse doth not delight
Me as she did before;
My hand and pen are not in plight
As they have been of yore.
. . .
The wrinkles in my brow
The furrows in my face,
Say, limping age will hedge him now
Where youth must give him place.[28]

Just as the ideal of youth has dual, negative and positive aspects, so does the archetype of old age. The astrological figure of Saturn, the wise old god identified with pastoral's Golden Age, is also represented by Kronos, or Father Time—the castrated and castrating ogre fiercely jealous of youth who consumes all that he has created.[29] Erikson alludes to the same dual aspect of the archetype when he defines the condition of old age as "a state of mind governed by struggle for Integrity versus a sense of Despair and Disgust. . ."[30]

The negative traits of old age—Despair, Disgust, Disdain and Dread—come to the fore in the anti-pastoral complaint of Wynken in the second eclogue of Drayton's *The Shepheardes Garland*. He replies to youth's mirth not by affirming the values of age but by regretting his own demise:

Indeed my Boy, my wits been all forlorne,
  My flowers decayd, with winter-withered frost,
My clowdy set eclips'd my cherefull morne,
  That Jewell gone wherein I joyed most.

My dreadful thoughts been drawen upon my face,
  In blotted lines with ages iron pen,
The lothlie morpheu saffroned the place,
  Where beuties damaske daz'd the eies of men. . .[31]

The negative, "saturnine" mood of this passage recalls the medieval poetry and inconography picturing old age as a gruesome *momento mori.* According to the theory of correspondances that dominated physiology and psychology until the seventeenth century, old age itself was identified with the melancholy disposition, since it was governed by the cold, dry melancholy humours of the body.[32] A person's outlook in the final stage of life could be assumed to be gloomy—at best one of pessimistic wisdom, but more likely an attitude of enfeebled despair:

Elde was paynted after this,
That shorter was a foot, iwys,
Than she was wont in her yonghede.
Unneth herself she mighte fede;
So feble and eke so old was she
That faded was al her beaute.
Ful salowe was waxen her colour;. . .
A fould, forwelked thyng was she
That whilom round and softe had be. . .

The tyme that eldeth our auncessours,
And eldith kynges and emperours,
And that us alle shal overcomen,
Er that deth us shal have nomen;
The time, that hath al in welde
To elden folk, had maad hir eelde. . .
These olde folk have alwey cold;
Her kynde is sich, whan they ben old.[33]

Traditional schemes of interpreting allegory attributed a specific eschatological meaning to such negative images of old age. They characterized the *vetus homo* or "old Adam" as the unregenerate human being who must undergo guilt and punishment for original sin until redeemed by Christ's sacrifice and rebirth.[34] Renaissance writers often exploited these negative connotations of old age with elaborate metaphorical paradoxes expressing anti-pastoral feelings of alienation in youth.

A typical design fitting this pattern is the multiple *adynata* in which positive youth is transformed into negative old age, while the garden is blasted into desert. Originally published in 1573, Phillipe Desportes' sonnet, "Je me veux rendre hermite et faire penitence," was translated by a number of English poets, including Sir Walter Ralegh. It expresses the passionate youth's intention to become a penitent hermit, but one who will gain neither peace, forgiveness nor wisdom:

Like to a Hermite poore in place obscure,
I meane to spend my daies of endles doubt,
To waile such woes as time cannot recure,
Where none but Loue shall euer finde me out.

My foode shall be of care and sorow made,
My drink nought else but teares falne from mine eies,
And for my light in such obscured shade,
The flames shal serue, which from my hart arise.

A gowne of graie, my bodie shall attire,
My staffe of broken hope whereon Ile Staie,
Of late repentance linckt with long desire
The couch is fram'de whereon my limbs Ile lay.
And at my gate dispaire shall linger still,
To let in death when Loue and Fortune will.[36]

The ideal of the old hermit's contemplative solitude here becomes a self-inflicted punishment, a symbol of the young man's saturnine desolation, guilt and despair. The negative hermit of this poem has a schematic relationship to the ideal of Milton's "Il Penseroso," discussed earlier. There the young man coming away to the hermitage finds a place which combines both pastoral ideals of youth and age in the neoplatonic *concordia discors* of the *puer senex.* But in Desportes' *discordia concors,* the same coupling of opposites expresses an amplified dissonance. I shall call this figure the *senex puer.* The young man, old before his time, rotten before he ripens, joins the negative aspects of both extreme stages of life into a logically and psychologically disturbing image that turns pastoral nature upside down:[37]

> As if my yeare were waste, and woxen old
> And yet alas, but now my spring begonne,
> And yet alas, yt is already donne.
> . . .
> All so my lustfull leafe is drye and sere
> My timely buds with wayling all are wasted:
> The blossome, which my braunch of youth did beare,
> With breathed sighes is blowne away and blasted.
> . . .
> My bloosmes that crowned were at firste,
> and promised of timely fruite such store,
> Are left both bare and barrein now at erst
> The flattering fruite is fallen to grownd before,
>   And rotten, ere they were halfe mellow ripe
>   My harvest wast, my hope away dyd wipe.[38]

It is with this conceit that Spenser opens *The Shepheardes Calender*. He uses the schematic reversal of rhetorical topoi, the double *adynaton* of *senex puer*. As I shall show in the final chapter of this book, this device not only portrays the protagonist's feeling of dislocation in the world, it also conveys to the reader a sense of time moving in two directions at once.[39]

* * *

The despair expressed by much pastoral poetry in reaction to its own utopian assumptions rarely sets the final tone of the Arcadian lyric, the eclogue or the collection. Even the most unrelenting of complaints usually ends on a note of resigned acceptance or future hope. The same natural rhythm that dictates "sun one day, rain the next," insures the eventual return of clear skies. Pastoral melancholy leads to two kinds of outcome, two ways the youthful or aged person alienated from his condition or environment can go. He can expend his lament and become reconciled to his place, or he can take counsel from grief and head elsewhere. Anti-pastoral sorrow is the prelude either to adjustment or to departure from the alternate world of Arcadia.

There are two basic phases to the emotional progression recently designated "the grief cycle."[40] First comes the sufferer's growing sensation of pain and isolation. The climax of that sensation issues in the expression of lamentation and mourning. Such expression often provides a feeling of release that allows for a sufferer's reverse movement of reintegration into his previous social and physical surroundings. Though the natural landscape of pastoral can neither supply the absolute nor undo the losses of amorous frustration, bereavement and the decline of powers in old age, it does provide a context in which the grief cycle can work itself out. As a setting of consolation that includes and absorbs sorrow, it regains the qualities of a chosen place, the virtues of a better world.

Ellen Zetzel Lambert has written about this process in a recent study of the genre of pastoral elegy:

> "The pastoral elegy. . .proposes no one solution to the questions raised by death, but rather a setting in which those questions may be posed, or better, "placed." It offers us a landscape. . .it remains a concrete, palpable world, a world in which the elegist can place diffuse, intangible feelings of grief and thereby win his release from suffering. . .it is the setting, the rural scene as it is composed by the poet and experienced by the herdsmen that consoles us."[41]

Death may assert its prerogatives in Arcadia, placing a tombstone upon the greensward, but the meadow surrounds it, and if not removing death's sting, at least can neutralize its venom. In his lament for Lycidas, Milton's speaker recites the traditional catalogue of flowers, and it is still the custom to lay bouquets on graves in expensively maintained parks. So appropriate is the natural landscape for mourning that the pastoral poet brings to it the most alien of beings, the apex of the *vita activa*: the king. And he dresses the royal corpse in shepherd's weeds to remind us of his common bond with all men and with the grass that withers.

The sorrow "placed" in the pastoral world is not only funereal, however. The herdsman's setting also consoles the pains of youth—love pangs, frustrated ambition, disillusionment; and the griefs of old age: exile, poverty, abuse and the approach of death. What about the landscape of rocks and trees and streams provides such solace? First, it is an escape from familiar reality—in Baudelaire's phrase, an "anywhere out of this world" where the distressed person constricted by pent-up feelings can find freedom to deliver his anguish. Since the worldly world clothes the nakedness of pain as well as pleasure with the garb of shame, grief, like erotic love, withdraws from the busy haunts of men to the privacy of the forest:

Oh Woods unto your walks my body hies,
To loose the trayterous bonds of tyring Loue
Where trees wher hearbs where flowers
Their native moisture poures
From foorth their tender stalks, to help mine eyes. . .
. . .
Thus weary in my walke, and wofull too,
I spend the day, fore-spent with daily greefe:
Each object of distresse
My sorrow doth expresse. . .[42]

And in addition to listening without offense, the natural setting, like a therapist or a friend, echoes back tormented feelings and assures the afflicted one he has been heard. Often such echoing goes further than mere passive reflection; it expresses total empathy, as nature joins the lament with its own display of turbulence:

Ah trees why fall your leaues so fast?
Ah Rocks, where are your roabes of mosse?
Ah Flocks, why stand you all agast?
  Trees, Rocks, and Flocks, what, are ye pensive for my losse?
. . .
Floods weepe their springs aboue their bounds,
And Eccho wailes to see my woe:
The roabe of ruthe dooth cloath the grounds,
  Floods, Eccho, grounds, why doo ye all these teares bestow?

The trees, the Rocks and Flocks replie,
The birds, the winds, the beasts report:
Floods, Eccho, grounds for sorrow crie,
  We grieve since Phillis nill kinde Damons loue consort.[43]

Pastoral's pathetic fallacy also gives solace to the elderly shepherd. The fading of light and warmth so often evoked at the end of pastorals of old age has the effect of a lullaby, changing fear of the dark into a welcoming of rest:

Still, you could take your rest with me tonight,
Couched on green leaves: there will be apples ripe,
Soft roasted chestnuts, plenty of pressed cheese.
Already roof tops in the distance smoke,
And lofty hills let fall their lengthening shade.[44]

This typical Vergillian conclusion, with its "surgamus" or invitation, "let us arise and go now," becomes the conventional manner of closing all later eclogues. Though the speakers have found no solution to their sufferings and conflicts, their encounter ends with a provisional reconciliation, a recognition of human contact in creature comfort.[45] By making the reader's point of view quickly recede from foreground to setting, this same device "places" the characters in a larger prospect like figures in a Chinese or Flemish landscape, reducing both their hopes and torments into proportion with the vast panorama that surrounds them.[46]

The pastoral setting consoles with instruction as well as sympathy. The pains of youth and age are due as much to the mental discomfort of disappointment and disorientation as to the actual deprivations of love, vigor or homeland. The sorrow of intellectual disillusionment is compensated by an awakened awareness of the necessity of cyclical change in the surrounding landscape. In observing the proportion between his own misfortunes and nature's decline, the sufferer learns the inevitability of loss, and hence is relieved of an accompanying sense of guilt or incongruity. Such relief can be equated with the familiar "consolation of philosophy." But pastoral solace itself is not so much a Boethian sense of the futility of all earthly things as a stoic and epicurean prescription of *amor fati*: an affirmation of what is inevitable and therefore ordered.

In the passage from "December" quoted earlier, Spenser makes Colin Clout an exemplum of this proportion between the inner life of man and the rhythms of nature. In mourning the decline from youth to age, from initiation to exile, from expectation to disappointment, and in equating these with the seasonal progression from spring to winter, Colin reveals the workings of nature within himself. There is no more obvious yet subtle evidence of the human being's place in nature and nature's place in the human being than the life cycle. An awareness that the states of our bodies, our behavior, our emotions and our ideas are all deeply conditioned by our ages is an awareness of our subjection to fate. The facts of life—birth, copulation and death—are the facts of the life cycle; and the life cycle, which includes death, is the underlying order of the pastoral world.

The consolatory wisdom of embracing one's fate is traditionally derived from the experience of old age. It emerges in the avoidance of becoming "the foreman of Fortune" that Spenser's Thenot has learned in his "thrice threttie years"; it is the humble "wisdom through suffering" of the old men and women in Aeschylus' and Sophocles' tragic choruses; it is the meagre glimmer of sense that rides out the brutal "natural" storm that swallows old Gloucester and Lear: "Ripeness is all." Erik Erikson arrives at the same notion of *amor fati* when he uses the word *integrity* to describe the critical achievement of the final stage of life, wherein ". . .may gradually ripen the fruit of all these seven stages. . .an experience which conveys some world order and spiritual sense, no matter how dearly paid for. . .the acceptance of one's one and only life cycle. . .as something that had to be and that by necessity permitted no substitutions."[47]

For those whose pastoral sorrows will not yield to an acceptance of their place in the cosmic order, the only alternatives are despair or departure. If the first and formative stirrings of the pastoralist's impulse takes expression as a seductive invitation to come away to the natural paradise, the final and most withering statements of antipastoral melancholy are songs of longing for escape from a rustic penal colony. One need not be as emphatic or specific as Eleanor Winston Leach in her assertion that "an ultimate turning back to the great world is the common denominator of pastoral literature," to recognize that forsaking the pastoral world is as conventional as going there.[48]

The death of youth lamented by the pastoral elegy leads a number of writers to seek an alternative to the natural cycle of generativity. As early as the second century B. C., Bion's "Lament for Moschus" complains that this cycle doesn't provide comfort for human mortality but instead a cruel reminder of the finality of death:

> Alas, when in the garden wither the mallows, the green celery, and the luxuriant curled anise, they live again thereafter and spring up another year, but we men, we that are tall and strong, we that are wise, when once we die, unhearing sleep in the hollow earth, a long sleep without end or wakening.[49]

Bion affirms human strenth and intellect as more precious than anything else in nature, and for that very reason more vulnerable. The perception of nature as inimical to the human leaves the shepherd narrators of neo-Latin pastoral elegies by Petrarch, Boccaccio, Castiglione and Sceve standing as separate, aloof and desolate as Vergil's Gallus in landscapes pictured as barren strands and rocky deserts.[50] Disenchanted with life on earth, they find some meagre hope in the prospect of reuniting with the deceased in the promised land beyond the grace:

> After he became wearied with the groves and the long toil, he was departed, never to return; with winged course he flies forth through trackless ways to the mountains. Thence from the highest summit he looks down and beholds our cares and our confusion, and how great is the distress of the wood that he once ruled. He speaks with Jove and to him entrusts the bereaved fold. Argus, farewell! Brief the delay, we shall all follow thee.[51]

But consolation of this sort only broadens the gulf between the good life and the shepherd's life in nature. The one who has departed is fortunate; those who remain behind have learned the lesson of the vanity of any earthly paradise, *vanitas, vanitatis*.

This is a characteristically medieval Christian application of the anti-pastoral theme. Disillusionment with what once appeared as an ideal place drives home the homiletic prescription not to store up treasures in this world where they are liable to rust and rot. Life in nature, like all mortal life, is fallen and corrupt; the only better world lies not in the peripheries but beyond them. Renaissance pastoral elegies preach the same moral. In both, the direction of movement is toward "the other groves and other streams" of the green pastures of heaven.[52]

A second destination of escape *from* the pastoral landscape is the golden eternity of works of art. Sidney proposes this alternative in Dicus' pastoral elegy—#75 in the "Fourth Eclogues" of the *Arcadia*:

Time ever old, and yonge is still revolved
Within it selfe, and never taketh ende:
But mankind is for aye to nought resolved.
The filthy snake her aged coate can mende,
And getting youth againe, in youth doth flourish:
But unto Man, age ever death doth sende.
The very trees with grafting we can cherish,
So that we can long time produce their time:
But Man which helpeth them, helplesse must perish.
Thus, thus the mindes, which over all doo clime,
When they by yeares' experience get best graces,
Must finish then by death's detested crime.
We last short while, and build long lasting places;

Ah let us all against foule Nature crie:
We Nature's workes doo helpe, she us defaces.
For how can Nature unto this reply?
That she her child, I say, her best child killeth?
Your doleful tunes sweete Muses now apply.[53]

Like Bion, Dicus rejects both pastoral ideals and consolations. Time, Nature and the life cycle all name the same malevolent opponent of the trapped human spirit. Not only does youth pass, never to return. Just when we are old enough to harvest the wisdom of experience, Nature steals our lives out from under us. Our only hope lies in the mind's ability to "climb over all" and "build long-lasting places" to compensate for Nature's defects; but she cruelly undermines those efforts. However, through the despair here emerges a set of values more substantial than a passing mood of depression. Counter to the pleasure principle of youth and old age's pastoral of the mean estate, they affirm the high aspiration of art and the monuments of civilization.[54]

The same sense of the futility of the life cycle coupled with the aspiration to escape from nature into art shapes the conclusion of *The Shepheardes Calender*. Following the *senex puer* Colin Clout's despairing farewell to a pastoral world that only disappointed all the hopes it raised in him, Spenser appends to the final eclogue the Horatian affirmation that ". . .all thinges perish and come to theyr last end, but workes of learned wits and monuments of Poetry abide for euer."[55] And Yeats' familiar "Sailing to Byzantium" contains a modern constellation of the same group of anti-pastoral motifs: the speaker forsaking the country of youth and old age in search for an elsewhere that will redeem its failures in the glories of art:

That is no country for old men. The young
In one another's arms, birds in the trees
—Those dying generations—at their song,
The salmon falls, the mackerel crowded seas
Fish, flesh and fowl, commend all summer long
Whatever is begotten, born and dies.
Caught in that sensual music all neglect
Monuments of unaging intellect.

An aged man is but a paltry thing,
A tattered coat upon a stick, unless
Soul clap its hands and louder sing
For every tatter in its mortal dress,

> Nor is there singing school but studying
> Monuments of its own magnificence
> And therefore I have sailed the seas and come
> To the holy city of Byzantium.[56]

Thus, we come full circle: after outlining pastoral ideals that identify nature, youth and old age with a utopian good life, here we find the green and golden worlds to be sundered and antithetical—just as they are in the passage from Sidney's "Defense" with which this study opened:

> Nature never set forth the earth in so rich tapestry as divers poets have done; neither pleasant rivers, fruitful trees, sweet smelling flowers, nor whatsoever else may make the too-much loved earth more lovely; her world is brazen, the poets only deliver a golden.

The young in one another's arms, the birds in the trees, the pleasant rivers, the sweet smelling flowers as well as the dying generations and the tattered coat upon the stick are all brazen; only the words of the poet deliver the Byzantine golden frieze. And yet the same inescapable ambivalence toward nature and art that permeates the pastoral-antipastoral dialectic manifests itself in both these passages. For green and golden worlds are ultimately interrelated and interdependent: what the poet sets forth in a rich tapestry is "the earth"; and what, "once out of nature" in the holy city, the golden bird sings of is "past, passing and to come."[57]

To the old man, like Yeats' speaker or Colin Clout, escape from the pastoral world implies transcendance: passage beyond the earth to a city of god or to the enamelled court of an eternal emperor. But the young shepherd has a third alternative. He can leave the countryside and make his way to an actual urban environment. This is the course that old Piers urges upon Cuddie in the "October" eclogue:

> Abandon then the base and viler clowne,
> Lyft vp thy selfe out of the lowly dust:

> And sing of bloody Mars, of wars, of giusts
> Turne thee to those, that weld the awful crowne
> . . .
> There may thy Muse display her fluttryng wing,
> and stretch herselfe at large from East to West. . .

As I have shown in chapter two, such departure from the countryside and entry into the central world of the *vita activa* coincides with youth's passage from childhood to adulthood. Though the transition from young love to adult marriage becomes explicit in the nuptial rites that mark the departure from Arcadia in works like *Daphnis and Chloe* and *As You Like It*, for the solitary young artist at the end of his childhood, the nature of the mature state he is about to enter remains undisclosed. The melancholy shepherd does, however, unmistakeably experience discomfort in the rustic environment of youth. The sense of the bucolic world's limitations expressed in anti-pastoral complaints—the frustration with its constriction, fragility and simplicity—may be a product of adolescent growing pains, but those pains are intense enough to feel more like the onset of death than of growth.

> Our Muses are perished; withered are our laurels. . .shepherds have lost their song; flocks and herds scarcely find pasture among the meadows and with muddying feet for scorn they roil the crystal springs; nor do they deign anymore, seeing themselves to lack of milk, to nourish their own offspring. Likewise the beasts abandon their wonted dens; the birds take flight from their sweet nests; the hard and insensate trees cast down their fruits upon the earth before their due maturity; and the tender flowers all together wither away throughout the saddened countryside.[58]

Thus at the end of his book, Sannazaro's young narrator leaves the woods on his way back to court, experiencing not so much the exuberance of commencement as the melancholy of valediction.

As Sidney places "Dicus #75" just before his company's final departure from Arcadia, and Spenser places the lament for Dido in the eleventh month, so Sannazaro sets a pastoral elegy immediately prior to this concluding passage. The repeated juxtaposition of the death of a young person and the with-drawel from the pastoral world suggests their possible ritual equality. Mircea Eliade states that "in scenarios of initiatory rites, 'death' corresponds to the temporary return to chaos; hence it is the paradigmatic expression of the *end of a mode of being*—the mode of ignorance and the child's irresponsibility." This identification is ". . .characteristic of archaic mentality: the belief that a state cannot be changed without first being annihilated. . .without the child's dying to childhood. . . In modern terms we could say that initiation puts an end to natural man and introduces the novice to culture."[55] Insofar as the eclogues are the product of a writer at the start of his career, the three alternative escapes from Arcadia proposed in bucolic poetry—passages from earth to heaven, from nature to art and from youth to maturity—all are equivalent metaphors for the end of the beginning and the start of the poet's "major phase."

This conclusion of the last three chapters' discussion of the connection among the rustic motifs of pastoral, its primitivistic ideals of happiness and its thematic preoccupation with youth and old age again highlights the importance of the mode's projection of temporal processes onto a spatial map. By postulating two contiguous worlds of city and country, pastoral conventions articulate a set of contraries out of which emerge a range of philosophical definitions and ethical judgements. The idea of human culture—what in the Renaissance was called the "artificial"—takes shape by being physically localized in a place opposite to the green world of nature. Once defined, each world is judged by reference to the other. Civilization is bad because it suppresses natural feeling or is dominated by Fortune; Nature is bad because it violates human aspiration and accomplishments embodied in civilization. The equally conventional pastoral dichotomy of periphery and center of the human life cycle enriches these definitions and judgements. The pastoral stages of youth and old age are distinguished from adulthood by their non-worldly pursuits, which are judged superior or inferior to its active, civilized life.

In addition to delineating opposition, the dichotomy of country and city worlds makes possible a commerce and communication across borders, with the result that a simple dualistic pattern yields to greater complexity. A dissatisfied person can travel from one world to another and thereby change his nature. Insofar as he rejects his home setting and longs for the opposite, he violates the separation between worlds at the same time as emphasizing it. As we have shown in this chapter, such dissatisfaction and leaning over the border is in many ways a consequence of the existence an alternative world where the grass is always greener, the gold always brighter.

The inevitability of movement between the two worlds of city and country suggest that the pastoral-anti-pastoral dichotomy is more than a dichotomy; it is analogous to the opposing extremes of a cycle of changes. Thus the metaphor of spatial separation requires modification. A succession of contraries interlocked with one another is better represented by a metaphor of temporal opposition, like the stages of the cycle. The contrary states of youth, maturity and old age carry their opposites within them; at any moment each is residual with the past, pregnant with the future. Like the other natural processes that provide its backdrop and like the emotional processes which it voices, pastoral's movement is by contraries, and out of its movement contraries emerge. The dialectic of pastoral-anti-pastoral conventions and its cycle of conflicting judgements about country and city is congruent with the debate-like retention and rejection of the past that characterizes all human aging and growth.

NOTES

[1] *Vergil's* Eclogues: *Landscapes of Experience* (Ithaca and London: Cornell University Press, 1974), p. 37. "Only" in this sentence is a broad exaggeration. In "The Renaissance Imagination: Second World and Green World," *Centennial Review* 9(1965):36-78, Harry Berger Jr. discusses the way all fictions have a tendency at their conclusions to destroy the "heterocosm" or other world of imaginary reality they create. In *Self-Consuming Artifacts* (Berkeley: University California Press, 1972), Stanley

Fish sees such dissolution of the poem's reality deliberately employed in seventeenth-century hieroglyphic and meditational verse. The self-negating dialectic of verse debate is further discussed in the next chapter of this study.

[2] "Sunday Morning," in *The Collected Poems of Wallace Stevens* (New York: Alfred A. Knopf, 1961), p. 66.

[3] *The Poems of Theocritus,* translated by Anna Rist (Chapel Hill: University of North Carolina Press, 1978), *Idyll* 4.43, p. 59. This passage's significance is pointed out by Ellen Zetzel Lambert in *Placing Sorrow: A Study of the Pastoral Elegy Convention from Theocritus to Milton* (Chapel Hill: University of North Carolina Press, 1976), p. xvii.

[4] "The Nimph's Reply," *England's Helicon,* ed. Hyder Edward Rollins (Cambridge: Harvard University Press, 1935) I, 185.

[5] *As You Like It,* II, v, 47ff.

[6] Sir Phillip Sidney, "Yee Gote-heard Gods, that love the grassie mountaines," *The Poems of Sir Phillip Sidney,* ed. William A. Ringler, Jr. (Oxford: Clarendon Press, 1962), pp. 81, 82.

[7] H. R. Patch has shown how the ideal world of pastoral is generated by a "negative formula"—a dialectical reversal of the description of the actual world. *The Other World According to Descriptions in Medieval Literature* (Cambridge: Harvard University Press, 1950), pp. 12ff.

[8] see, for instance, Erik H. Erikson, "Youth: Fidelity and Diversity" in *Youth: Change and Challenge,* ed. Erik H. Erikson (New York: Basic Books, 1963), pp. 15ff.; Kenneth Kenniston, "Youth as a 'New' Stage of Life," *American Scholar,* 1970, pp. 636-650; James Hillman, "Senex and Puer," in *Puer Papers,* ed. Cynthia Giles (Irving, TX: Spring Publications, 1979), p. 23ff.

[9] "The Stages of Life," from *Modern Man in Search of a Soul* (London and New York, 1933) reprinted in *The Portable Jung,* ed. Joseph Campbell (New York: The Viking Press, 1971, reprinted by Penguin Books, 1976), p. 9.

[9a] Harry Berger Jr. develops an analogous conceptual approach in "Mode and Diction in *SC.*" He sees "the paradise principle"—the longing for paradise—as the "psychological basis of the pastoral retreat." Corollary to this is the "have-not principle," which accounts for the hostility and depression of those characters who expect to find paradise in the pastoral world and then suffer the frustration of disillusionment. (*Modern Philology* 67 (1969) p. 145)

[10] Barnabe Googe, *Eglogs, Epytaphes, and Sonettes,* ed. E. A. Arber (London, 1871), "Egloga tertia," p. 42.

[11] *The Singer of the* Eclogues: *A Study of Vergilian Pastoral* (Berkeley: University of California, 1979), p. 133.

[11a] Anonymous, "Eclogue intituled Cuddy," in *English Pastoral Poetry,* ed. Frank Kermode (New York: Barnes and Noble, 1952), p. 165.

[12] translation of Anna Rist, p. 33.

[13] Ernst Robert Curtius, *European Literature and the Latin Middle Ages* (New York, 1963), pp. 94-98, discusses the history of the figure's uses.

[14] 11. 35-43. This and the following passage (11. 50-54) translated by Paul Alpers, *The Singer of the* Eclogues (Berkeley: University of California Press, 1979). All later citations from *The Eclogues* are from this translation.

[15] *The Poems of Sir Phillip Sidney,* p. 43.

[16] p. 147.

[17] p. 25.

[18] Erwin Panofsky, "*Et in Arcadia Ego*: Poussin and the Elegaic Tradition," in *Meaning in the Visual Arts* (New York: Anchor, 1955), pp. 295-320.

[19] Vergil's Daphnis in Eclogue V has been traditionally supposed to represent Julius Caesar. Marot, Sceve and Ronsard each wrote elegies lamenting the death of royalty. See Lambert, pp. 107-124.

[20] Alpers translation, p. 11.

[21] Wordsworth took this image of goats hanging on a crag to illustrate the creative powers of the imagination in the Preface to the 1815 edition of his *Poetical Works*, edited by Ernest de Selincourt, vol. 2 (Oxford, 1944) p. 436. Cited by Alpers, p. 94.

[22] Alpers translation, (I, 74-78), p. 15.

[23] Idyll I, 122-128, trans. Anna Rist, p. 32.

[24] Alpers translation. (IX, 51-55), p. 57.

[25] G. R. Coffman, "Old Age from Horace to Chaucer," *Speculum*, IX, 1934, pp. 249-278.

[26] Paul Alpers, "The Eclogue Tradition and the Nature of Pastoral," *CE*, 34, 1972, p. 365-366.

[27] "December," 11. 127-155 in *The Works of Edmund Spenser: A Variorum Edition; The Minor Poems*, eds. Charles Grosvenor Osgood and Henry Gibbons Lotspeich (Baltimore: Johns Hopkins Press, 1943), I, 117-8. All later references to this edition.

[28] Thomas, Lord Vaux, "The Aged Lover Renounceth Love," *The Poems of Lord Vaux*, ed. Larry P. Vonalt, (Denver: Alan Swallow, 1960), p. 29.

[29] James Hillman, p. 16; also R. Klibansky, E. Panofsky, and F. Saxl, *Saturn and Melancholy* (London: Nelson and sons, 1964).

[30] Erik H. Erikson, "Reflections on Dr. Borg's Life Cycle," in *Adulthood* (New York, Norton and Co. 1978), p. 16.

[31] *Works of Michael Drayton*, vol. V., ed. Kathleen Tillotson and B. H. Newdigate (Oxford: Oxford University Press, 1961), p. 50, 11. 13-20.

[32] Lawrence Babb, *The Elizabethan Malady: A Study of Melancholia in English Literature from 1580 to 1642* (East Lansing: Michigan State University Press, 1951), pp. 11-13.

[33] *The Romaunt of the Rose*, 11. 349-412, translated by Geoffrey Chaucer in *The Works of Geoffrey Chaucer*, ed. F. N. Robinson (Boston: Houghton Mifflin, 1957), pp. 568-9.

[34] Robert P. Miller, "The Scriptural Eunuch and Chaucer's Pardoner," in Schoek and Taylor, *Chaucer Criticism* (Terre Haute: University of Notre Dame Press, 1960), p. 221.

[36] *The Poems of Sir Walter Ralegh*, edited by Agnes Latham (Cambridge: Harvard University Press, 1962), p. 11.

[37] The reversal of the pastoral of solitude is a traditional bucolic pattern. Sidney's Dorus hints at the possible drawbacks of this perfect place in the refrain to his song of praise quoted earlier: "No danger to thy selfe if be not in thy selfe." Petrarch, who originated "the pastoral of self" in his *Life of Solitude* later described the morbid self-obsession and hopeless longings for his beloved that invaded the peace of his sheltered retreat. The isolation which at first brought him into closer rapport with God and nature soon turned to sloth and despair:

> Why, do you not see that if a man bears his wound with him, a change of scene is but an aggravation of his pain and not a means of healing it?. . . In whatever place you are, to whatever side you turn, you will behold the face, you will hear the voice of her whom you have left. . .do you imagine that love is to be

extinguished by subterfuges like this? Believe me, it will rather burn more fiercely.

Petrarch's Secret or the Soul's conflict with Passion, trans. William H. Draper (London, 1911), pp. 141, 143, cited in Judy Zahler Kronenfeld, "The Treatment of Pastoral Ideals in *AYLI*," Stanford Diss. 1970., p. 213.

[38] "December," 97-108.

[39] Studies by Babb, Saxl and Kronenfeld have all shown that the negativity of these melancholy characters was itself a popular Renaissance ideal. The saturnine temperament and mood was often considered a badge of genius, especially in neoplatonic circles. Indeed the melancholy posture became not only an expression of real emotional distress but a fashionable affectation. English observers attributed the trend to the corrupt influence of continental models, and often satirized it, as in this dialogue between Rosalind and Jaques in *AYLI*:

Ros.: They say you are a melancholy fellow
Jaques: I am so: I do love it better than laughing. . .
. . .Why, 'tis good to be sad and say nothing. . .
. . .it is a melancholy of mine own, compounded of many simples, extracted from many objects, and indeed the sundry contemplation of my travels, in which my often rumination wraps me in a most humorous sadness. . .
Ros.: Farewell, Monsieur Traveller. Look you lisp and wear
strange suits; disable all the benefits of your own country; be out of love with your nativity, and almost chide God for making you that countenance you are; or I will scare think you have swam in a gondola. . . (IV, i, 2-34).

In practise then, the contrast between the *puer senex* and the *senex puer* was often blurred. By indulging himself as the latter, the young man aspired to reach the heights of the former.

[40] See Robert Jay Lifton, *The Broken Connection: On Death and the Continuity of Life* (New York: Simon and Shuster, 1979), pp. 195-99.

[41] *Placing Sorrow,* pp. xii-xiv.

[42] Ignoto, "The Sheepheards sorrow for his Phaebes disdaine," *England's Helicon,* p. 108.

[43] Thomas Lodge, "The Sheepheard *Damons* Passion," *England's Helicon,* p. 91.

[44] Eclogue I, conclusion, Alpers translation, p. 15.

[45] In *Vergil's Pastoral Art: Studies in the Eclogues* (Princeton: Princeton University Press, 1970), Michael Putnam argues that this consolatory conclusion is to be taken ironically. Putnam claims that the fortunate Tityrus' failure to sincerely commiserate with Meliboeus' suffering forces us to read the first eclogue as bitter satire. (pp. 12, 329). But such a reading is only partial no matter how admirably defended. Our sympathy toward Meliboeus, like our sympathy for other Vergillian victims of historical conflict, does not mean that we take sides. The injustice of the two old men's portions and the inevitability of the approaching doom of one of them adds a poignant intensity to the crepuscular scene—an indifferent beauty like that of nature itself.

[46] This is the same tone that concludes Steven's "Sunday Morning," a poem that takes most of its themes and images and Vergillian tone from the pastoral elegy.

[47] *Childhood and Society* (New York: Norton, 2nd ed. 1963), p. 268. This wisdom of age is quite close to the ideals of experience outlined in the previous chapter. Depending on context, it is either a positive affirmation of the special value and prerogative of old age, or, it is, as here a more tentative resignation and acceptance of it.

[48] *Landscapes of Experience*, p. 37.

[49] *Greek Bucolic Poets*, ed. and trans. A. S. F. Gow (Cambridge, Eng., 1953), p. 134.

[50] Lambert, *Placing Sorrow*, pp. 51 ff.

[51] Petrarch, *Bucolicum Carmen*, second eclogue, 11. 115-21, cited and translated by Lambert, p. 59.

[52] But they usually conclude with a second reversal of tone which conveys a less pessimistic outlook toward life on earth. In "Lycidas," for example, the apotheosis of the lost friend not only heightens Christian faith in the hereafter, it also redeems the fallen world:

> So Lycidas, sunk low, but mounted high
> Through the dear might of him that walk'd the waves,
> Where other groves, and other streams along
> With *Nectar* pure his oozy Locks he laves. . .
> Now Lycidas the Shepherds weep no more;
> Henceforth thou art the Genius of the shore,
> In thy large recompense, and shalt be good
> To all that wander in that perilous flood.

By dissolving the isolation of the mourner, reaffirming the community of survivors, and declaring the continuity between natural and eternal life, this final resolution of his grief allows the mourner to go on living "with eager thoughts. . .tomorrow to fresh woods and pastures new." And so, once the death of Spenser's Dido has warned the shepherds of "the trustlesse state of earthly things," she becomes the tutelary deity of Arcadia. In the final stanzas of the elegy, her benevolent influence resurrects fallen nature with a new dispensation, transposing the "carefull verse" of complaint into the "ioyfull verse" of celebration.

[53] *The Poems of Sir Phillip Sidney*, p. 127.

[54] This same answer to the aging process is stated by the young-old narrator of Shakespeare's sonnets 63-73.

[55] Translated or glossed thus by E. K. The actual text of the final emblem remains conjectural. *The Minor Poems*, I, 467.

[56] *The Collected Poems of William Butler Yeats* (New York: MacMillan, 1956), p. 191.

[57] Yeats, p. 192

[58] Ralph Nash, ed. *Arcadia and Piscatorial Eclogues* by Jacopo Sannazaro, (Detroit: Wayne State Press, 1960), p. 152-3.

[55] Mircea Eliade, *Birth and Rebirth: The Meanings of Initiation in Human Cultures*, trans. Willard Trask (New York: Harper Bros. 1958), pp. xiv-xv.

4

"Youthe and Elde are often at Debaat": Medieval *Conflictus* and Renaissance Pastoral Debate

Upon his first arrival in Arcadia, Spenser's Sir Calidore delivers an after-dinner speech in praise of "the happie life/Which shepheardes leade, withoute debate or bitter strife."[1] Addressing his rustic hosts on a full stomach, he declaims the familiar outsider's conception of the pastoral world as a place of unperturbed pleasures and simple satisfactions, a fantasyland of heart's desire.[2] But the author of *The Faerie Queene* then subjects the young knight to a series of debate-like encounters and inner conflicts within the confines of the green world that correct this callow conception of bucolic life. Likewise, much recent criticism has moved beyond a simple, idyllic notion of the genre and has come to recognize the central role played by the juxtaposition of opposing points of view in all pastoral; indeed scholars have often used the term "debate" to characterize the structure of statement and counter-statement typical of pastoral works:[3]

> The moral debates are real and exploratory, not staged, debates between pastoral perspectives of varying but plausible legitimacy. . .It is the major purpose of the moral debates, therefore, to explore the conflict of perspectives and meanings that, by the time of the Renaissance, pastoral was fitted to express.[4]

Indispensable as the term has become to analyze, say, the pastorals of Spenser or Marvell, practically no attention has been paid to its literal meaning or its derivation.[5] The word "debate," as it is used loosely here to name a literary dialogue between opposing speakers, descends from *debat* or *debaat,* a Middle English word which refers specifically to a formal poetic convention. This convention evolved out of the classical eclogue, became widely popular during the middle ages, and then lost its generic identity, but continued to survive during the Renaissance in the guise of pastoral debate. This essay argues that the explicitly articulated structure of medieval verse debate remains an essential formal model for Elizabethan pastoral poetry, first because that particular structure expresses the mode's inherent thematic antinomies, and second, because that same structure embodies the conflict of opposites that Renaissance writers found to be the formal principle of all human experience.[6] An implication of this thesis guides the essay's analysis of particular poems: knowledge of the rules governing medieval verse debate can illuminate the practice and intentions of Renaissance pastoralists.

Although there are no modern critical studies of pastoral debate per se, the genre was held in great esteem by Tudor writers—as attested by its ubiquity in song books and collections of eclogues. Its most celebrated example, the shepherd-nymph dialogue by Marlowe and Ralegh, first appeared in an anthology containing twenty-eight additional pastoral debates. Sidney's *Arcadia* includes eighteen; and, out of the twelve eclogues of *The Shepheardes Calender,* five follow this convention.[7] Shakespeare's purest pastoral work, *As You Like It,* is filled with dramatic debates, and its overall structure has reminded many readers of the debate's balanced consideration of topics from opposing points of view.

In order to focus inquiry into such a large genre, I have limited my sampling of pastoral debates to the thematically defined subgroup of conflicts of youth and age. But this essay's analysis of formal structure is drawn from and applies to pastoral debates on other subjects as well: summer vs. winter, body vs. soul, passion vs. reason, ambition vs. humility, leisure vs. work, city vs. country, or to bed vs. not to bed. Of all these topics, youth vs. age is the most familiar of traditional rhetorical topoi, and it also brings into sharpest relief the central thematic concerns of pastoral.[8]

* * *

"Amant alternae camenae"—the muses love alternating songs—says Vergil's Palaemon, inviting his companion to share in the composition of poetry inspired by the landscape.[9] The ensuing amoebic contest, in which the singers try to outdo each other as they trade symmetrical lines, has been a familiar feature of the pastoral eclogue since Theocritus. J.C. Scaliger, the sixteenth century scholar, saw in this bucolic convention a literary imitation of the verse debates of primitive peoples.

Scaliger surmised that all later poetry evolved from elements of these contests.[10] His speculations were echoed by the Romantic critics, Uhland and Grimm, who found the ultimate source of the lyric in the ritual songs sung during folk festivals of *Renouveau* celebrating the passing of winter and the rebirth of spring.[11] Such songs represent the oscillations of the seasons and other natural polarities as a battle of mythical creatures.

In light of those subsequent developments, however, a crucial generic distinction needs to be drawn between the purely playful and stylistic nature of the amoebic contests and the more serious conceptual and ethical content of true pastoral debate. E.K., the commentator of *The Shepheardes Calender,* makes such a distinction, calling the former "recreative" and the latter "moral" eclogues.[12] Nowhere in classical pastoral can such a real debate be found. Rather the first literary precedent for moral eclogues appears in one of Aesop's fables, a verbal battle of winter and spring. "Winter scorns spring because of its mildness and amiability, while before him people must tremble; Springtime takes this condemnation as praise, since the very characteristics for which he is scorned make him beloved by people, whereas winter is hated."[13] Here we find generic features absent in Theocritus and Vergil: the articulation of systematically matched lists of contraries, the emphasis on abstract qualities rather than individuals, a logical sequence of statement and refutation, and an interest in the relativity of perspectives stemming from descriptions of the same reality from opposite points of view.

Plato's *Phaedrus* also provides a structural model for the pastoral debate.[14] It opens with a panoply of bucolic motifs: a young man and an old come away from the city to a rural landscape, a *locus amoenus* that provides the leisure for both erotic dalliance and detached contemplation. Such a retreat is conducive to the dialectical consideration of abstract issues—in this case conflicting concepts of eros associated with body and soul, passion and reason, rhetoric and philosophy.[15] As Wesley

Trimpi has observed, pastoral retains this function as the setting for exploratory debate throughout the middle ages and the Renaissance:

> The part that the *locus amoenus* plays in the discursive activities of the Muses, whether in the *Phaedrus,* the *De Oratore,* or the *Decamerone,* is not primarily as a setting for physical comfort as opposed to discomfort, but for the contemplative as opposed to the active life.[16]

Such withdrawal into a green world permits the mind to play with conflicting ideas and values without the necessity of arriving at a conclusion or of finally taking sides. This method of considering and arguing issues impartially from both sides of the question—*in utramque partem*—became, under the influence of the Platonic Academy, a basic principle of the later humanist tradition.[17]

The earliest extant medieval eclogue was written at the ninth-century court of Charlemagne by Alcuin, a monk who also produced a seminal treatise on dialectic.[18] But though his *Conflictus Veris et Hiemis* was intended as pastoral—another title is *Vergilis de Hime et Vere*—in tone, structure, atmosphere and characterization, this poem is unlike anything in Vergil or Theocritus. Instead of a slice of rural life and a subtle dramatization of the interaction between rustics, the work presents a systematic discussion of a single subject, in formal symmetrical speeches by allegorical figures. The *Conflictus* is an early example of a new medieval genre, the verse debate, or *Streitgedicht*—a convention that metamorphosed out of the classical eclogue. For the Carolingean poet like Alcuin or the author of *Ecloga Theoduli,* "pastoral" has lost the sense of concrete physical place so strong in classical writers. The "other world" becomes mythical and formulaic, the territory of dream vision and allegory, a rhetorical more than a geographic topos. This change may be partially due to the deurbanization of medieval society, which, during the ninth century was unlikely to provoke nostalgic yearnings for a less civilized mode of existence. It can also be attributed to the anti-mimetic, formalistic and disputatious tendencies of all medieval culture.

By the high middle ages, the idea of continuity with classical pastoral has been forgotten, and the verse debate comes into its own as a distinct genre. It grows in popularity both as a Latin and a vernacular form, bearing a babel of different names throughout Europe: Altercatio, Conflictus, Dialogus, Disputatio, Certamen, Causa, Colloquium, Comparatio, Contentio, Judicum, Lis Pugna, Rixa, Controversia, Jeu parti, Partimen, Tenso, Serventes, Lauda, Pastourelle, Streitgedicht, Streitrang, Pregunta, Debaat, Flyting and Ressonyng.[19] The opposition of youth and age, spring and winter, innocence and experience remain the most popular of themes, but the genre accomodates every possible issue on which two sides can be taken: Judaism vs. Christianity, thrift vs. generosity, wine vs. water, divine vs. human love, heterosexual vs. homosexual love, lentil soup vs. lentil puree.[20] And yet, though the debate's ancestry is forgotten, a trace of its lineage remains. For whether in grand doctrinal disputes like *Winnour and Waystere* or in the brief stark encounter of "The Ressonyng betuix Aige and Yowth," the poet always sets the scene of the verbal battle with a springtime trip into the country.

With few exceptions, modern scholarship has failed to recognize this process of literary evolution and has instead assumed that the pastoral mode and the eclogue form died out during the middle ages, only to be reborn suddenly with the Renaissance revival of the classics.[21] In line with this theory, Petrarch is accurately described as the first modern pastoralist, for his twelve *Aeglogae* recapture some of the spirit and texture of classical bucolic verse in their evocation of particulars of the Italian countryside.[22] But ignoring the continuity between classical eclogue and medieval debate has caused a number of critics to credit—or debit—Petrarch with first introducing satirical moral concerns, a debate structure and a querulous tone into the Arcadian realm.[23] Rather than introducing it, however, Petrarch was in fact drawing back from the argumentative style which he had inherited from his predecessors; it was this very de-emphasis on argument that made his pastoral innovative. Nevertheless, despite his conscious attempt to revive the classical form of pastoral, six of Petrarch's twelve eclogues retain the form of debate, bearing closer resemblance to the *Theoduli* than to Vergil. Here, as elsewhere, Petrarch's combining of classical and medieval uses of genre results in the characteristic synthesis of "Renaissance" style. He is the inventor of true pastoral debate.[24] From Boccaccio and Petrarch to Mantuan; from Mantuan to Barclay, Googe and Spenser; from Spenser to Sidney, Drayton, Milton, Marvell and Blake, that fundamentally medieval structure of debate retains an underlying presence throughout the pastoral tradition, rendering the mode a particularly apt vehicle for exploring abstract and conflicting ideas.

While the union of classical pastoral and medieval debate develops into Renaissance pastoral debate, the genre of *conflictus* itself loses popularity; by the start of the sixteenth century the verbal battle between allegorical creatures has already become a rare and conscious anachronism, as for instance Marvell's "Dialogue of Body and Soul." Even a poem like Lorenzo de Medici's *Altercazione,* which retains the title and tone of medieval debate, is immediately recognizable as an eclogue in which real people discuss issues related to the dichotomy of town and country—in this case the nobleman's idealization of rural life vs. an actual shepherd's account of its hardships.[25] The patterns of this historical development suggest that the classical pastoral conventions revived in the Renaissance reabsorbed the structures and functions of the *conflictus* and thereby denied the medieval genre any niche within the system of literary kinds where it could survive.[26]

* * *

As the vestigial presence of earlier evolutionary forms can demarcate the components and define the functions of a later, more complex structure, so the buried presence of the extinct genre of medieval *conflictus* within Renaissance eclogue illuminates the design and strategy of pastoral debate. The remainder of this essay develops a formal model that the medieval and Renaissance genres have in common. It also highlights the changes that verse debate undergoes in its historical development from one period to another. In order to provide coherent interpretations of complete poems, this discussion focuses on two specific examples: Robert Henrysson's fourteenth century *debaat*, "The Ressonyng betuix Yowth and Aige," and Edmund Spenser's sixteenth century eclogue, "Februarie."

Verse debate has four structural components: elaboration of setting in a pleasant natural landscape; articulation of contrary principles that are to engage in battle; dramatization of the conflict; outcome of the battle, including judge's verdict. In cumulative sequence these components conduct the reader from a simple idealized world and a sensation of relaxed harmony to an increasingly complex and dissonant awareness. This formal structure and its affective strategy is congruent with pastoral's thematic concerns about innocence and experience. Starting in an earthly paradise, the debate poem moves to a fall into division and strife, and ends with a recognition of the failure of human capacities to fulfill human needs.

The introduction to the verse debate frames the later action in a specified dramatic context. It establishes a mode of pleasureable escape to a happier world, of springtime exuberance, of festive entertainment and of protection from the hostile elements and from the dangerous consequences of subversive ideas. The setting is often invoked with lush imagery, such as in the opening of Henrysson's "Rekknynge":

> Quhen fair flora, the godes of the flowris,
> Baith firth and feildis freschely had ourfret,
> And perly droppis of the balmy schowris
> Thir widdis grene had with thair water wet,
> Movand allone in morning myld I met
> A mirry man, that all of mirth cowth mene,
> Singand the sang that richt sweitly was sett:
> "O yowth, be glaid in to thy flowris grene."[27]

Or it can be sketched with mere formulaic allusion, as at the beginning of Spenser's *The Shepheardes Calender*:

> A Shepheardes Boy (no better do him calle)
> When Winters wastful spight was almost spent
> All in a sunneshine day, as did befall,
> Led forth his flock, that had been long ypent.[28]

The second component of verse debate is the articulation of contraries. It introduces the contest to come by disposing the world into a symmetrical system of corresponding dichotomies. This dualistic vision, like the appearance of the snake in Eden, divides the homogeneous unity of the *locus amoenus*, but it maintains a simple and stable picture of the world. Pastoral thrives on simple juxtapositions of opposites: day-night, sun-rain, summer-winter, play-work, youth-age. The pastoral muses' love for alternate songs manifests itself in the antithetical pairings of Shakespeare's dialogue of the owl and the cuckoo that concludes *Love's Labour's Lost*, in Milton's "L'Allegro" and "Il Penseroso," in Blake's *Songs of Innocence and Experience*.[29] In many bucolic lyrics, the articulation of contraries fulfills the primary function of the poem:

> Crabbed Age and Youth
> Cannot live together:
> Youth is full of pleasance,
> Age is full of care;
> Youth like summer morn,
> Age like winter weather,
> Youth like summer brave,
> Age like winter bare
> Youth is full of sport
> Age's breath is short.
> Youth is nimble, Age is lame:
> Youth is hot and bold,
> Age is weak and cold,
> Youth is wild, and Age is tame,
> Age, I do abhor thee.
> Youth, I do adore thee;
> Oh, my Love, my Love is young!
> Age, I do defy thee—
> O sweet shepherd, hie thee,
> For, methinks thou stays too long.[30]

In longer, more complex works, like the *The Shepheardes Calender*, an elaborate system of parallel contraries provides the thematic principle by which the poet designs the work and by which the modern critic comes to grips with it:

> With youth, Spenser associates susceptibility to love, freedom from care, delight in song, ambitious striving. With maturity and age come

pain and disillusionment in love, a profound sense of responsibility, rejection of pleasure, disappointment in life's harvest. From eclogue to eclogue these subsidiary contraries receive greater or less emphasis, yet each recurs often enough to give unity to the whole.[31]

This binary schema of opposition is an obvious feature of the medieval debate. It makes its presence felt not only in the title and the verse form of the genre, but in a component of structure. The anonymous author of "The Parlement of the Thre Ages" gives the articulation of contraries a local habitation and a name:

Now hafe I rekkende yow theire araye, redely the sothe
And also named you thaire names naytly there-aftaire,
And now thaire carpynge I sall kythe, knowe it if yowe liste.[32]

He differentiates the actual argumentative content—the "carpynge" in which the characters speak for themselves—from his own presentation of the contestants and their allegorical qualities—his "rekkenynge."

Robert Henrysson introduces the principals of his "Ressonyng" with another such descriptive "reckkenynge" of contraries:

Movand allone in morning myld I met
A mirry man, that all of mirth cowth mene,
Singand the sang that richt sweitly was sett:
"O yowth, be glaid in to thy flowris grene."

Aige

I lukit furth a litill me befoir
And saw a cative on ane club cumand,
With cheikis clene and lyart lokis hoir;
His eine was how, his voce was hess hostand,
Wallowit richt wan, and waik as ony wand,
Ane bill he beure upoun his breist abone,
In Letteris Leill but lyis, with this legand,
"O yowth, thy flowris fedis fellone sone."[33]

Reminiscent of the figure of the old crone emerging from Hansel and Gretel's candy house or Vergil's "cold snake hiding in the grass," this emotionally chilling juxtaposition of extremes gratifies the reader's desire for symmetry and correspondence. As the poem proceeds, he enjoys matching the names and physical descriptions with the opposing styles of speech, behavior and attitude that emerge through the later dramatic characterization of the contestants. Yowth is brawny as a boar; his breast is burly and broad; the old man has bare cheeks and a stringy chin-beard. The young man boasts of health—clean lineaments and complexion, robust heart, liver and spleen. Aige, the stern reeve, or reckoner, admits he is a loathly presence and lists his diseases and disabilities: fevers and failing strength, drooping muscles, atrophy of the senses. Their manners reflect the contrast. Yowth is noisy, petulant, exuberant and full of braggodocio. He dresses and swaggers like a dandy when he goes to court to impress the ladies. Aige is bitter, self-critical, and crabby. Though closed-mouthed at the opening, when antagonized by Yowth, he strikes back with a merciless, acerbic wit. He carries a sign upon which is permanently engraved the emblematic statement of his philosophy of life: "O youth, your flowers fade full soon." Yowth sings a transitory melody whose refrain expresses the outlook of his state: "O youth enjoy your flowers green."

The disposition of reality into a system of polarities is an essential function of the genre of pastoral debate—a function conspicuously absent from the classical eclogue. In addition to reflecting the medieval proclivity for dualism and allegory, the articulation of contraries in the verse debate exemplifies a more basic cognitive process: "most human things go in pairs."[34] According to Aristotle, this statement by Alcmaeon summarizes the outlook of all the Presocratic philosophers: "They identify all the principles with the contraries, although they give no reasons for doing so, but are, as it were, *compelled by truth itself*."[35] Modern historians have identified the polarity thinking that patterns the debate's articulation of contraries as an early stage in the evolution of philosophy—a stage intermediary between myth and scientific reasoning. As such, it is particularly appropriate to the natural landscape and the primitivistic world of Arcadia.

In his own investigations, Aristotle himself usually reasons by contraries, isolating extremes to arrive at a mean. For example, in his study of applied psychology in *The Rhetoric*—"the various types of human character in relation to the emotions and the moral qualities"—he proceeds by articulating the polarity of youth and age:

> Young men look at the good side rather than the bad, not having yet witnessed many instances of wickedness. They trust others readily, because they have not yet often been cheated. They are sanguine; nature warms their blood as though with excess of wine; and besides that they have as yet met with few disappointments. . . .They disobey Chilon's precept (nothing in excess) by overdoing everything. . .They think they know everything and are always quite sure about it. . .They are fond of fun and therefore witty, wit being well-bred insolence.
>
> The character of Elderly Men. . .may be said to be formed for the most part of elements that are the contrary of all these. They have lived many years; they have often been taken in, and often made mistakes; and life on the whole is a bad business. They 'think' but they never 'know' and because of their hesitation they always add a 'possibly' or a 'perhaps,' putting everything this way and nothing positively. They are cynical. . .their experience makes them distrustful and therefore suspicious of evil. . .their temperament is chilly; old age has paved the way for cowardice; fear is, in fact, a form of chill. . .Their fits of anger are sudden but feeble. Their sensual passions have either altogether gone or have lost their vigour; consequently, they do not feel their passions much, and their actions are inspired less by what they do than by the love of gain. Hence, man at this time of life is supposed to have a self-controlled character; the fact is that their passions have slackened, and they are slaves to the love of gain. . .They are querelous, and not disposed to jesting or laughter—the love of laughter being the very opposite of querelousness.[36]

The third component of verse debate is the dramatized conflict of the contestants or "carpynge." It unfolds as a game whose rules are determined by the principles of competitive oratory. Appealing to the reader's enjoyment of any spectator sport, this argumentative section also tests the validity of philosophical arguments and reveals the interaction of logical, emotional and circumstantial factors as they affect human perception and discourse.[37] The effect of this third section on the reader is to further disrupt the order previously established. Its bickering tumult unveils two irreconciliable but equally true views of the reality so neatly disposed by the articulation of contraries.

Aristotle's *Rhetoric,* the root text of the rhetorical tradition, provides a schematic guide by which to analyze the "carpynge."[38] Discussing the epeidictic "ceremonial oration of display,"[39] whose purpose is to convince the audience that the subject under consideration merits either praise or blame, Aristotle distinguishes the orator's three modes of appeal: logical (*logos*), emotional (*pathos*), and ethical (*ethos*).[40] The first persuades by means of "lines of argument," also known as "chains of enthymemes" or "topoi." The second persuades by "stirring the emotions of the reader" with "rhetorical" devices. The third persuades by means of "evincing a personal character which will make his speech credible,"—by dramatizing the speaker as a reliable authority. This schema outlines the ensuing structural analysis of the verse debate's argument.

Henrysson's Youth and Aige follow typical "lines of argument" or chains of enthymemes as they proceed to spar:

> This yungman lap upoun the land full licht,
> And mervellit mekle of his makdome maid;
> "Waddin I am," quod he, "and woundir wicht,
> with bran as bair, and breist burly and braid;
> na growme on ground my gairdone may degraid,
> nor of my pith may pair of wirth a prene;
> My face is fair, my fegour will not faid;
> O yowith, be glaid in to thy flowris grene."
>
> This senyeour sang bot with a sobir stevin;
> schakand his berd, he said, "my bairne, lat be;
> I was within thir sextie yeiris and sevin
> Ane freik on fold, als forss and als fre,
> als glaid, als gay, als ying, als yaip as yie;

Bot now tha dayis ourdrevin ar & done;
Luke thow my laikly luking gif I lie:
O yowth, thy flowris fadis fellone sone."[41]

Like many proponents of the pastoral of youth, Henrysson's Yowth asserts the praiseworthiness of his state with the "innocent" reasoning of the bucolic inventory. Essentially descriptive, his encomium appeals to the logic of the senses. Here, he says, in the beauty of these concrete details lies my virtue; to respond to my poetry is to assent to my proposition. Even after a challenge to the validity of those sensations, youth reaffirms the same abstract principle simply by adducing more details. When he exhausts the fund of fresh examples, the encomium's line of argument terminates.

Aige's rebuttal, as familiar and obvious as the medieval cliche of *ubi sunt,* conceals a philosophical distinction that merits closer attention. Aige points out that his antagonist has committed what Aristotle calls "the eristical fallacy"—has asserted "the spurious enthymeme of confusing what is absolute [or universal] with what is particular."[42] Conceding that the qualities of the universal condition of youth are indeed praiseworthy, Aige insists that in any particular person, the value of those youthful qualities is vitiated by their transience. Yowth's praise of youth—the particular's praise of the absolute—depends on the assumption that the absolute will remain in the particular. But Aige's own experience of the metamorphosis from youth to age proves that assumption false. This disposes of Yowth's encomium of himself. Aige disposes of youth, the universal with an implication. Since the universal quality confers benefits that are perishable in any particular, it is no more praiseworthy than any particular in which it temporarily resides.

The same line of argument is taken by Old Age in *The Parlement of the Three Ages.* The fact that it is addressed by one allegorical figure to another in these medieval debates gives the argument a special involuted richness, for the speakers themselves are both universals and particulars. When the argument reappears in Renaissance pastoral debates by Drayton and Sidney, the allegory is deemphasized, but the metaphysical resonance remains. Thus Geron (or old man) to young Phillisides, who has just delivered a vituperation against old age:

> But fondlings fonde, know not your owne desire
> Loth to die yong, and then you must be olde,
> Fondly blame that to which yourselves aspire.[43]

The paradox is not merely verbal; it is ontological, like the riddle of the sphinx. Youth confronting age confronts itself.

In the *debat* of Spenser's "February" eclogue, age defends itself and attacks youth with another revealing line of argument—a refutation of childish wishful thinking. Typical of the pastoral of age's assertion of the "reality principle" over the pleasure principle, Thenot's second speech begins with the *topos* of "Reply," a parody of the encomium of youth:

> So loytring live you little heardgroomes,
> Keeping your beastes in the budded broomes;
> And when the shining sunne laugheth once,
> You deemen, the Spring is come attonce.
> Tho gynne you, fond flyes, the cold to scorne,
> And crowing in pypes made of greene corne
> You thinken to be Lords of the yeare.
>
> (35-41)

The encomium is false, asserts Thenot, because it rests on an infantile, self-oriented, subjective apprehension. "You demen. . .You thinken. . ." Confusing your own desires with actuality, you think you are beautiful and powerful because you want to be, or because you appear that way in your own eyes. But thinking doesn't make it so. Thenot sums up childish vanity with the word, "Surquedrie"—blind arrogance and presumption, the hybris that old age perennially deplores.

Thenot supports his contention with the observable fact that, time and again, the real world intrudes upon youth's dream world and destroys it:

> But eft, when ye count you freed from feare
> Comes the breme winter with chamfred browes,
> Full of wrinckles and frostie furrows:
> Drerily shooting his stormy darte,
> Which cruddles the blood and prickes the harte.
>
> (42-6)

When reality disproves their naive, rosy assumptions, the young must suffer; that suffering is both testimony and punishment for youth's failure to face facts—a sign of its blameworthiness.

> Then is your careless corage accoied,
> Your carefull heards with cold bene annoied.
> Then paye you the price of your surquedrie
> With weeping and wayling and miserie.
>
> (47-50)

The extended personification of Winter and old age functions as a rhetorical scare tactic to frighten Cuddie into submission. But it also argues that youth's folly is easily unmasked. The "breme Winter" is a fierce old man who can defeat youth's lordly aspirations and destroy his fatuous illusions. Having lost his innocence through this encounter, Cuddie himself will grow up; by virtue of the forced confrontation with the reality that is old age, Cuddie himself will pass out of youth and into maturity.

Spenser then allows youth a counter-rebuttal of equal length and symmetrical structure—a reply to the reply, which turns Thenot's argument on its head by pointing out the same logical fallacy in the critical reasoning of age. In the self-protective pessimism of its self-proclaimed realism, Cuddie finds an equally distorting application of wishful thinking. Thenot's argument, he declares, suffers from the very faults it condemns. Age's perceptions are the ones distorted by deficiencies of vision, by a refusal to face reality—in this case, the reality of pleasure, beauty and springtime. Cuddie supports his claim with two lines of argument that mirror Thenot's. First, the old man's views are distorted by a combination of senility and envy:

Ah foolish old man, I scorne thy skill,
That wouldest me, my springing youngth to spil,
I deeme, thy braine emperished bee
Through rusty elde, that hath rotted thee
Or sicker thy head veray tottie is,
So on thy corbe shoulder it leanes amisse.
Now thy selfe hast lost both lopp and topp,
Als my budding branch thou wouldest cropp:
(50-59)

Rather than accepting the old man's precautionary advice against hybris as a February pruning of excess growth, Cuddie takes it as a Saturnian threat of castration.

His second line of attack argues that the old man's views are fallacious because they too are liable to reversal, given a change of circumstance. Like Thenot's earlier argument, it postulates a hypothetical encounter with a figure representing the opposed principle:

But were thy yeares grene, as now bene myne,
To other delights they would incline.
Tho wouldest thou learn to caroll of Love,
And hery with hymnes thy lasses glove.
(59-62)

Now Cuddie teasingly evokes his own youthful pleasures to lure his opponent away from the defenses of age's limited world-view. He destroys the protection of Thenot's comfortable pessimism and stings him with the memory of joy he can no longer possess:

Tho wouldest thou pype of Phyllis prayse:
But Phyllis is mine for many dayes:
I wonne her with a gyrdle of gelt,
Embossed with buegle about the belt.
(63-66)

The old man's resulting pain proves the reality and value of youthful delights and shows the fallacy of their repudiation. Cuddie rests his case with a projection that mirrors Thenot's earlier one: his opponent metamorphosed into an opposite state:

> Such an one shepheards woulde make full faine:
> Such an one would make thee younge againe.
> (67-68)

After this exchange, Thenot essentially gives up on logic, for he has discovered that the boy debates with a skill well in advance of his years. Instead, the old man follows Aristotle's advice to the orator who cannot proceed successfully using chains of enthymemes: he stops arguing logically and introduces a fable. In so doing he shifts ground from the dialectical to the rhetorical level of persuasion.[45]

Though rational and emotional methods of persuasion usually accompany one another, Aristotle clearly distinguishes them and advises the orator to practice the two skills separately.[46] Authors of verse debate use rhetorical devices in two ways: to reinforce the lines of argument with ornamentation of style, and to replace the lines of argument with other forms of verbal competition: lyrical outbursts, vituperation, fable. Cuddie and Thenot both clinch their arguments with traditional rhetorical figures: old man Winter and the young shepherdess are introduced to produce fright or envy, to decorate the poem, and also to display the poet's ability to work with the familiar literary models that make up his stock and trade.[47]

Rhetorical power is often exhibited through unrestrained excesses of praise and abuse in the verse debate, such as this passage from *The Owl and the Nightingale*:

> "A loathsome creature, base and foul"
> Monster," she said, "away, take flight;
> I sicken at your very sight;
> When you your croaking noises make
> I faint and must my song forsake;
> My heart is weak, my voice distressed

When you are close beside me pressed
Twere better vomit than to sing
Because of your vile muttering."[48]

But it also operates in more subtle maneuverings of tone that can affect both opponent and spectator as strongly as the most incisive argumentation. In Henrysson's "Ressonyng" for instance, the speaker demonstrates the strength of old age by recounting his own history with a marvelous mixture of alliteration, rhythmic fracturing of the line, and parallelism.

I was within thir sextie yeiris and sevin
Ane freik on fold, als forss and als fre,
Als glaid, als gay, als ying, als yaip as yie.
(27-32)

Fable is the most common substitute for dialectic. When his argument flounders in "February," Thenot reverts to the fable of the Oak and the Briar to rescue his persuasive purpose, the praise of age and dispraise of youth. What E.K. calls this "Icon or Hypotyposis of disdainfull Younkers" succeeds in drawing attention away from the logical contest and enlisting the audience's sympathy on the side of old age.

Thenot achieves his intent largely through the pose of disingenuousness: the indictment of rhetoric by rhetoric. Throughout the tale, the old oak doesn't say a word; he is a benign and yielding victim of youth's malevolent jealousy. The voluble, honey-tongued Briar proliferates "Painted words. . .as usen most Ambitious folke:/ His colowred crime with craft to cloke." (11. 160-162) The Briar's success at hoodwinking the husbandman into destroying the oak evokes an indignation in the reader that is intensified by the account of the slow, agonizing death of the tree:

The Axes edge did oft turne againe,
As halfe unwilling to cutte the graine:
Semed, the sencelesse yron dyd feare,
Or to wrong holy eld did forbeare. . .

. . .fiercely the good man at him dyd laye
The blocke oft groned under the blow,
And sighed to see his neare overthrow.
In fine the steele had pierced his pith,
Then downe to the earth he fell forthwith:
His wondrous weight made the grounde to quake,
Thearth shronke under him, and seemed to shake.
There lyeth the Oake, pitied of none.
(195-220)

And that sympathy leads to the reader's satisfaction in the Briar's eventual self-inflicted punishment. Once the oak is gone, the proud and now unshadowed young Briar has to face Winter without protection. Bowed down by the weight of snow on his foliage, he is trodden into the dirt by indifferent cattle. Cuddie's advantage at the logical level of the argument gives way to the vindication of old age at the level of the audience's emotional response.

Aristotle's orator achieves the most compelling force of persuasion by establishing his own credibility as a person. Success ultimately depends on his ability to control the audience's natural tendency to move from what he says and the way he says it to the speaker himself:

> Persuasion is achieved by the speaker's personal character when the speech is so spoken as to make us think him credible. We believe good men more fully and more readily than others. . .This kind of persuasion, like the other, should be achieved by what the speaker says, not by what people think of his character before he begins to speak.[49]

Only by creating the impression of himself as a believable character can he finally gain their trust and respect; and that impression, though separate from his speech, nevertheless arises out of it.

In the genre of verse debate—the fictional imitation of a real verbal contest—the audience's interest in the orator extends beyond a concern with the credibility of what he says. The reader looks for character per se, for a sense of immediacy and veracity apart from the truth value or the persuasiveness of his statements. Indeed, the most exciting aspects of character may be those which undermine the speaker's reliability and show more of him than he wishes to expose.[50]

In Henrysson's "Ressonyng," the individual characters of Yowth and Aige reveal themselves through shifts of subject and mood. Yowth, for instance, jumps from extolling his bodily health to his prospect of dalliance at the court, after Aige's warning about corporeal decay. Frightened by the threat, he seeks to comfort himself with the prospect of secretive sexual play; and at the same time he tries to prick the old man with envy:

> Ane uthir verss yit this yungman cowth sing:
> "At luvis law a quhle I think to leit,
> In court to cramp clenely in my clething,
> And luke amangis thir lusty ladis sweit;
> Of mariage to mell with mowthis meit,
> In secreit place, quhair we ma not be sene,
> And so with birdis, blythly my bailis beit:
> O yowth, be glad in to thy flowris grene."[51]

The barb takes hold. Aige's dramatic response is stated explicitly by the author's stage direction, but it comes across more intensely in his change of tone from warning to curse:

> This awsterne grief anssuerit angirly:
> "For the cramping thow salt baith cruke & cowre;
> The fleschly lust thow salt also defy,
> And pane the sall put fra paramour;
> Than will no bird be blyth of the in bouir;
> Quhen the manheid sall wendin as the mone,
> Thow sall assay gif that my song be sour
> O yowth, thy flowris fedis fellone sone."[52]

As the contest proceeds, the antagonism between the characters deepens, manifested in the way each goes for the other's soft spots. The young man rubs in the elder's suffering by flaunting his own vitality; the old man brandishes his experience to terrify the youth. Each gains compensation for his own inadequacy by attacking the opposite inadequacy of his antagonist:

> This mirry man of mirth yet movit moir:
> "My corps is clene withowt corruption
> My self is sound, but seiknes or but soir,
> My wittis fyve in dew proportioun,
> My Curage is of clene complexioun,
> My hairt is haill, my levar, and my splene;
> Thairfoir to reid this roll I haiv no ressoun:
> O yowth, be glaid in to thy flowris grene."
>
> The bevar hoir said to this berly berne:
> "This breif thow sall obey, sone be thow bald;
> Thy stait, thy strenth, Thocht it be stark and sterne,
> The feveris fell and eild sall gar the fald;
> Thy corps sall clyng, the curage sall wax cald,
> Thy helth sall hynk, and tak a hurt but hone,
> Thy wittis fyve sall vaneis, Thocht thow not wald:
> O yowth, thy flowris fadis fellone sone."[54]

The reader's attention moves from the competition of ideas and stylistic virtuosity to the dramatic display of frightful human hostility.

Yet though the conflict of character makes the genre an incipient form of theatre, in medieval verse debate this level of the argument remains clearly subordinate to the dialectical and rhetorical levels of meaning.[55] In the evolution from medieval *conflictus* to Renaissance pastoral debate, this emphasis changes. The primacy of "thought" or theme recedes before the ascendance of character and situation; the rigid stanzaic structure gives way to a pattern of verse paragraphs. The "not obvious" features of the speakers—their inner reactions and motives—take control of the plot. And as character becomes thus "interiorized," it frees itself from the abstraction that identifies it; it develops the ability to change.[56] This historical shift of generic emphasis toward dramatic conflict clearly presents itself in Spenser's "February," despite the author's attempts to give the poem an archaic medieval flavor. Its overall movement is psychological rather than logical. The switch from dialectical to rhetorical contest results from unstated dramatic interactions of character. Cuddie's pounding rebuttal softens Thenot's tone, and leads to the old man's show of appeasing the boy with the offer of a story "cond of Tityrus in my youth." In their mutual admiration of this figure from the past (who represents Chaucer) there seems to be a basis of reconciliation. The old man concedes: "Many meete Tales of Youth did he make, and some of love and some of chevalrie." The boy accepts: "They been so well thewed, and so wise, whatever that good old man bespake." (90-100)[57]

But, as mentioned earlier, the tale in fact doesn't end the conflict; it is Thenot's gambit to regain the initiative. Breaking the argument with a gesture that seems friendly, he deviously steals victory from Cuddie, who has naively put down his guard. At the moment the sword strikes home in the moral of the fable, Cuddie interrupts with irritation but without realizing that he has lost the battle. The words of his final outburst identify him with the exposed and punished Briar:

> Now I pray thee shepheard, tel it not forth:
> Here is a long tale, and little worth.
> So longe haue I listened to thy speche,
> That graffed to the ground is my breche:
> My hartblood is welnigh frorne I feele,
> And my galage growne fast to my heele:
> But little ease of thy lewd tale I tasted.
> Hye thee home shepheard, the day is nigh wasted.

The movement away from medieval allegory toward greater emphasis on the realistic conflict of individuals continues with Drayton's treatment of the convention of the pastoral debate of youth and age. His "Eclogue Two"—which imitates and alludes to Spenser's second month—has a similar plot outline: a proud young man lords it over an old one, whose pessimistic wisdom succeeds by stratagem in destroying youth's innocence. But the structure of debate, the antagonism of adversaries, and the thematic implications are disguised here by the amiable aesthetic competition of the singing contest.

At the opening, young Motto tries to "raise up" old Wynken from his melancholy brooding with joyful song. But mirth is no match for saturnine gloom, and by the end of his first speech, Motto is forced to concede the limitations of his state by recognizing the strength of the opposing one:

> Might my youths mirth delight thy aged yeeres,. . .
> Now would I tune my miskins on this Greene. . .
> But melancholie grafted in thy Braine
> My rimes seems harsh, to thy unrelisht taste. . .(1-10)[57a]

Wynken replies with a woeful complaint about this decline from Youth; Motto responds with a commiserating "reflection" in which he takes pains to thoroughly dissociate himself from any such concerns:

> Even so I weene, for thy old ages fever,
> Deemes sweetst potions bitter as the gall,
> And thy colde Pallat having lost her savour,
> Receives no comfort in a Cordiall. (33-37)

Wynken's reply recapitulates Henrysson's "eristical argument" about particular and universal. In a lovely extended version of the old age elegy he tries to erode youth's optimism:

> As thou art now, was I a gamesome boy,
> Though starv'd with wintred eld as thou do'st see,
> And well I know thy swallow-winged joy,
> Shalbe forgotten as it is in me.
>
> When on the Arche of thine eclipsed eies,
> Time hath ingrav'd deepe characters of death,
> And sun-burnt age thy kindlie moisture dries,
> Thy wearied lungs be niggards of the breath. . .
> . . . .
> Remember then my boy, what once I said to thee.

To give more evidence of the inevitable fall of youth, Wynken quotes an idealistic encomium written by Rowland, Wynken's hero, before that cynosure of pastoral poets lost his innocence. But in doing so, Wynken knows that he is once again luring his naive antagonist into exposing his vulnerable optimism. The rhetoric of the encomium intoxicates Motto; he ignores the *memento mori* context and responds with his own panegyric:

O divine love, which so aloft canst raise,
And lift the minde out of this earthly mire,
And do'st inspire the pen with so hie prayse,
As with the heavens doth equal man's desire. . .

He has taken the second bait. "O foolish boy," Wynken replies as soon as Motto finishes. Rowland himself was trapped by the sentiments in that poem of youthful flight, but his actual experience of life, of the inevitable disappointments of love and the failures of ambition taught him to repent, to break his pipe, to retire to a cave in solitude, becoming like Desportes' speaker or Molière's Alceste, a typical *senex puer*. Hearing Wynken recite Rowland's "dolefull elegy" as proof of the hero's fall, Motto renounces his youthful innocence and accepts the experience of age:

Woes me for him that pineth so in payne,
Alas poore Rowland, how it pities me
So faire a baite should breed so foule a bayne,
Or humble shewes should cover crueltie. (131-4)

Age's favored line of argument surfaces here—the one refuting wishful thinking and asserting "the reality principle." But it has not been explicitly stated; instead it emerges through the dramatic interaction by way of Wynken's trick.[58] By retaining the medieval debate's argumentative structure and thus reversing its subordination of character to principle, Drayton and other Renaissance pastoralists subject the reasoning process itself to the most sceptical kind of scrutiny.

Sidney was particularly interested in the way pastoral debate's structural conventions lent themselves to that scrutiny. In the second book of the *Arcadia,* he grouped a series of six pastoral debates under the thematic rubric of "Reason vs. Passion," and subsumed the conflict of youth and age within it. In Eclogue 9, "Phillisides and Geron," the very standard of dialectical debate is at issue; the rules of the game become the subject of the contest. Although Geron, the old man, can retort to every line of Philisides' argument with a rationally convincing reply, the value of his objectivity and rationality is never accepted by his opponent. The old man, the man of reason, as Pascal later avers, can never convince by reason the youth, the man of the heart. The man of passion, no matter how intense and abusive his onslaught, will never succeed in showing the man of reason the reality of the force that has him in its grip.

As the exchange in Eclogue #9 proceeds, each opponent becomes more and more absorbed in his own mode of thinking. By the end, Geron's astute critique of Philisides' self-indulgent and delusion-generated passion degenerates into a series of irrelevant old saws advising Georgic pursuits to cool the young man's ardor. Philisides' expression of idealism and intensity in the meantime deteriorates into sordid abuse. Each character only hears himself and has ceased to apprehend the intended meaning of the other's words:

> Hath any man heard what this old man hath said?
> Truly not I who did my thoughts engage
> Where all my paines one look of hers hath paid.[59]

Both logical and rhetorical debate have given over to pure dramatic confrontation. Philisides, like Spenser's Cuddie, interrupts his opponent's speech just before it concludes. But his rude departure while Geron is talking neither claims victory nor concedes defeat. It silences the old man and confounds the reader.

The indeterminate ending of "Geron and Philisides" typifies the fourth and final structural component of verse debate.

Rather than leading to the declaration of winner and loser—the goal of most competitive games—the poem usually closes with a stalemate.[60] Such an outcome thwarts the epideictic purposes of both orators: neither achieves his intended allocation of praise and blame. And though the readers are pressed to make a judgment by the speaker's tactics, by the end of the poem their awareness of those tactics and the evenness of the match have removed rather than supplied grounds for decision. To confirm this lack of logical, emotional and dramatic closure, a debate convention provides a commentator or a motto. Thus the last four lines of Sidney's "Geron and Philisides" are spoken by a bystander:

> Thus may you see, howe youthe esteemeth aige
> And never hathe therof arightlye deemede
> While hote desyres do Raigne in fancie's rage
> Till aige it self do make it self esteemde.

The same kind of inconclusiveness necessitates the intervention of judge, referee or observer to terminate the allegorical *conflictus*, usually with a similar Solomonic verdict.[61] Henrysson's "Ressonyng" clearly displays the tension between the expected ending of a contest and the verse debate's characteristically "suspended"conclusion. Aige takes the last word in the exchange, and Yowthe, finally affected by his dire warnings, leaves the scene thoroughly chastized.

> This gowand grathit with sic gret greif,
> He on his wayis wrethly went but wene
> This lene awld man luche Not, but tuk his leif. . .[62]

The old man takes neither glory nor solace in his victory. Then the narrator reenters the scene and addresses the reader with a moral:

> And I abaid under the levis grene:
> Of the sedullis the suthe quhen I had sene,

Of trewth, me thocht, thay triumphit in thair tone:
"O yowth, be glad in to thy flowres grene!"
"O yowth, thy flowris faidis fellone sone!"[63]

The dispute he just witnessed has raised a deadly serious issue and left it hanging. Persuaded by both opposing orators, he can choose neither, and therefore concludes with a logical impossibility: the assertion of two contrary statements.

Such a disturbing assertion of paradox as outcome prevents the reader from putting down the poem with a feeling of satisfaction and completion. Instead, the poem stays with him as an open question. Henrysson develops this affective strategy with two devices. First, he emphasizes the riddling effect on the narrator by making him meditate on the dilemma in the contemplative shade of the green tree. There the speaker awaits the solace and wisdom that nature provides those who suffer from mortal limitations. Second, Henrysson expresses the logical, rhetorical and dramatic contradiction by suggesting a shift out of the discursive medium of language into another mode of perception that can better accomodate contradiction—in this case the polyphonic harmony of two melodies.[64] Spenser also ends his debates with a demonstration of the limitations of all discursive thought and language. The failure of both dialectic and rhetoric to reach their goals in debate leads to a conclusion consisting of paired "Emblemes"—contradictory maxims that can be absorbed by the mind only as a *visual* experience to which the law of contradiction does not apply:

Thenot's Embleme
Iddio perche e vecchio,
Fa suoi al su essempio.
Cuddie's Embleme.
Niuno vecchio
Spaventa Iddio.[64a]

* * *

The ambivalent moral of the verse debate's final structural element recapitulates the binary symmetry of the introductory articulation of contraries. But here, at the end of the poem, the reader no longer perceives the dualistic system of dichotomies as a way of sorting the world into neat categories and correspondences. Instead, that dualism has become a source of scepticism and self-doubt.

This change has occurred in the course of the argument proper, the "carpynge." In this middle section of the poem, the author has blurred the simple order of opposition by articulating two contrary articulations of contraries. By changing the metaphysical status of his characters from objects to subjects, he has disclosed alternate visions of the same world from the two perspectives generated by the opposites. These perspectives have taken on more reality than anything objective in the reader's field of vision. And the two perspectives of the characters are themselves occupied not by objects, so much as by the comparison of perspectives. Using the debate technique of rebuttal—stating, discrediting and parodying the opposite point of view—youth defines his own position by criticizing age's view of him, and age does likewise. Such use of interlocking rebuttals subjects the reader to the kind of disorientation that results from standing between two mirrors.

Moving the reader in this way from the simple clarity of thinking by polarity to the mind's reflexive confrontation with its own subjectivity constitutes the verse debate's overall affective strategy. The reader's progression through the structural components of the genre, from garden setting to primitive articulation of contraries to sophisticated relativity of perspective—from a condition "without debate or stryfe" to a constant tension between opposing points of view—is a kind of mental fall from Eden. It corresponds to the typical emotional trajectory of pastoral: the search for innocence that ends in experience.[65]

This overall generic form of pastoral debate has a number of analogies. Stanley Fish has traced back to the *Phaedrus* itself a convention of "Self-Consuming Artifacts," in which literary structure works to make the reader's sensation of movement through the text from beginning to end feel illusory: "The reader passes through doors only to find himself in rooms he just left."[66] In dialogue, essay, sermon or poem, the writer following this convention uses the instruments of logic and rhetoric first to seduce and engage the reader and then to confound him with a demonstration of their fallaciousness. Thus the reader is brought by the work's own reflexive invalidation from a state of understanding and enjoyment to a condition of confusion and discomfort. Fish maintains that the purpose of such a destructive strategy is to open the reader to religious illumination—some intuitive insight that can arrive only when the rational discursive mind has relinquished its grip on consciousness. This technique of evoking epiphanies—similar to that of the Zen koan or the Sufi parable—is used by devotional poets like Donne and Herbert and preachers like Andrewes and Thomas Browne as well as by philosophers like Pascal, who argue the reader to the verge of all argument and then invite him to take the leap of faith.

But though the critique of reason embodied in such structures often leads to conversion, just as often it can lead to a kind of phenomenological self-questioning and suspension of judgment that remains in the service of the intellect. As a method of empirical inquiry, the sceptical exploratory stance cultivated by the strategy of the verse debate was associated with the rhetorical tradition back to Cicero. His use of the dialogue form, unlike Plato's, ended not with the leap to a higher form of cognition but with a question mark or an open mind. During the middle ages, the technique of looking at the question from both sides without arriving at a determination was the habit of mind of orators, lawyers and scholastic theologians as well as of writers of the *Streitgedicht*. During the Renaissance, the endless questioning implied in the relativity of perspectives characterized both the method and the conclusions of much humanist thought. Montaigne's escutcheon displayed a pair of balanced scales under the motto, "Que sais-je". In this passage from his lengthy defense of the

Sceptics (Pyrrhonians) in the *Apology for Raymond Sebond,* Montaigne describes inconclusive debate as the closest approach to truth:

> The profession of the Pyrronians is to waver, doubt and inquire, to be sure of nothing, to answer for nothing. . .Their expressions are "I establish nothing; it is no more thus than thus, or than neither way; I do not understand it; the appearances are equal on all sides; it is equally legitimate to speak for and against. . .Their effect is a pure, complete and very perfect postponement of judgement. They use their reason to inquire and debate, but not to conclude and choose.[67]

Whether one sees it as reason's dead-end or as the beginning of the experimental method, whether as a source of *angst* or a source of *sprezzatura,* the relativity of perspectives is a major preoccupation of Renaissance thought. Claudio Guillen has demonstrated the connection between the practise of Quatrocento painters, who discovered in the study of optical perspective a means to create the appearance of truth to nature, and theories of Descartes and Leibnitz, who saw reality itself as a function of the point of view.[68] This concern was most emphatically strengthened by the period's repeated discovery of hitherto unknown points of view—whether those of heliocentric universe or of new world natives—points of view that stood in debate-like relation to traditional attitudes they could deny but not replace.

This epistemological concern with point of view often becomes explicit within the art of the period:

> ". . .in works where the metaphor of perspective appears. . .there is ultimately an important concentration not on the content of a given theme but on how it can be known. . .The artist in such cases is fundamentally concerned with how human experience can be perceived or known, and this in turn affects or enters the structure of the work of art.[69]

In the Elizabethan sonnet, as well as in other Petrarchan forms of poetry, the interest in perspective manifests itself in the shifting moods of the narrator—his persistent bewilderment at how he and his mistress can maintain identity and yet go through radical and discontinuous change:

> The Petrarchan speaker's rhetorical strategy of alternating and suspending contrarieties within his own ethos in fact generates structural transformation in each poem. His expression of joy and lament, hope and despair, certitude and doubt, characteristically balance thesis against antithesis, statement against counterstatement, and reversal against counterreversal, allowing a dialectical unity to evolve out of multiplicity through patterns of shading and contrast, challenge and fulfillment, assertion and negation.[70]

In the structure of poetic debate, these same oscillations are projected as two opposing voices. The absence of a central consciousness in the poem draws the reader himself into the structure as the monitor of the shifting points of view and makes him the subject rather than the observer of epistemological relativity. In Drayton's "Eclogue 7," for example, perspective becomes the literal subject of debate, as the author shifts the topic from the ethical values of youth and age to their competing judgments of the aesthetic value of two poems included within the eclogue. That shift pushes the genre's affective strategy to its limits by inducing a controlled sequence of oscillations of perspective within the reader and then making him aware of his own inconsistent responses.

The relativity emerges at the outset in the overlapping articulations of contraries. What appears to Borrill as a contented Sheepcoate protected from the wind, for Batte is a "loathsome Cave." What Batte describes as "shepheardes frolicke" Borrill experiences as "Golden Slavery." The *carpynge* then proceeds with paired, overlapping rebuttals—refutations of defensive pessimism and of wishful thinking—each of which adopts and then mocks the opposing perspective:

(Batte)
Like to the curre, with anger well neere woode,
   who makes his kennel in the Oxes stall,

And snarleth when he seeth him take his foode,
  and yet his chapts can chew no hay at all.
Borrill, even so it fareth now with thee,
And with these wisards of thy mysterie

(Borrill)

. . . .Ah foolish elfe, I inly pittie thee,
  misgoverned by thy lewd brainsick will:
The hidden baytes, ah fond thou do'st not see,
  nor find'st the cause which breedeth all thy ill:
Thou thinks'st all golde, that hath a golden shew,
And art deceiv'd, for it is nothing soe. (55-72)

The dialectical contest then shifts to the purely rhetorical level as Borrill offers a fable of the fly and the flame, illustrating the dangers and silliness of youthful love. Batte counters with an ornamental *descriptio* of an elaborate scene he plans to carve on his staff, illustrating the grandeur of love and the nobility of its "canonized" saints. Borrill counterthrusts with a formal *vituperatio* of Love—"Oh spightful wayward wretched love. . ."; and is then answered by Batte's *confirmatio*—"Love is the heaven's faire aspect."[71]

But Drayton goes beyond the decorative embellishments of the typical "delectable controversie" when he extends the singing contest by interlacing the poems with reviews—critiques of substance and style by the opposing speaker:

Borrill, sing on I pray thee let us heare,
That I may laugh to see thee shake thy beard
But take heede Borrill that thy voyce be cleare,
Or by my hood thou'lt make us all afeard,
Or els I doubt that thou wilt fright our flockes,
When they shall heare thee barke so like a foxe.
(121-126)

Batte's derisive preface skews the reader's response to the song itself. After such an introduction it is hard to regard the crude alliteration and the alternating masculine and feminine endings of Borrill's lines as anything but ridiculous:

O spightfull wayward wretched love,
Woe to Venus which did nurse thee
Heavens and earth thy plagues do prove,
Gods, and men have cause to curse thee.
(127-130)

And the youth's sarcastic comment at the close of the old man's song reinforces the reader's suspicion that the author intends it as a burlesque:

Ah worthy Borrill, here's a goodly song,
Now by my belt I never heard a worse:
(151-2)

But instead of dismissing it with a laugh, Batte rails on, revealing that in fact it has affected him more seriously:

Olde doting foole, for shame hold thou thy tongue,
I would thy clap were shut up in my purse.
It is thy life, if thou mayst scolde and braule:
Yet in thy words there is no wit at all.
(153-6)

Now the reader is prompted to reconsider his contemptuous response and to regard the poem from a different perspective. He may discover that as a ritualized curse in the spondaic style of Barnabe Googe, it does possess a measure of saturnine power and eloquence:

Thoughts griefe, hearts woe,
Hopes paine, bodies languish,
Envies rage, sleepes foe,
Fancies fraud, soules anguish,
Desires dread, mindes madnes,
Secrets bewrayer, natures error,
Sights deceit, sullen sadness. . .
(131-8)

Batte's song receives similar treatment. From the perspective created by Borrill's caustic introduction, Batte's "Love is the Heaven's Faire Aspect" appears a laughable bit of fluff, especially in its last stanza:

Love is my life, life is my love
Love is my whole felicity,
Love is my sweete, sweete is my love,
I am in love, and love in me.
(189-192)

Borill's hostile reaction at the poem's conclusion elicits the reader's guffaw:

Is love in thee? alas poore sillie lad,
Thou never coulds't have lodg'ed a worser guest. . .
(193-4)

However, if the reader rejects the antagonistic critique and changes his point of view to share the one from which the poem is uttered—that of a young man intoxicated with Petrarchan rhetoric, neo-Platonic philosophy, the smells of earth on a May morning and the eyes of a remote "shepherdesse"—his response and aesthetic judgment will alter dramatically. Appreciating its childlike simplicity of thought and its elvish tinkle of sound, he will enjoy the pastoral charm of a *chanson innocente*.

By manipulating these shifting reactions to his text, Drayton thoroughly mobilizes the resources of the genre. Not only does he demonstrate the relativity of perspectives in the conflict of his characters, he steers the reader into switching positions himself, and hence into observing his own reversals of judgment. Such use of the pastoral debate of youth and age yields compelling proof of the indeterminacy of knowledge that Montaigne argued with the evidence of a similar example: "Do you think the verses of Catullus or Sappho smile to an avaricious and crabbed old man as they do to a vigorous and ardent youth?"[72]

This opposition of youth and age traditionally serves to illustrate the inconsistency and contingency of human knowledge—from the passage in Aristotle's *Rhetoric* cited early in this essay to Mutability's epideictic carpynge against Jove on Arlo Hill:

> And men themselves do change continually
> From youth to eld, from wealth to poverty
> From good to bad, from bad to worst of all
> Ne doe their bodies only flit and fly
> But eeke their minds (which they immortal call)
> Still change and vary thoughts, as new occasions fall.

As such an embodiment of the relativity of perspectives, youth-and-age makes a particularly apt subject for the formal convention of verse debate. Youth-and-age also constitutes an essential theme of the pastoral mode, since idealized and negative conceptions of these peripheral stages of the life cycle correspond to pastoral's vision of an "other" world on the peripheries of civilization. Thus, the topos of youth-and-age itself emerges as a node of convergence between content and form, between theme and structure, between pastoral and debate. From this node sprouts the pastoral debate of youth and age—a "minor poetic genre" with the richness and vitality that flows from a great root system.

As You Like It, Shakespeare's most fully realized pastoral work, is also the one that devotes most attention to the theme of youth-and-age. As the title hints, it is also the most debate-like and debate-ridden in structure. When Touchstone, Rosalind and Celia arrive in Arcadia, their first discovery locates them at the crossroads of thematic mode and formal genre:

> Well, this is the Forest of Arden. . .
> Look you who comes here:
> A young man and an old in solemn talk.

After this ceremonial introduction, the reader joins them as a spectator at the *conflictus* of two local natives:

Corin: That is the way to make her scorn you still.
Silvius: O Corin, that thou knews't how I do love her!
Cor: I partly guess; for I have lov'd ere now.
Sil: No. Corin, being old, thou canst not guess,
Though in thy youth thou wast as true a lover
As ever sigh'd upon a midnight pillow.
But if thy love were ever like to mine,—
As sure I think did never man love so—
How many actions most ridiculous
Hast thou been drawn to by thy fantasy?
Cor: Into a thousand that I have forgotten.
Sil: O, thou didst then n'er love so heartily!
If thou rememb'rest not the slightest folly
That ever love did make thee run into,
Thou hast not lov'd;
Or if thou hast not sat as I do now,
Wearing thy hearer in thy mistress' praise,
Thou hast not lov'd
Or if thou hast not broke from company
Abruptly, as my passion now makes me,
Thou hast not lov'd.
O Phebe, Phebe, Phebe!
(II, iv, 21-42)

This is an obvious parody of a set-piece: the debate between Corydon and Montanus which occurs in Shakespeare's chief source, Lodge's *Rosalynde,* and which itself closely imitates Sidney's "Philisides and Geron."[73] A seizure of passion drives the young man to break off the discussion and exit suddenly, as it did Philisides and Montanus in the earlier versions. But Silvius won't go without first drawing attention to the demonstrative significance of the gesture:

Or if thou hast not broke from company
Abruptly, as my passion now makes me,
Thou hast not lov'd.

The elder shepherd Corin, like his predecessors, tries to help his companion by offering remedies. Instead of Geron's or Corydon's abstract maxims he offers the young man the benefit of his worldly experience by giving practical advice about tactics in courtship: "That is the way to make her scorn you still."

But more important than parody is the way Shakespeare focuses his treatment of the genre on the central issue of ways of knowing, the issue of relativity of perspective. Instead of simply asserting the respective claims of passion and reason, youth and age both make the more sophisticated claim of relativity itself. They compete for a point of view that includes both their own and their opponents' perspective. In response to Silvius' remark that he doesn't know what love is, the old man states he can "partly guess," since he has loved in the past so often that he has been drawn into a thousand follies. But the deliberate rendering of his experience as no longer present—as safely behind him and forgotten—implies a claim of superior authority for his distant detached "perspective" on both youth and love. The long view of his many years has granted him the typical wise old shepherd's ability to sift reality from illusion and sense from foolishness, to forget those things he judges not worth remembering. Covertly though it is stated, this claim is not lost on Silvius. His reply, having predictably reverted to the topic of love, still deals with the real issue of innocent vs. experienced ways of knowing. Silvius counters that Corin's paradoxically forgotten memory of love is no knowledge at all. He implies that the experience which puts love into perspective destroys real understanding, which is available only in the present "proof."

Here Shakespeare gives the argument some new twists. To demonstrate that his present-oriented point of view has as much depth as age's binocular vision, Silvius shows that he too can see things from both sides of the question:

> Or if thou hast not sat as I do now
> Wearing thy hearer in thy mistress' praise,
> Thou hast not lov'd.

He can see himself—and his own tiresome behavior—from Corin's point of view. Knowing that Corin was once young, he also knows that he himself will some day be old. And yet he retains his passion. A kind of adolescent romantic irony makes innocence less ignorant than age would like to think it. Like Rosalind and all the young lovers in *As You Like It*, Silvius affirms the logical absurdity of his feelings and conduct; the more foolish love makes him look, the stronger it manifests its springtime force. The old man's wisdom can teach him nothing; their opposed positions can never be reconciled in language for they are functions of the natural aging process itself.

By thus revealing the limitations of rhetoric—taking the word in its very broadest sense as the deliberate control of language—even the most sophisticated version of pastoral debate displays its own primitive origins in folk festivals and seasonal rituals. In the setting of tree, field and stream, it subordinates the argumentative, logical conflict of ideas to the larger oscillations of the life cycle. Like Sidney, Shakespeare demonstrates the dominion of nature over discourse by breaking the conversation rather than bringing it to closure. But in place of Sidney's instance of rude inclivity, the dramatist ends his pastoral debate of youth and age with an utterance of bird song: "O Phebe, Phebe, Phebe."

NOTES

[1] *The Works of Edmund Spenser: A Variorum Edition*, ed. Edwin Greenlaw *et* al., (Baltimore: Johns Hopkins Press, 1938) VI, 106 (Book VI, ix, 18).

[2] See, for instance, Renato Poggioli, *The Oaten Flute* (Cambridge: Harvard University Press, 1975; Thomas Rosenmeyer, *The Green Cabinet* (Berkeley: University of California Press, 1969); Bruno Snell, "Arcadia: The Discovery of a Spiritual Landscape," in *The Discovery of the Mind* trans. J. G. Rosenmeyer (Berkeley: University of California Press, 1953), pp. 282-308. This view of pastoral as essentially and exclusively idyllic was widely maintained in the 18th century, as shown by J. E. Congleton in *Theories of Pastoral Poetry in England*, 1684-1798 (Gainesville: University of Florida Press, 1952).

[3] Patrick Cullen, *Spenser, Marvell and Renaissance Pastoral* (Cambridge: Harvard University Press, 1970), pp. 1-2. See also Edward W. Tayler, *Nature and Art in Renaissance Literature* (New York: Columbia University Press, 1964); Harold Tolliver, *Pastoral Forms and Attitudes* (Berkeley: University of California Press, 1971); Eleanor Winston Leach, *Vergil's Eclogues: Landscapes of Experience* (Ithaca and London: Cornell

University Press, 1974); Donald Friedman, *Marvell's Pastoral Art* (Berkeley: University of California Press, 1970); Leo Marx, *The Machine in the Garden: Technology and the Pastoral Idea in America* (New York: Oxford University Press, 1964); Raymond Williams, *The Country and the City* (New York: Oxford University Press, 1973), especially chapter 2: "Pastoral and Counter Pastoral."

[4] Patrick Cullen, pp. 29-31.

[5] Donald Friedman sees the debate as an underlying principle of all Marvell's poems. In his excellent second chapter, "Forms of Debate," however, he dismisses any significance of the connection between pastoral and *debat*: "Marvell's recurrent choice of the *debat* form for pastoral poems, both plain and philosophical, needs no comment." (p. 31). This undocumented assertion seems to assume that some study like the present one had already been completed. Cullen, whose reading of Spenser has enriched my own, makes no mention of medieval *debat* at all, and instead sees Spenser's use of debate as an innovative combining of two diverse pastoral traditions, which he calls "the Arcadian" and "Mantuanesque." It seems to me this is proliferating entities. The opposed perspectives in Spenser's debates are juxtaposed in all pastorals as the conflicting visions of youth and age. The opposition itself is that of the medieval *conflictus*.

[6] The effect of traditional rhetorical practices of disputation on the structures of various Renaissance genres has been thoroughly explored in a number of full-length studies. Madeleine Doran's *Endeavors in Art: A Study of Form in Elizabethan Drama* (Madison: University of Wisconsin Press, 1954) and more recently, Joel Altman's *The Tudor Play of Mind: Rhetorical Inquiry and Elizabethan Drama* (Berkeley: University of California Press, 1978) apply it to drama. C. J. Kennedy *Rhetorical Norms in Renaissance Literature* (New Haven: Yale University Press, 1978) and Rosalie Colie in *Paradoxia Epidemica* (Princeton: Princeton University Press, 1966) show its effect on the lyric. In "The Quality of Fiction: The Rhetorical Transmission of Literary Theory," *Traditio* XXX (1974), Wesley Trimpi shows how it affects the development of all genres of fiction. Only Trimpi and Doran mention the *debat*, which distills and demonstrates this influence, but they do so merely in passing.

[7] B. H. Bronson observes that the majority of texts in the Playford song collections are pastoral dialogues and debates. "The Dialog Song or Proteus Observed," *PQ*, 54: 117-136.

[8] Pastoral is usually defined by reference to theme and motif, and is thereby referred to as a *mode*. In this essay I consider pastoral as a structural convention. Following Frye, I refer to structural convention or "analogue of form" as *genre*, and here use "pastoral" to signify a cluster of genres as well as a mode. Northrope Frye, *Anatomy of Criticism* (Princeton: Princeton University Press, 1959), pp. 95 ff.

[9] Sing, while we sit here on the soft grass
Now all the fields and all the trees are blossoming;
Now the woods are greening; now the year has reached its
  height of beauty
Begin Damoetas, then you follow, Menalcas
You will sing in turn; the Muses love alternating songs.

III, 55-9. trans. Michael Putnam, *Vergil's Pastoral Art* (Princeton: Princeton University Press, 1970), p. 126. All later citations of Vergil in this chapter are to this translation.

[10] *Poetics*, trans. F. M. Padelford (New York: 1905), pp. 21-22, cited by Hallett Smith in *Elisabethan Poetry* (Cambridge: Harvard University Press, 1952), p. 14. Singing

contests of this nature remain an important feature of many present day cultures. Salient examples are the *cantraversias* sung by Puerto Rican farmers and the "rapping" sessions popular among Afro-Americans. See Roger Abrahams, *Deep Down in the Jungle* (Chicago: Aldine Publishing Co., 1970).

[11] These speculations are mentioned by Hans Walther in *Das Streitgedicht in der lateinischen Literatur des Mittelalters* (Muenchen: C. H. Becksche Verlag, 1920), p. 34. This book remains the standard treatment of the medieval *debat.*

[12] Charles Grosvenor Osgood and Henry Gibbons Lotspeich, *The Minor Poems,* vol. 1 (Baltimore: Johns Hopkins Press, 1943), p. 12. All later citations of *The Shepheardes Calendar* are to this volume.

[13] Hans Walther, p. 5 (my translation).

[14] The form he used to explore and dramatize the clash of philosophical ideas most probably influenced Theocritus and Vergil. (Adam Perry, "Landscape in Greek Poetry," *Yale Classical Studies* XV (1957), 29.) The *Phaedrus* in particular inspired the imitation of the many Renaissance platonists who considered themselves pastoralists. Pico della Mirandola thought of this dialogue as a version of pastoral because of its particular combination of setting and theme. (Richard Cody, *The Landscape of the Mind* (Oxford: Oxford University Press, 1969), pp. 4-6.) On pastoral and platonism, see also Edgar Wind, *Pagan Mysteries in the Renaissance* (Harmondsworth: Penguin Books, 1967).

[15] Phaedrus and Socrates present contending ideas on the two intertwined subjects of rhetoric and love. Phaedrus maintains Lysias' position that both love and rhetoric are most effective in achieving their goals when played as a game, when separated from their subjects' true feelings and desires. Socrates sees both love and rhetoric as a means of aspiration and of realizing the subjects' highest goals. Eventually the discussion moves to the topic of the opposition of body and soul. The contention between them is reflected in the dramatic struggle of the two speakers. Below the surface of the discussion, Phaedrus tries to use the attraction of his youthful body to seduce Socrates physically, while Socrates tries to use the attraction of his mind to seduce Phaedrus into the appreciation of higher things. (This reading is borne out by the analogous encounter between Alicibiades and Socrates in the *Symposium* and by passages like this:

> Phaedrus: There's shade there and a bit of a breeze and grass to sit on, or, if we like, even to lie in. . .isn't if from somewhere around here, from the Ilissus, that Boreas is said to have carried off Oreithyia?)

Within the terms of this struggle, the pastoral setting plays a correspondingly ambivalent role. In connection with the erotic theme, its natural beauty is either a stimulus to the young man's dalliance or an emblematic foretaste of the philosopher's paradise. In connection with the rhetorical theme, the green pleasance represents both a spontaneous appeal to the innocent simplicity of a natural retreat, and a sophisticated attempt to manipulate the listener with what by this time had already become a conventional topic for the bravura display of eloquence. (See Adam Perry, pp. 15-17 and Ernst Robert Curtius, *European Literature in the Latin Middle Ages* [New York: Pantheon Books, 1953], p. 187.

[16] Wesley Trimpi, p. 82.

[17] According to Cicero, most of the questions people face cannot be determined by absolutes, but exist in the realm of probability. "Since true sensations are associated

with false ones closely resembling them,. . .they contain no infallible mark to guide our judgment and assent. . ." Thus the "sole object of our discussion is by arguing both sides to draw out and give shape to some result that may be the nearest possible approximation to the truth." Cited by Trimpi, p. 45 and by Joel Altman, p. 69.

The method of debate, arguing both sides of the question, was used by medieval and Renaissance educators to sharpen their students' skills of inquiry and oratory. Such a method, which by its own nature questioned orthodoxy and authority, would be safe to pursue only in an environment at once detached and protected:

> So long as the Senecan exercises were merely preparatory for the actual encounters of the forum, they could remain in the cool and shaded protection of the declamatory halls and gardens. The young *declamator* might there enjoy the leisure of the *umbrosi loci* until, as an *orator,* he must face the dust, heat, and noise in the full sun before a real judge instead of an appreciative audience.
>
> Trimpi, p. 82.

Trimpi notes that the pastoral introduction to medieval debate works as an analogous shelter:

> The engagement in fictional debate, where umbratical *quaestiones* offer their shaded amenities to the excursions of wit, corresponds to an entrance into a walled garden or a dream vision, or even to the departure on a quest or pilgrimage. All offer a period of artistic immunity before demanding a return to the moral reality of the listener's world. This moral suspension is the most characteristic license of medieval fictions, its freedom from historical and philosophical proscriptions as Sidney was later to describe them.

Trimpi here (p. 82) alludes to the passage in Sidney's *Defense* describing poetry itself as a golden pastoral world, removed from the actual. Throughout the middle ages and the Renaissance this removal makes the shepherd's world a natural setting of fictional debate. The notion of the "Poem as Pastoral Enclosure" is developed by Tolliver, pp. 11 ff. and by Harry Berger Jr. in "The Renaissance Imagination: Second World and Green World," *Centennial Review* 9 (1965), pp. 36-79.

[18] My account of the evolution of debate from the eclogue follows James Holly Hanford's "Classical Eclogue and Medieval Debate," *Romantic Review* 2 (1911) pp. 16-31, 129-143. His theory was attacked by Betty Nye Hedberg in "The *Bucolics* and the Medieval Poetical Debate," *Transactions and Proceedings of the American Philological Association,* vol. 75 (1944), pp. 47 ff. But her point that there were other classical forerunners of verse debate in addition to the eclogue doesn't affect my use of Hanford's hypothesis.

[19] "Poetic Contests," in *Encyclopedia of Poetry and Poetics,* ed. A. Preminger (Princeton: Princeton University Press, 1965), pp. 626 ff.

[20] Walther, pp. 35 ff.

[21] W. W. Greg, *Pastoral Poetry and Pastoral Drama* (London: 1906; rep. New York: Russell and Russell, 1959). "During the middle ages the stream of pastoral production though it nowhere disappears is reduced to the merest trickle." p. 18.

[22] W. Leonard Grant, *Neo-Latin Literature and the Pastoral* (Chapel Hill: University of North Carolina Press, 1965), p. 76 ff.

[23] "The allegorical pastoral turns the praise of pastoral life to an indictment of bad shepherds of the church. . .Petrarch and Mantuan develop this "negative analogy" out of all proportion, turning it to a genre of its own." Poggioli, pp. 94-5.

[24] Many of the poets who follow Petrarch exhibit similar mixtures of purpose and style in their uses of genre. In the thirteenth of his series of sixteen *Bucolium Carmen*, Petrarch's friend Boccaccio sets out to present an amoebic singing contest modelled after Vergil's third eclogue. But the habits of thought of the rhetorical tradition of debate are so entrenched that partway through the poem he strays from his amoebic model and reverts to systematic allegorical argument, contrasting the virtues and vices of poetry with those of wealth. (Grant, pp. 97-100) As in the medieval *debat*, philosophical theme returns to dominate idyllic setting and dramatic character. In medieval poetry, formal organization appears on the surface of the work, containing content rather than being contained within it. Renaissance literature shows the opposite tendency: substance contains and even hides structure; mimesis supplants abstraction. A similar historical contrast applies to affective strategy. In keeping with the highly rhetorical nature of most medieval literature—its persuasive, instrumental approach to audience—the author's intentions and reader's expected response are often evident, or supposed to be evident to the informed critic. (D.W. Robertson's *A Preface to Chaucer: Studies in Medieval Perspectives* (Princeton: Princeton University Press, 1962) represents such "rhetorical" criticism. See Curtius, p. 148, on the domination of poetry by rhetoric during the middle ages.) Renaissance literature on the other hand, because of its more realistic and expressive tendencies, rarely prompts such confident assertions about intention and response. These two elements of a poem—formal structure and affective strategy—define and are defined by genre; by the time of the Renaissance, the concept of genre of "kinde," which had organized literary theory and practice during the middle ages, was itself losing some of its ruling force, as writers experimented with new mixtures and with using old forms in unconventional ways. (Rosalie Colie, *The Resources of Kind: Genre Theoery in the Renaissance* (Berkeley: University of California Press, 1973), p. 8. Claudio Guillen, *Literature as System: Essays Toward the Theory of Literary History* (Princeton: Princeton University Press, 1971).

This greater clarity in notions of genre may partly explain why there have been numerous critical studies of the medieval *Streitgedicht*, while Renaissance pastoral debate has escaped consideration as a genre altogether, despite critics' frequent use of implicitly generic notions of debate in discussions of Renaissance pastoral. Writers on medieval debate agree that the convention has a number of distinct structural features and rhetorical effects, but there has been no agreement on what these features are, nor has anyone offered a hypothesis explaining how the parts of the structure combine to generate a unified overall effect. (M. R. Bossy, "The Prowess of Debate," unpub. diss., Yale, 1970, discusses four "traits" of the *debat*: "1) the respectful acceptance of verbal skill as an honorable endowment; 2) the confrontation of antagonists evenly matched at the outset of the discussion; 3) the concern for polarities of value. . . 4) the awareness of the semiotic ambivalence of language." p. 8. D. E. Lampe, "Middle English Debate Poems," diss. Minnesota, 1969, somewhat tentatively mentions "the three or four essential elements of the debate genre." (p. 1) The first is pastoral setting, the second is "the establishment of the allegorical identities of the participants," third is the "plait or pleading," i.e., the actual argument, and fourth is the presence of the narrator.)

[25] Lorenzo de Medici, *Tutti le Opere* (Milan, 1958) III, 11. 12, 15. Cited and partly translated by Judy Zahler Kronenfeld, "The Treatment of Pastoral Ideals in *As You Like It*: A Study in Convention and Traditional Renaissance Dichotomies," Stanford diss. 1970. p. 126.

[26] Another parallel but separate evolution of pastoral and debate conventions from classical through medieval to Renaissance periods deserves brief mention here. Spread by the troubadors of Provence throughout Europe between the year one thousand and fourteen hundred, the genre of *pastourelle* most likely is a courtly refinement of a peasant folk-song genre. Governed by a strict formal pattern, the *pastourelle* begins with a knight's account of his "outriding" to the country, where he comes upon an attractive young shepherdess. It continues as a dramatic dialogue between the two, hinging upon his attempts and her graceful, witty or abusive refusal. Though not specifically allegorical, the *pastourelle* explores the contrast of noble and peasant, male and female, carpe-diem/anti-carpe diem outlooks analogous to the debate of youth and age. Robert Henrysson's "Robin and Makeyne" is a familiar Middle English version. "The Passionate Sheepheard" and "The Nymph's Reply" combine the conventions of *pastourelle* with those of the *conflictus.* See W. P. Jones, *The Pastourelle* (Cambridge: Harvard University Press, 1931) and W. D. Paden, "The Medieval *Pastourelle*—A Critical and Textual Reevaluation," Diss. Yale, 1971.

[27] (When fair Flora, the goddess of the flowers
Both groves and fields all freshly had bespread
And the pearly drops of balmy showers
The trees so green had with their water wet
Walking alone one morning mild I met
A merry young man there, of mirthful mien
Singing a song that was right sweetly set:
"O youth enjoy yourself in flowering green.")

My translation. Text is from *The Poems and Fables of Robert Henrysson,* ed. H. Harvey Wood (Edinburgh: Oliver and Boyd, 1933), p. 179. All later references are this edition, except where noted.

[28] Admittedly, "February" begins with young Cuddie's protest against the harshness of his landscape and against Spring's late arrival. But this very complaint implies the expected norm of the idyllic pastoral setting, a norm established at the opening of January, throughout the other eclogues of *SC,* and later in "Februarie" itself.

[29] "The magic of 'When daisies pied. . .' and of 'When icicles. . .' (the *debat* which concludes *Love's Labor's Lost*) is partly that they seem to be merely lists. . .and yet each song says, in a marvelously economical way where people are in the cycle of the year, the people who live entirely in the turning seasons. The only syntax that matters is 'When. . .Then. . .' . . .not folk songs, consciously pastoral, sophisticated enjoyment of simplicity." C. L. Barber, *Shakespeare's Festive Comedy: A Study of Dramatic Form and its Relation to Social Cutom* (New York: Meridian, 1959), p. 117.

[30] "The Passionate Pilgrim" 11. 157-68 in *The Complete Poems and Plays of William Shakespeare,* Ed. William Allan Neilson and Charles Jarvis (Cambridge, Mass.: Houghton Mifflin, 1942). This poem, though included in a collection attributed to Shakespeare, was, according to most editors, not written by him.

[31] William Nelson, *The Poetry of Edmund Spenser* (New York: Columbia University Press, 1963), p. 39.

[32] edited by M. Y. Offord (London: Early English Text Society, Oxford University Press, 1959), vol. ii, lines 166-168.

[33] (I looked beyond him but a little way,
And saw a shape approaching with a cane
His cheeks were bare, his hoary locks were gray
His eye hollow, his hoarse voice coughed with pain
Withered he was and weak as a twig under strain
Upon his breast he bore a message of doom
Which said in letters small that did not feign
"O youth your flowers will fade now precious soon.")
Poems and Fables of Robert Henrysson, p. 179.

[34] G. E. R. Lloyd, *Polarity and Analogy: Two Types of Argument in Early Greek Thought* (Cambridge: Cambridge University Press, 1966), p. 65.

[35] cited by Lloyd, p. 15.

[36] Aristotle, *Rhetoric*, trans. W. Rhys Roberts (New York: Modern Library, 1954), pp. 121-5.

[37] The term "debate" stems from Latin *battuere* or "battle." The heat of this battle is the source of the convention's vigor, assimilating to poetry the attractions of competitive sport. As Castiglione observed:

> And forsomuch as our mindes are very apte to love and to hate: as in the sights of combats and games. . .it is seene that the lookers-on many times beare affection without any manifest cause why, into one of the two parties, with a greedy desire to have him get the victorie, and the other to have the overthrow.

(Castiglione, *The Courtier*, trans. Sir Thomas Hoby (1561) in *Three Renaissance Classics*, ed. Burton Milligan (New York: Scribners, 1953), p. 273.) Verse debate survives widely as a form of verbal folk art—in the *flytings* hurled during Celtic folk festivals, in the "dozens" and "raps" exchanged in ghetto streets, and in the improvised *contraversia* sung by Puerto Rican peasants. But the form of poetic contest I am concerned with here is the product of literary culture. It has more significant analogues in the late Roman *controversia*, the fictional trial that pitted two orators in hypothetical litigation for the entertainment of a theatrical audience.

[38] For a full study of Renaissance applications of these three levels of discourse, see C. J. Kennedy, *Rhetorical Norms in Renaissance Literature*. How much direct influence Aristotle's *Rhetoric* had on later writers is open to question. But the rhetorical tradition carried forward by Cicero, Quintillian and Aphthonius, who supplied the actual texts in the schools, was heavily enough based in Aristotle's *Rhetoric* to make his treatment an appropriate paradigm for this study.

[39] *Rhetoric* 1358b, p. 32.

[40] *Rhetoric* 1356a, pp. 24-5.

[41] (As this young man leapt lightly on the land
I marvelled much to mark his mighty zest.
"Superb I am," said he, "a superman
With boar's brawn, broad and burly breast
Who'd dare deny the boon with which I'm blessed
Or of my doughtiness a dot demean.
My face is fair, my form can stand time's test
O youth, enjoy yourself in flowering green."

This old man sang with sober voice and slow
Shaking his chin beard, "Boy," he said, "let be
I was, but sixty seven years ago
A champion on the earth, as strong and free
As glad, as gay, as green, as glib as ye
But now those days o'erdriven are and done
Look at my loathly shape and there truth see
O youth, your flowers will fade now precious soon.")

42 *Rhetoric* 1402a, p. 159.

43 *The Poems of Sir Phillip Sidney*, ed. William A. Ringler, Jr. (Oxford: Clarendon Press, 1962), p. 24, lines 102-4. All later references are to this edition.

44 *Rhetoric*, 1394a, p. 134.

45 Rhetorical interpolations sometimes take up more space in the verse debate than the argument itself. In the *Parlement of Thre Ages*, Youth embarks on a long formulaic digression on the joys of falconry, while Old Age devotes more than half of the poem to a series of exempla illustrating the fall of pride.

46 *Rhetoric*, 1354a, p. 19. In order to succeed in this, the orator must have knowledge of human character—as it is manifested not only in the *persona* of the speaker he creates but in the audience to whom he wishes to appeal. Such knowledge includes an understanding of the emotions, their separate natures, relationships and causes. Of the many emotions displayed in the drama of *conflictus*, anger is the most prevalent. And since anger is one of the strongest emotions that the orator stimulates, Aristotle provides a lengthy analysis of its forms and causes that guides the orator as dramatist:

> Anger may be defined as an impulse, accompanied by a pain, to a conspicuous revenge for a conspicious *slight* directed without justification towards what concerns oneself or one's friends. . .It must always be attended by a certain pleasure—that which arises from the expectation of revenge. . .There are three kinds of slighting—contempt, spite and insolence. . .you feel contempt for what you consider unimportant. . .Spite. . .is a thwarting another man's wishes, not to get something yourself but to prevent his getting it. . .Insolence is also a form of slighting, since it consists in doing and saying things that shame the victim simply for the pleasure involved. . .The cause of the pleasure thus enjoyed by the insolent man is that he thinks himself greatly superior to others when ill-treating them. That is why youths and rich men are insolent. . .(*Rhet.* 1378b)
> People afflicted by sickness or poverty or love or thirst or any other unsatisfied desires are prone to anger and easily roused: especially against those who slight their present distress. . .thus a lover is angered by disregard of his love. . .(*Rhet.* 1379a)

This passage describes the forms and causes of anger discoverable in the pastoral debates of Age and Youth.

47 Their use also provides employment for literary critics like E. K.:

> But eft when) A verye excellent and lively description of Winter so as may bee indifferently taken, eyther for old Age, or for Winter season. . .Phyllis) The name of some unknowen, whom Cuddie, whose person is secrete, loves. The name is usuall in Theocritus, Vergile and Mantuane.
>
> (*Minor Poems*, I, 27)

[48] Translated by Braydon Eggers (Durham, N.C.: Duke University Press, 1955) 11. 32 ff. H. Haesler provides an exhaustive list of such rhetorical devices in "*The Owl and the Nightingale* und die literarischen Bestrebungen des 12. und 13. Jhts," (Frankfurt-am-Mein, 1942).

[49] *Rhetoric*, p. 52.

[50] In this connection, it is relevant to look at Aristotle's definition of character in the *Poetics*:

> Character in a play is that which reveals the moral purpose of the agents, i.e., the sort of thing they seek or avoid, *where that is not obvious*. . .(italics mine). Thought, on the other hand, is shown in all they say when proving or disproving some particular point or enunciating some universal proposition.
>
> (Translated by Ingram Bywater (New York: Modern Library, 1954), 1450b, p. 232)

In this passage, which illuminates the overlap between the disciplines of poetry and rhetoric, character is again distinguished from the content of speech and located somewhere behind the words: "the sort of thing they seek or avoid, where that is not obvious." Character must be inferred by the reader; or, in those cases when drama is staged—the *Streitgedicht* was often performed by jongleurs and minstrels—it must be *interpreted* by the actor.

[51] Another stanza this young swain did sing
"Now's time, I think, to partake of love's treat
At court, of course. I'll swagger, strut and swing
And look for one amongst the ladies sweet
Whose mouth with mine will mix in marriage meet
In secret places where we wont be seen
And there that bird will love to cool my heat
O youth enjoy yourself in flowers green."

[52] Then angrily replied the austere Reeve
"For your swagger you shall croak and cower
Your fleshly lust will some day make you grieve
And pain will pull you from your paramour
And then will no bird love you in the bower
When lo, your manhood's waned just like the moon
And then you'll learn if this my song's too sour:
O youth, your flowers wither precious soon."

[54] The merry man of mirth still argued more
My body's clean without trace of corruption
My spirit's sound—it's neither sick nor sore
My senses five maintain their due proportion
My mind is in a perfect clear condition
My heart is hale, and so's my liver and spleen
Therefore I will not need your admonition
O youth enjoy yourslef in flowers green."

The greybeard answered thus the burly boy
"You'll serve this sentence; soon you'll lose your hair
The stature and the strength you now enjoy

Old age and fevers foul away will bear
Your heat will cool, your body will outwear
With failing health you'll surely come to ruin
Despite your wish, time won't your senses spare
"O Youth your flowers wither precious soon."

[55] Following the usual pattern of characterization in medieval literature, the particular is secondary, descended from the universal, while the reader's view of the characters' subjective existence—their interior reality—remains subordinate to his sense of them as objective embodiments of the contraries. Like the physical setting of the debate, the psychological reactions of the principals appear only as ornaments or *colores* to enliven the demands of theme, plot and a priori structural pattern.

(Trimpi, p. 27)

[56] "The Renaissance and Reformation were crucial stages in the process of 'interiorization' of European culture." Claudio Guillen, p. 307.

[57] Their choice is ironically appropriate. Chaucer's Miller the one who observes that "Youthe and Elde are often at debaat." Not only his Prologue and Tale, but that of the Reeve, the Merchant, the Pardoner, the Wife of Bath and the Clerk all have as a central theme the conflict of youth and age.

[57a] *The Shepherd's Garland* in *The Works of Michael Drayton,* ed. J. W. Hebel, vol. V, ed. Kathleen Tillotson and B. H. Newdigate (Oxford, Oxford University Press, 1961), p. 50. All later references to this volume.

[58] The Drayton's tactics are suggested by Quintillian: "Ethos includes the skillful exercise of feigned emotion or the employment of irony and sometimes even a feigned submission to our opponents." Cited by W. J. Kennedy, pp. 10-11.

[59] *The Poems of Sir Phillip Sidney,* p. 26, 11. 135-7.

[60] This generalization needs qualifying. Though most debates end as stalemates, a considerable number do conclude with one side's triumph. Examples of these are the early "Ecloga Theoduli," the debate between Wine and Water (won by Wine), Drayton's second eclog, Milton's debate between the lady and Comus, and Marvell's debate between the resolved soul and created pleasure. Such "didactic" works have a different affective strategy from the "exploratory" poems that end in stalemate. (This pair of categories is proposed by Altman, p. 7 ff.) They expose both sides of the question in order to refute error and lay it to rest, in order to confirm a single homiletic message and support one side in a controversy. Renaissance Puritan satires took the form of such debate dialogues. See L. H. Smith, "The Elizabethan Debate Dialogue," diss. University of Minnesota, 1974. However, in some cases the intended or at least stated effect is lost, and the reader sides with the wrong contestant—as did Blake with Milton's Satan.

In some of the debates considered here, the question of the nature of the outcome of the argument has itself become a vexed *altercatio.* Scholars like Lampe (*Middle English Debate Poems*), and Douglas Peterson ("*O and N* and Christian Dialectic") insist for instance that the *Owl and the Nightingale,* the *Owl and the Cuckoo* and other *debats* that seem to be exploratory, in fact are didactic, since contemporary "rules" of disputation or of Christian Doctrine would force the reader to side with one side and see the fallacy of the other. Other scholars, like Bossy (*The Prowess of Debate*) and *Speirs* (*Middle English Poetry*) insist that poems like "*Parl. of Thre Ages*" that seem to have a didactic outcome, in fact are open, in that their 'holy' speakers partially discredit themselves on the dramatic level.

[61] In the Carolingean "Conflictus Hyemis et Estatis," after Winter tries a trick similar to Thenot's in "February," Dame Theology enters from above, counsels Summer and Winter to cease their quarrelling, and advises that continuation will lead to their mutual destruction while reconciliation will take them both to heaven. (Walther, p. 209) In "The Owl and the Nightingale," the royal wren convinces the two birds to stop squabbling, not by adjudicating their claims, but by referring them to another judge. And in the allegorical *debat* in the *locus amoenus* on Arlo Hill between Change and Constancy that concludes Spenser's *Faerie Queene*, Dame Nature validates and criticizes the arguments of both parties, predicting the moment when all debate shall finally cease.

[62] This gallant groaned with a grievious heave
And soon departed sadly from the scene;
The old man didn't laugh, but took his leave. . .

[63] And I remained under the leaves so green
Until the worth of each one's words I'd seen
And knew that truth wove through their crossing tune
"O Youth take hold of joy in flowers green!"
"O Youth your flowers will wither precious soon."

In one of the Ms. editions of Henrysson's poems published by the Early Scottish Text Society, the word "triumphit," for which no suitable definition has been found, is replaced by the word "trevist"—i.e., "traversed" or "kept intersecting." I have used this variant in my translation.

[64] Sidney creates an analogous conclusion of musical harmony out of mental contradictions at the end of a pastoral debate that introduces his first series of eclogues in Arcadia:

[The dance of the Arcadian shepherds]

[A] We love, and have our loves rewarded.
[B] We love, and are no whit regarded.
[A] We finde most sweete affection's snare,
[B] That sweete, but sower despairfull care.
[A] Who can despaire, whom hope doth beare?
[B] And who can hope, who feeles despaire?
[AB] As without breath, no pipe doth move,
No musike kindly without love.

(*The Poems of Sir Phillip Sidney*, p. 14)

[64a] "Februarie" (translation: God, because he is aged, makes those he loves like himself . . . No old man fears God.)

[65] In *Dialectical Criticism and Renaissance Literature* (Berkeley: University of California Press, 1975), Michael McCanless draws a contrast between an "either-or" and a "both-and" picture of reality that corresponds to my opposition between the articulation of contraries and the relativity of perspective. His definition of "dialectic" provides an involuted but accurate description of what happens to the reader of pastoral debate:

> Dialectic occurs when men attempt to force on a "both-and" reality an "either-or" reading of it. . .Agents attempt to resolve conflicts and contradictions between antinomial concepts, ideological positions and doctrines by reducing

these antinomies to one conflicting side and ignoring or denying the other. In so doing, they only invite back on themselves the attacks of other men (or concepts or ideologies). . .A discourse that commits itself to antinomial categories as its key terms is. . .a verbal action the end of which is to extricate itself from the dialectical logic implicit in these categories. This dialectical logic asserts itself in proportion to the argumentative force directed at escape from it. . .dialectic becomes inevitable to the exact degree that dialectic is denied. (p. 11)

[66] Stanley Fish, *Self Consuming Artifacts* (Berkeley: University of California Press, 1972), p. 51. see also his *The Living Temple: George Herbert and Catechizing* (Berkeley: University of California Press, 1978).

[67] *The Complete Essays of Montaigne,* trans. Donald M. Frame (Stanford: Stanford University Press, 1965), p. 372.

[68] The word "perspective" originates with Latin, "Perspiccere," meaning "to see clealry," "examine," "regard mentally," The term first gained currency when used by quattrocento painters to refer to the technique of creating the illusion of three dimensional space on a two dimensional surface. This was done by the painter's organizing the canvas as a pyramid of coordinates whose base was the point of view of the observer and whose apex was a calculated "vanishing point." (Claudio Guillen, *Literature as System,* p. 291). At the same time as supplying an instrument for the representation of truth, however, perspective was regarded as a mode of trickery and deception, and was both treasured and distrusted as such. It was a sign of the virtue and the danger of an expertly rendered scene in perspective that the beholder might not be able to distinguish between it and actually looking out the window. The word "perspective" thus also referred to illusionary devices like "anamorphic" paintings.

> Like perspectives, which rightly gazed upon Show nothing but confusion—eyed awry Distinguish form.
>
> (Shakespeare, *Richard II,* II,ii, 14-16, cited by Guillen, p. 309)

The very accuracy of the perspective representation depended on the fact that it was produced from a single, frozen location of the perceiver. But this rigid viewpoint also called into question the "truth" of the painting's representation. For the sizes and relationships of objects portrayed would appear wholly different from another vantage, raising serious doubts in the viewer's mind about the ability of the sense of sight—the noblest of the senses—to determine what was really there. In Guillen's words, "the concept and metaphor of perspective can readily be associated with growing epistemological dualism, the rigorous split between subject and object, as in the Cartesian distinction between mind and res *extensa*". (p. 292) This Cartesian epistemology is made explicit in Marvell's famous *conflictus,* "The Dialog of the Body and Soul," but the questioning that leads to it is implicit in the Relativity of Perspectives that characterizes the genre as far back as Marvell's medieval sources. (see H. Walther, 63 ff.) In Leibnitz' philosophy of the Monad, developed late in the 17th century, this notion of the relativity of perspectives, which permeates the Tudor *Weltanschauung* and which is generically implicit in the verse debate, is articulated into a full-blown epistemology and metaphysics. Starting with the premise that different perceptions of reality contradict each other and yet have their own validity i.e., "That the relations between perceiving units and perceived objects are at once different and 'truthful'," Leibnitz took the outrageous leap of postulating the point of view itself as the only true reality:

a non-material substance that he compared to a center of a sphere and called a monad. Leibnitz defined "perspective" as "the order imposed by the mind on the representations it receives" and drew the conclusion that there is no truth apart from the perceiver at all; and as a corollary that all the contradictions that we experience in "debate" are simply expressions of the different perspectives of the monads. According to Leibnitz, all the perspectives are collectively harmonized in the totality of viewpoints which is God.

[69] Guillen, p. 310.

[70] Kennedy, p. 21.

[71] See Altman, p. 45, for a compendium of these rhetorical devices.

[72] Montaigne, p. 424.

[73] Thomas Lodge, *Rosalynde, or Euphues' Golden Legacy* ed. Edward Chauncey Baldwin (Boston: Ginn & Co., 1910), pp. 41 ff. The set piece extends back to Theocritus' Idyll X, in which an old and young laborer briefly discuss love.

5

The Backstretched Connexion: Youth and Age in *The Shepheardes Calender*

This chapter proposes an interpretation of *The Shepheardes Calender* which places the debate of youth and age at the work's core. Spenser used both the thematic content and the formal structure of this minor bucolic convention as the central shaping principle of his major pastoral work. Such emphasis was particularly appropriate, first because pastoral's rural settings on the periphery of civilization correspond to the peripheral states of the human life cycle, and second, because pastoral's projection of dual worlds inspires debate-like comparisons of perception and judgment.

But Spenser did not simply reprocess these essential elements of the pastoral tradition. Rather he modified and enriched his conventional models by disclosing the debate of youth and age through the viewpoint of a narrative persona, a viewpoint which shifts in the course of the poem from identification with youth to identification with age. That is to say, Spenser used the pastoral debate of youth and age as a means by which to externalize the inner conflicts of past and future, of regression and maturation, endemic to adolescence. By patterning his series of eclogues with a phased succession of such debates, Spenser allowed the reader to participate in the reversal of perspective that constitutes the subjective transformation of boy into man. Moving from premises about the psychology of pastoral and about the philosophy of debate laid down previously, this chapter arrives at the conclusion that *The Shepheardes Calender*—a product of its author's youth and addressed to youthful readers—has as its deepest unifying subject the life stage of youth itself.

* * *

The mysterious "E.K." 's introductory epistle, "argvments," and glosses, which have traditionally provided the starting point of critical discussion of the *Calender,* focus upon the pervasive theme of youth vs. age. The friend of the poet draws attention to its appearance in obvious places like "Febvarie," where the young and old shepherd and their fabulist counterparts engage in generational battle, or like "Maye," where two old men dispute the issue of youthful pleasure vs. aged prudence. In the "argvment" that precedes "December," E.K. remarks on the way Colin's old age elegy conflates the seasonal and human life cycles:

> Wherein as weary of his former wayes, he proportioneth his life to the foure seasons of the yeare, comparing hys youthe to the spring time, when he was fresh and free from loues follye. His manhoode to the sommer, which he sayeth, was consumed with greate heate and excessive drouth. . .by which hee meaneth loue. . .His riper yeares hee resembleth to an unseasonable harueste wherein the fruites fall ere they be rype. His latter age to winters chyll and frostie season, now drawing neare to his last ende.[1]

Later scholars have often quoted this charming passage of critical prose as a guide to the largest movement of the *Calender*. It suggests the contrast between the early eclogues—"Febrvarie," "March," "April," and "Maye"—and the later ones—"September," "October," "November," and "December," a contrast between the seedtime of childlike innocence sown in the rites of spring and the harvest of sombre experience reaped in care, disappointment and resignation.[2]

Along with supplying the topic of specific eclogues and determining the largest thematic contrast of the sequence, youth vs. age appears in some guise in every one of the twelve months. When its presence is not evident, E.K. alerts us to its whereabouts with the motif-hunter's delight in discovery:

> Hereby is meant, that all the delights of Loue, wherein wanton youth walloweth, be but folly mixt with bitterness, and sorrow sawced with repentaunce. . .euen the selfe things which best before vs lyked, in course of time and chaung of ryper yeares, whiche also therewithall chaungeth our wonted lyking and former fantasies, will then seeme lothsome and breede vs annoyaunce, when yougthes flowre is withered, and we fynde our bodyes and wits aunsere not to such vayne iollitie and lustful pleasaunce. (p. 35)

Despite its tendentious relation to the text, this gloss on the "March" emblem correctly calls attention to the contrast and progression between youth and age as the *Calender's* typical configuration, an identifiable watermark on every page of the poem.

Spenser draws together the diverse components of his set of eclogues by linking the polarity of youth and age with the extremes of mood between which any segment of the poem oscillates. E.K. names these extremes of celebration and mourning "recreative" and "plaintive," dividing the twelve months into "Rankes" according to which mood dominates. But he also observes that "to this division may everything herein be reasonably applied." (p. 12) At the beginning of "March," for instance, the tone modulates suddenly from plaintive to recreative:

Thomalin, why sytten we soe,
As weren ouerwent with woe,
Vpon so fayre a morow?
The iouous time now nigheth fast,
That shall alegge this bitter blast,
And slake the winters sorowe.

THOMALIN

Sicker Willye, thou warnest well:
For Winters wrath beginnes to quell,
And plesant spring appeareth.
The grasse nowe ginnes to be refresht,
The Swallow peepes out of her nest,
And clowdie Welkin cleareth.
(1-12)

And then later in the eclogue it drops off once again into complaint:

But he, that earest seemd but to playe,
A shaft in earnest snatched,
And hit me running in the heele:
For then I little smart did feele:
But soone it sore encreased.
And now it ranckleth more and more,

And inwardly it festreth sore,
  Ne wote I how to cease it.
(95-102)

Throughout the *Calender* these momentary modulations of mood are equated with changes in weather and season and with a fall from innocence to experience that parallels the maturation process. Spenser measures the ebb and flow of emotion at many different intervals with the same oscillating pendulum that clocks the minutes, months and decades.[3]

In organizing his poem with the polarity of youth and age, Spenser made use of the elaborate schemata which dominated traditional conceptions of the natural world—the setting of pastoral. He found one of these systems of correspondence in the *Kalendar of Shepherds,* the peasant almanac which had recently been published in a translation from the original French.[4] He also incorporated elements of the popular psychology of the humours, which presupposed significant relations among elements, passing moods, general temperaments, conditions of the body and the ages of man. According to this theory, youth was naturally sanguine—hot, wet and merry—while age was naturally melancholic—cold, dry and depressed.[5] Such a set of norms supplied Spenser with a matrix against which variations and change could be plotted. In "Januarie," for example, he heightens the pathos of his central figure, Colin Clout, by portraying the sad youth's condition as a disruption of the natural order of correspondences:

Such rage as winters, reigneth in my heart,
My life bloud friesing with vnkindly cold:
Such stormy stoures do breede my balefull smart,
As if my yeare were wast, and woxen old.
And yet alas, but now my spring begonne,
And yet alas, yt is already donne.
. . .
All so lustfull leafe is drye and sere,
My timely buds with wayling all are wasted:

> The blossome, which my braunch of youth did beare
> With breathed sighes is blowne away, and blasted.
>
> (25-40)

The inverted sequence of this *adynaton*—the rhetorical figure of nature turned upside down—typifies the traditional bucolic pattern of contrasts by confessing negative, anti-pastoral feelings in the midst of a world postulated as ideal.

While Spenser subordinated all the other themes of *The Shepheardes Calender* to the distinctly Arcadian concern with youth and age, he chose pastoral debate as the work's predominant formal structure. Five of the *Calender's* twelve eclogues—those E.K. refers to as "Moral: which for the most part be mixt with some Satyrical bitterness"—transmute "recreative" and "plaintive" moods into ideological positions. Here the oscillation of extreme feelings is mirrored in the alternation of opposed arguments, rhetorical appeals and manipulative gambits of antagonistic orators. "Febrvarie's" confrontation of young Cuddie and old Thenot sets the pattern for the rest. Like "Maye," "Ivlye," "September," and "October," it superimposes layer upon layer of social, ethical, educational, aesthetic, political and religious issues; and it often hides or reveals the specifics of those issues under the universal rubric of generational conflict.

Because Spenser presented these disputes in extremely serious, vehement tones, many early twentieth century critics assumed that he was using the moral eclogues to propagandize his readers, and they expended a great deal of effort proving or disproving that his view was expressed by one side or the other.[6] That critical endeavor turned out to be largely self-cancelling however, and more recent scholars have concurred in the opinion that Spenser rather intended fully to air both sides of the question without arriving at a final conclusion. "Suspension" has thereby become the last critical word on the moral eclogues—the same word so widely applied to the eclogues of Vergil. In "The Eclogue Tradition and the Nature of Pastoral," Paul Alpers comments that the most important achievement of

Patrick Cullen's book on the *Calender* is displaying the truth of William Nelson's remark that Spenser uses dialogue to show (in Nelson's words) "a valid disagreement in which speakers explore what may best be said on either part."[7] Echoing thus through recent criticism like a pastoral topos itself, Nelson's phrase unconsciously locates the formal conventions of the moral eclogues squarely within the generic boundaries of the medieval *conflictus* or verse debate—boundaries I have delineated in the preceding chapter. The terms of his description of Spenser's purpose—"Explore what best may be said on either part"—allude to the "exploratory" rather than didactic nature of the Ciceronian dialogue, and also translate the motto of the tradition of rhetorical inquiry that produced the verse debate: *et utramque partem.*[8]

Nelson's approach has led other critics to observe that the problematic unity of the complete *Calender* can be extrapolated from the five moral debates. Patrick Cullen, for instance, sees the "central purpose and technique" of the entire work in "a juxtaposition of different perspectives whereby pastoral experience is evaluated."[9] If we accept this view of Spenser's intentions, the four-part paradigm of allegorical verse debate I have offered earlier supplies a reading of the whole collection of twelve eclogues. Its initial setting is always the *locus amoenus* of the recreative landscape. Each eclogue articulates contraries that in some way can be equated with youth vs. age. The wrangling arguments in the five moral eclogues combine with the oscillation of moods in the other seven eclogues to make up the *Calender's* "carpynge." And the ambivalent, inconclusive ending of the sequence—with its premature despair, its missing final emblem, and its palinodal *envoi*—confronts the reader with the relativity of perspectives. Thus, *The Shepheardes Calender* itself is a version of *debat.*[10]

* * *

And yet, having supported the balanced, exploratory interpretation of Spenser's first published work by adducing its medieval generic pedigree, as a reader I am still left searching for a deeper unity by which to apprehend the poem. In studying a book of this scale and power, I am not satisfied to conclude with a system of dichotomies, ambivalences or "suspensions," no matter how extensive or subtle. Instead, I seek what Heraclitus called "the backstretched connexion" that lies concealed beneath the ceaseless strife of opposites animating all existence ". . .as in the bow or the lyre."[11] I seek a confrontation with the text not only as a timeless pattern of themes and structures, but as the expression of an individual human being, a writer who communicates his own coherent sense of the world through the evolving point of view of a protagonist and through the temporal sequence of a story.[11a]

The key to discovering the central consciousness and the elusive plot line of *The Shepheardes Calender* lies within other stipulations of genre. The Vergilian "perfecte paterne of a poete" specifies the shepherd-pastoralist as ephebe, as a young man on the brink of psychosocial and artistic adulthood. In the "Dedicatory Epistle," E.K. refers to this convention to explain both the origin and the end of the work:

> His unstayed youth had long wandred in the common labyrinth of love in which time to mitigate and allay the heate of his passion, or else to warne the young shepeherds S. his equalls and companions of his unfortunate foly, he compiled these xij Aeglogues. . .
>
> (p. 10)

Elaborating this idea, E.K. refers to the *Calender* as "the maydenhead of this our common friend's Poetrie." (p. 11) The gesture of offering a maydenhead distills the ambivalent significance of youth's position in the life cycle, its suspension between past and future. Looking toward the past, that gesture marks the nadir of a downward movement, the irrecoverable loss of virginity—and with virginity, the loss of innocence. The powerful nostalgia accompanying this loss has always generated poetry: both the pastoral of youth's idyllic fantasies of an Edenic past and the elegaic complaints of the anti-pastoral of melancholy. But looking forward to the future, the youth's offer of a maydenhead represents the beginning of ascent—the moment of emergence, of growing up, of entering and being entered by the world.[12] By focussing such intense scrutiny on youth's place in the life cycle, Spenser chronicles the passage from childhood to maturity in *The Shepheardes Calender.* In so doing, he molds the central convention of pastoral, the debate of youth and age, into a prototype of the *Bildungsroman.* In both content and form, this set of eclogues bears significant resemblance to books with titles like *The Prelude, Great Expectations, The Way of All Flesh,* and *Portrait of the Artist as a Young Man.*[13]

Spenser creates the protagonist of this narrative with the semi-allegorical device of employing a variety of characters to represent different facets of a single "Young Man." Cuddie, Thomalin, Diggon, Willie and Perigot take the traditional social roles of the young bucolic *pastor*—the bumpkin, the singer, the lover, the fledgling governor or priest. The first among equals in the group of *pueri* is Colin Clout, Spenser's portrait of the artist. But it is Immerito, the shady persona of the narrator, who encompasses all these facets in himself, and thus becomes the hero of the work: the person who actually grows up.[14]

When one thinks of the whole *Calender* as a story of Immerito's maturation, one's sense of the poem's structure alters. The unstable, tensive endings of each eclogue and the dissonant conclusion of the whole sequence propel the story forward and force the reader beyond the characters' perceptions of themselves—force him to take a larger view that reveals those conflicts as momentary manifestations of a single being's change through time. Thus the pervasive dualism of debate turns into the dialectic of development; the polarity of youth and age is no longer static; it generates the voltage which sets the growth process in motion. As Blake writes in *The Marriage of Heaven and Hell,* "Without Contraries, there is no Progression."[15] Regarded in this way, "Youth" is no longer the first phase in the sequence of "Youth, Adulthood, Old Age," as it has been regarded earlier. Instead, it becomes the middle phase in the sequence, "Childhood, Youth, Maturity." "Youth" in this sense, is the age of man that, in the words of Kaspar Naegele, "drives a wedge into the continuity of the life cycle."[16]

This Janus-faced quality of orientation toward both past and future defines the concept of youth within many frames of reference. In the physical sense, youth is the period of life when sexual differentiation and desire are dramatically emergent yet incompletely developed, when the voice cracks between soprano and bass, when skin glows and also blemishes. In the emotional sense, youth is the period of struggle between awakening urges and weakened parental imperatives. In the mental sense, youth is the period when the brain first becomes subject to "the onset of epistemological dualism. . .the awareness of a multiplicity of truths, from which the individual must choose 'commitment within relativism.' "[17] As a stage of cognitive development, youth is the period of "thinking about thinking; of hyperawareness of the inner processes and states of consciousness."[18]

A corresponding ambivalence also besets youth's social being. During this period, the person's roles are subjected to diametric reversal, since it "*necessarily* coincides with the transition period from the family of orientation to that of procreation. . .from the receiver to transmitter of cultural tradition."[19] Indeed, while the person undergoes this "crucial change of individual age roles. . .two age definitions still interact within him."[20] Thus conceived, youth becomes the arena of the "debate" of childhood and maturity. Hence, the pastoral debate of youth and age hearkens back to one of the rites of passage which mark the transition from childhood to maturity in traditional societies. This consists of "the dramatization of the encounter between different generations, a dramatization which may take the form of a fight, or a competition."[21]

In fact, all rites of passage ceremonialize the intensification of conflict and the breakdown of structure and meaning that occur at such transitional periods:

> Those undergoing the rite of passage are betwixt and between the established states of politico-jural structure. They evade ordinary cognitive classification too, for they are neither this nor that, here nor there. . .the most characteristic midliminal symbolism is that of paradox, of being *both* this *and* that. . .androgenous, both living and dead, human and animal, ground down into homogeneous social matter, to be refashioned anew.[22]

With this in mind, we read "Febrvarie," for instance, not only as an allegory of the eternal battle of youth and age, winter and spring, passion and reason or pleasure and reality principles. We can also understand it as a young man's projection of the war in his own soul between the claims of past and future, child and parent. In addition to accounting for the unexplained intensity of hostility between the principals, such a reading confirms the text's repeated hints that the antagonists are actually mirror images of one another.[23] Thus, the debate of youth and age in *The Shepheardes Calender* is not merely a vehicle for expressing the clash of literary pastoral ideals or of "traditional pastoral perspectives." Instead, it represents the immediate reality of the confusion, the turmoil, and the incessant interior squabble of conflicting points of view that plague the person coming of age. Using the poetic debate genre to thoroughly immerse the reader in these conflicts, Spenser at the same time dramatizes youth's dilemma with an almost clinical detachment.

Erik Erikson has diagnosed this dilemma as "Role Confusion" which the person negotiating the transition from childhood to maturity must resolve by passing through an "Identity Crisis"—a crisis that issues in an integrated sense of who he is. Indeed, establishing an adult identity can be seen as the overarching task of the stage of youth itself, its end, its teleological definition:

> "Ego Identity" is the creation of a sense of sameness, a unity of personality now felt by the individual and recognized by others as having consistency in time—of being as it were, an irreversible historical fact.[24]

Spenser shows this crisis coming to a head with adumbrations of death and rebirth in the later months of the *Calender*. He demonstrates the resolution of the crisis at the very end of the poem in the surfacing of Immerito as narrator and author. Immerito integrates the diverse and conflicting roles that have battled their way through the sequence. His is the "unity of personality" whose single voice at different moments has taken the inflections of young and old, recreative and plaintive, wise and foolish. Immerito speaks directly to the reader with self-confident resonance that subsumes and absorbs the variety of months, seasons and ages. To recognize that speaker not only at the end, but in all the voices of the *Calender* is to discover the unity of the poem.

* * *

Ego identity coalesces during emergence from childhood retreat into the exposure of history. To define himself, the individual finds public figures and ideological positions to which to attach loyality—or what Erikson calls "Fidelity." But despite his inner imperative for public involvement, the adolescent lacks the coherent sense of self and the set of priorities necessary for serious participation in the *vita activa*. Young people are therefore often allowed or even encouraged to express rapid and radical shifts of loyalty as an exploratory prelude to more permanent identification. This status of relative immunity from the consequences of positions strongly taken has been labelled youth's "moratorium"—a term that suggests the conventional use of the pastoral setting as a protected enclosure for the heated but nevertheless tentative expression of opinions on both sides of controversial questions.[25] By presenting public issues within the Arcadian *locus amoenus*, the moral debates of the *Calender* contain those issues within the framework of youth's quest for identity and fidelity.[26]

The dissolution of the essential social distinction between child and adult during youth which causes stress and confusion in the individual undergoing it also threatens the integrity of the whole framework of social roles, distinctions and meanings. For this reason in traditional societies, that transition is guided by patterns of highly ritualized behavior handed down from the past.[27] But in a society bereft of formal rites of passage, or in a historical period—like our own—when traditions themselves are being ground down and refashioned, the consciousness of youth is likely to become a primary arena for the battles between old and new, "Ancient and Modern," orthodox and innovative that generate the historical process itself.[28] The energy given off by such battles frequently takes the form of generational strife, in which youth asserts itself and forges identity by rejecting adult figures of authority, while age insists on protecting its prerogatives and privileges with self-righteous rigidity. In this sense, the altercation between Cuddie and Thenot in "Februarie" dramatizes a specific historical struggle.

According to one historian, this form of the debate of youth and age dominated politics in the era of Spenser's youth. Generational struggle heats up during periods of rapid social change, when the models and values of the older generation are not strong enough to withstand the challenge of the young or not flexible enough to accommodate it.[29] This phenomena arose in the late sixteenth century England. The Queen and her closest counsellor, William Cecil, Lord Burleigh belonged to what Anthony Esler has called "The Elizabethan Older Generation."[30] Formed amidst the chaotic revolutionary ferment of the middle Tudor decades, their social attitudes crystallized into rigid caution and conservatism—an ideological insistence on the observance of order and degree and on the evils of pride and ambition that verged on the fanatic. Politicians, preachers and poets promulgated this official propaganda with appeals to Christian humility, to the myth of the wheel of fortune, and to the pastoral ideals of old age—the glorification of the mean estate and the rejection of the aspiring mind.

This ideology served Elisabeth well in holding together a shaky commonwealth by centralizing power in the hands of her trusted advisors. But by the last two decades of the century, as her generation grew into their sixties and the generation of the 1560's—including Ralegh, Marlow, Sidney, Essex and Spenser—approached adulthood, both the ideology and the practise it justified came under fire. During these "bottleneck years," young men of spectacular talent and energy found themselves stymied by the unyielding prejudice of the old folk firmly ensconsed in power. Their frustrated drives to find preferment manifested themselves in bursts of adventurism or turned inward into pathological melancholy.[31] Among these young men, aspiration upward became a charged and ambivalent idea—an expression of both loyalty and rebellion, a source of both promise and punishment.

As a member of this younger generation, Spenser was subjected to suppression by Burleigh and his contemporaries. He responded to the double bind with an appropriately schizoid reaction. In Thenot's Tale of the Oak and the Briar, he presents the kind of cautionary fable that the older generation preferred: a story of upstart youth, who, jealous of age's prerogatives and wisdom, deviously plots to topple his elder and then is justly punished. But as noted earlier, the sympathy for old age evoked by this tale is reversed once we discover that the old Oak's pious virtue conceals the old narrator's subtle stratagem against Cuddie, the cowherd boy. In a later poem, Spenser completes this reversal with a direct attack on Burleigh as another old oak shadowing youth:

> O grief of griefs, o gall of all good hearts
> To see that virtue should despised be
> Of him, that first was raised for virtuous parts
> And now broad spreading like an aged tree
> Lets none shoot up, that nigh him planted be.[32]

Spenser employs the unresolved dualistic structure of pastoral debate to set forth the dilemma of aspiration vs. humility throughout the later eclogues of the *Calender.* It surfaces in "Ivlye" 's argument between the ambitious upland goatherd and the humble shepherd of the dale. And it returns again in "September" and "October," when downhearted young men who have attempted to strive upwards return to pastoral vallies discouraged by the lack of room at the top. In all three of these moral eclogues, the polarity of youth and age serves not only to organize literary topoi and psychological states, but also to "glance at" the "graver matters" of state confronting the young men whose life history begins to intersect with social history.

While the February eclogue focusses on what E.K. calls "the reverence due to old age," or what might be designated the problem of the older generation, "Maye" concerns itself with the problem of the younger generation, as seen by two old shepherds. Just as the climate of February was a foe to young Cuddie, so the month of Maying and of the pastoral of youth is out of season for Palinode and Piers. Their dispute over how to come to terms with the rites of spring resembles the argument between the two men of Chaucer's "Merchant's Tale" counselling their friend January how to deal with the young girl, May.[33] The two old men also represent aspects of the young man's maturing self. Palinode voices the retrospective nostalgia of leaving childhood behind, while Piers expresses youth's impatience with the past—its need to set childishness aside and take on self-control and responsibility.

"Maye" begins with an evocative pastoral of youth, Palinode's description of the festival of regreening—*reverdie* or *renouveau*:

> Is not thilke the mery moneth of May,
> When loue lads masken in fresh aray?
> How falles it then, we no merrier bene,
> Ylike as others, girt in gawdy greene?
> Our bloncket liueryes bene all to sadde,
> For thilke same season, when all is ycladd
> With pleasaunce: the grownd with grasse, the Woods
> With greene leaues, the bushes with bloosming Buds.
> Yougthes folke now flocken in euery where,
> To gather may buskets and smelling brere:
> And home they hasten the postes to dight,
> And all the Kirke pillours eare day light,

With Hawthorne buds, and swete Eglantine,
And girlonds of roses and Sopps in wine.
(1-14)

In accord with the usage of pastoral debate, Piers counters the invitation with a withering reply:

For Younkers *Palinode* such follies fitte,
But we tway bene men of elder witt.

The month most appropriate for recreative pastoral—according to the *Kalendar of Shepherds,* the month of "hot love"—is the one containing Spenser's most bitterly satiricial sentiments.

From the initial confrontations of pastoral perspectives of youth and age, the conversation shifts to the social issue of the relation of the generations—here, the question of how adults should raise their children. Piers introduces this topic with a brief animal tale to illustrate the way parents, particularly mothers, dote excessively upon their offspring:

Sike mens follie I cannot compare
Better, then to the Apes folish care,
That is so enamoured of her young one,
(And yet God wote, such cause hath she none)
That with her hard hold, and straight embracing,
She stoppeth the breath of her youngling.
So often times, when as good is meant,
Euil ensueth of wrong entent.
(95-102)

In his later fable of Fox and Kid, Piers attributes this harmful doting to adults' failure to recognize the values of experience—their own childish indulgence in the pastoral of youth. The Kid is lovingly described through its mother's eyes as a creature of the May:

Shee set her youngling before her knee,
That was both fresh and louely to see,
And full of favour, as kidde mought be:

His vellet head began to shoote out,
And his wrethed hornes gan newly sprout.
The blossomes of lust to bud did beginne,
And spring forth ranckly vnder his chinne.
(182-188)

The "old gate," his mother is a "waylefull widow" whose husband's death has left her full of carefull thoughts about the son she must raise herself. But though experience has alerted her to the dangers of the world, it has not yet taught her to guard and to school her son with sufficient vigilance—nor to resist the blandishments of youth and springtime herself. Sparing the rod that the father would wield, she is captivated by the kid's physical beauty, which reminds her of the sexual attraction of her late husband:

Of my old age haue this one delight,
To see thee succeede in thy fathers steade,
And florish in flowres of lusty head.
For euen so thy father his head vpheld,
And so his hauty hornes did he weld.
(202-206)

She forgets that the father was betrayed by treachery when she voices the hope that the son will succeed him. Then she leaves the child by himself and goes to the green wood to play the merry widow. In her innocent indulgence and deluded narcissism, the old woman fails to restrain what Piers in "October" refers to as "the lust of lawlesse youth." Once she leaves, the fox comes and convinces the credulous and charitable kid to open the door to a "sybbe"in need. He distracts the young goat with baubles and infatuates his victim with a mirror that exhibits his springtime loveliness. At the height of enjoyment, he pops the kid in a basket and takes him home for supper. Like many cautionary fairytales aimed at children, this story warns us to beware of love, pleasure and the pastoral of youth.

Spenser refers to the young kid who lacks a father's stern adult-oriented guidance as an "Orphane." E.K. glosses this word to mean "A youngling or pupill, that needeth a Tutour and a governour"—drawing a connection between inadequate parenting and deficient schooling.[34] The same connection is amplified in the conversations between two old men in another pastoral debate of youth and age, "Eclogue X" in Sidney's *Arcadia*. Here Mastix also finds the source of youth's unruliness in the immaturity of their elders:

> What marvaile if in youth such faults be done,
> Since that we see our saddest Shepheards out
> Who have their lesson so long time begonne?
> . . .
> As for the rest, howe shepeheardes spend their daies,
> At blowe point, hotcocles, or els at keeles
> While, "Let us passe our time" each shepeheard saies.
> So small accompt of time the shepeheard feeles
> And doth not feele, that life is nought but time
> And when that time is paste, death holdes his heeles.
> To age thus doe they draw there youthfull pryme,
> Knowing no more, then what poore tryall showes,
> As fishe sure tryall hath of muddy slyme.
> This paterne good, unto our children goes,
> For what they see their parents love or hate
> Their first caught sence prefers to teachers blowes.
> These cocklinges cockred we bewaile to late,
> When that we see our ofspring gaily bent,
> Woman man-wood, and men effeminate.[35]

Like Spenser's Palinode, Sidney's Geron counters this speech by accusing his old companion of excessive severity and self-righteousness.

Renaissance educators repeatedly addressed themselves to such issues of child discipline in treatises like Ascham's *Scholemaster* and Elyot's *The Governour*. Like Spenser's own teacher, Richard Mulcaster, these writers advocated a middle way—a balance between the extreme positions of Piers and Palinode, Mastix and Geron. Ascham idealized the life-stage of youth—"Youth is fittest to all goodness, surely nature in mankind is most beneficial and effectual in his behalf." But he qualified this praise by asserting the importance of proper training and control by age. Parents are too indulgent, he says; English youth are allowed too much rein, especially in the dangerous years of early manhood.[37]

The significance of "Maye" 's debate over youth and the rites of spring extends by way of questions of child-rearing to encompass the broadest political and religious controversies. According to Lawrence Stone, in the Catholic countries of Europe, "animal spirits of youth were siphoned into religious confraternities, processions and other rituals. . .order was maintained by periodic days of social inversion, when the young were allowed to lord it over their elders."[38] Youthful high spirits were tolerated quite widely and both sexual abandon and immoderation of eating and drinking were considered as part of the normal process of growing up. This relatively lenient attitude was reflected in the Italian humanists' notion of the innate purity and innocence of the child. But with the "drive for moral regeneration" accompanying the Reformation and Counter-Reformation, both the laxness toward youth and the seasonal festivities that accompanied it was replaced by a strongly authoritarian approach. At this time the idea came into fashion that the essence of upbringing was breaking the child's will, and only during the sixteenth and seventeenth century did flogging of children become standard practise.[39] This attitude toward children had its most extreme manifestation among the Puritans of the Massachusetts colony, where the death penalty was imposed for disobedience to adults.[40]

Not all the Puritans were this harsh, but they did agree on the intrinsic spiritual danger of the stage of youth itself and on the importance of adult guidance for young people at this "most unsettled age wherein the mind behaves for a long time like the wavering scales, rising and falling, going and coming ere it can settle."[41] This description, from one of the many sermons especially directed toward youth by Puritan preachers, displays a clear understanding of the vacillations of the adolescent mind reflected in the oscillating structures of Spenser's *Calender*. Indeed, E.K.'s account of the poem as a testament of the author's unfortunate wanderings in the "common labyrinth" of youth offered as a warning to other young men assimilates the work to the tradition of Puritan spiritual autobiography.

On the basis of the polemics in "Maye," Spenser has often been supposed to be a Puritan; but in fact there is no conclusive evidence that he was any more committed to Piers" position regarding childhood and Maying than to the "palinodal" position of his antagonist. Like the other debates in the *Calender,* "Maye" lays bare the irreconcilable alternatives that face the young person in quest of his own identity. Piers' conception of the pastoral of youth as Circean, Satanic temptation is that of the radical Protestants. To the establishmentarians of the monarchy, the aristocracy and the Church of England, these bucolic motifs served as banners of allegiance. By incarnating herself as the virgin queen of the May, Elisabeth used pastoral ideals of innocence to capture the imaginations of both peasants and poets and thereby strengthened her myth of commonwealth.[42] The landed aristocracy, which was responding to economic and social pressures from the rising urban middle class by robbing the peasantry of their ancient rights and dignity, found in those same ideals an expression of their own nostalgia and a source of conveniently obfuscating propaganda.[43] And in the seventeenth century, the pastoral cult of childhood emerged as a form of inner emigration for devout Anglicans—a product of the "cultural despair" wrought by the prospect of deepening civil strife.[44] Despite the appeal of the Puritan perspective, Spenser retained his devotion to these ideals of innocence. Though always qualified and checked, his attachment to the springtime world of pastoral festivity appears not only in Palinode's lovely verses, but throughout the *Calender.* Indeed, the "Aprill" eclogue achieves what many have seen as the poem's redeeming and crowning vision with a recreative song of praise for "Eliza queene of Shepheardes all."

"Maye" ends with a pair of emblems that balance these points of view: "Who doth most mistrust is most false. . .what fayth then is there in the faythlesse?" This conclusion emphasizes the eclogue's organization of polarities around the young man's dilemma of placing trust. In order to realize identity, he must recognize the presence of forces both in himself and outside that will betray him, that are not to be trusted. But at the same time, he must find a repository of fidelity, a central object of loyalty. If one challenge of youth is to pass beyond the innocent gullibility of Cuddie, Thomalin or the Kidde, another obstacle it must overcome is "faythlessness"—the excessive disillusionment that strips the person of ideals and aspirations and leaves him cynical, floundering and lost to himself.

Diggon Davie of "September" and the Cuddie of "October" both suffer this youthful malaise. They languish from what Erikson calls a "spoiled moratorium"—an extended identity crisis wherein the world's failure to provide adequate objects of fidelity combines with the individual's excessive demands for perfection to yield a "pathognomic picture which all sick youth have in common":

> This picture is characterized first of all by a denial of the historical flux of time. . .the sick adolescent thus gradually stops extending experimental feelers toward the future; his moratorium of illness becomes an end in itself and thus ceases to be a moratorium.[45]

"September" and "October" both portray the failure of youth's first "experimental feelers toward the future"—its fledgling attempts to claim an adult identity beyond pastoral, in the world of the *vita activa*. In the fall of the year, by the logic of anti-pastoral, the bucolic landscape has turned from utopia to a prison that its young inhabitants are seeking to escape. But disoriented by their exposure to the great world, both Diggon and Cuddie retreat back to Arcadia, the mean estate and their aged companions. Their disappointment and outrage echoes the satirical wisdom of the old men, but it lacks authenticity and smacks of neurotic self-pity. Afflicted with premature disillusionment, Diggon and Cuddie are both associated with the *adynaton* of the barren harvest, the fruit that rots before it ripens. "Inopem me copia fecit" states the emblem of "September": "Riches make me poor."

The riches which have impoverished Diggon are those of experience. He has had too much, too soon. His journies abroad, like those of many a young "unfortunate traveller," seem to have broadened his horizon at the cost of his fortune and his emotional stability. Along with his innocence he has lost his very sense of self:

> Hobbinoll: Diggon Davie, I bidde her god daye:
> Or Diggon her is, or I missaye.
>
> Diggon: Her was her, while it was daye light,
> But now her is a most wretched wight.
> For day, that was, is wightly past,
> And now at earst the dirke night doth hast. . .
> The iolly shepheard that was of yore,
> Is nowe nor iollye, nor shephearde more.
> In forrein costes, men sayd, was plentye
> And so there is but all of miserye.
>
> (1-29)

After unsuccessfully seeking the "high way of Fame and Fortune, he returns to the country with a sense that foxes and wolves are lurking behind every tree. Now having learned the advice of Piers in "Maye," he feels the need to constantly "liggen in watch and ward from soddein force (his) flocks for to gard." But this reversal of youth's idealistic optimism to a pessimistic paranoia also suffers from extremity. Through most of the eclogue, Diggon seems to take refuge in righteous outcries against the hypocrisy and abuses of those in high places, but at the end he turns to his old friend and admits that he has become unravelled by the failure of his great expectations. He has no idea where to turn next:

> Ah but Hobbinoll, all this long tale,
> Nought easeth the care, that doth me forhaile.
> What shall I doe? what way shall I wend,

My piteous plight and losse to amend?
Ah my good Hobbinol, mought I thee praye,
Of ayde or counsell in my decaye.
(242-247)

Sounding like the old and exiled Meliboeus in Vergil's first eclogue—after which the close of "September" is modelled—Diggon feels as if his life is ending along with his youth. It takes old Hobbinoll's extended temporal perspective to recognize that there is a future as well as a past, to convince the boy that a new life still awaits him:

Now by my soule, Diggon, I lament
The haplesse mischief, that has thee hent
But if to my cotage thou wilt resort,
So as I can, I wil thee comfort:
There mayst thou ligge in vetchy bed,
Till fayrer Fortune shewe forth her head.
(248-257)

Hobbinoll's wisdom of experience finds expression in a topos often associated with the pastoral of old age: the understanding and acceptance of the wheel of fortune's turns. Old Thenot invokes that image of inevitable rise and fall in "Febrvarie," in order to bring young Cuddie down a peg. But in "October," the companion piece to "September" 's dialogue of Diggon and Hobbinoll, old Piers tries to elevate youth's depressed spirit. With the revolution of the year, the wheel of fortune has brought young Cuddie low, fulfilling Thenot's earlier prediction. Now old age, in the person of "Maye" 's puritannical parson, predicts the same wheel's rise and urges youth upward from complaint to recreation:

Cuddie, for shame hold vp thy heauye head,
And let vs cast with what delight to chace,
And weary thys long lingring *Phoebus* race.
Whilome thou wont the shepheards laddes to leade,

In rymes, in ridles, and in bydding base:
Now they in thee, and thou in sleepe art dead.
(1-6)

Cuddie shows the symptoms of what psychologists of adolescence have called the pathology of the *puer eternus*. One of its manifestations is an abnormal lethargy and a tendency to sleep.[46] This common syndrome exhibits the pastoral ideal of *otium* gone otiose, the moratorium gone spoiled, the harvest turned rotten. Like modern therapists, old shepherds in numerous pastoral debates of youth and age prescribe responsible work as the primary cure for this condition.[47] For in work, youth can grow up enough to take the social role of adult for which he is biologically ready. Thus, when Cuddie responds that he is tired of singing the "dapper ditties, that I wont devise/ To feede youthes fancie, and the flocking fry,/ Delighten much," Piers urges him to stop writing poetry as a form of childish play and to treat it as a man's job, for which he will receive the adult reward of fame:

Abandon then the base and viler clowne,
Lyft vp thy selfe out of the lowly dust:
And sing of bloody Mars, of wars, of giusts,
Turne thee to those, that weld the awful crowne
To doubted Knights, whose woundlesse armour rusts,
And helmes ynbruzed wexen dayly browne.
There may thy Muse display her fluttryng wing
And stretch herselfe at large from East to West.
(37-44)

This kind of work is different from the georgic pursuits of agricultural labor often urged upon young herdsmen by their elders. It is the work of the artist. For the budding poet like Cuddie, work represents not only the purgation of childish play but also the adoption of adult vocation. He is entering the final stage of the identity crisis, which aims toward integrating the individual and society in the form of a tangible productive role, a career.[48] For Cuddie, to grow up means to find his calling as a poet. This involves leaving the pastoral world of youth and age and taking up residence at the central world of the court, writing the major genre of epic.

Cuddie resonds to the old man's exhortation by saying that he would like to rise out of the lowly dust, fly high, stand tall and sing with the voice of trumpets. But he lacks the courage, the confidence and the faith to commit himself. He attributes this lack to the plight of the younger generation at the Elisabethan court:

> But ah *Mecoenas* is yclad in claye,
> And great Augustus long ygoe is dead;
> And all the worthies liggen wrapt in leade,
> That matter made for Poets on to play:
> . . .
> But after vertue gan for age to stoupe,
> And mighty manhode brought a bedde of ease
> The vaunting Poets found nought worth a pease
> To put in preace emong the learned troupe.
>
> (61-70)

His identity fails to crystallize because of a failure of aspiration; since he has found no repository of fidelity, he prefers to remain in the humble shade. The official propaganda rejecting ambition and praising the mean estate takes on overtones of bitter defeat when espoused by the young man:

> And if that any buddes of Poesie,
> Yet of the old stocke gan to shoote agayne:
> Or if mens follies mote be forst to fayne,
> And rolle with rest in rymes of rybaudrye:
> Tom Piper makes vs better melodie.
>
> (73-78)

Piers offers new encouragement with another line of argument: if there is no worthwhile career for the poet at court, youth can find himself by aspiring still higher, to a heaven of neoplatonic illumination: "Then make winges of thine aspyring wit,/ And, whence thou camst, flye backe to heauen apace."

But once again Cuddie is brought low, in a dramatic sequence revealing that he still does not truly want to grow up. The young man claims he cannot rise out of the "loathsome mire" on the wings of lofty love, for love's Tyranny has sapped the powers of the poet, as testified by the hopeless case of his friend Colin Clout. This, of course, is not the same platonic love that Piers recommends to elevate his spirit. Rather it is "the lust of laweless youth," straining and sickening at its own Arcadian limits of "carnal perfection." Cuddie continues to gainsay Piers with his own idea of a platonic theory of poetic composition:

> Who euer casts to compasse weightye prise,
> And thinks to throwe out thondring words of threate:
> Let powre in lauish cups and thriftie bitts of meate,
> For *Bacchus* fruite is frend to Phoebus wise.
> And when with Wine the braine begins to sweate,
> The nombers flowe as fast as spring doth ryse.
> Thou kenst not *Percie* howe the ryme should rage.
> O if my temples were distaind with wine,
> And girt in girlonds of wild Yuie twine,
> How I could reare the Muse on stately stage,
> And teache her tread aloft in buskin fine,
> With queint *Bellona* in her equipage.
>
> (103-114)

E.K. and other commentators have missed that fact that this is a parody of the platonic doctrine of *enthousiasmous*—a version of divine inspiration appropriate not to the genuine initiate, but to the *puer eternus*. His adolescent method of "getting high" means taking a ride rather than flying on his own wings, means evading identity rather than forging it. Spenser makes this quite clear when he shows Cuddie's intoxicated, Coleridgean vision leading him not upward and out toward the future, but downward and back toward the past, toward a pastoral existence that has become cynical and cowardly:

> But ah my corage cooles ere it be warme,
> For thy, content vs in thys humble shade:

Where no such troublous tydes han vs assayde,
Here we our slender pipes may safely charme.

(115-118)

In the final winter eclogues, Spenser's account of the sorrows of youth deepens in gloom and contracts in focus as the year descends to the period of longest night. Since the *Calender's* opening in "Ianuarye," its young shepherds have been accumulating losses. Spring brought the departure of sexual innocence; summer saw the destruction of simple trust in people, ideas and institutions; autumn yielded the disappointment of great expectations and the letdown attendant upon intoxication. Now, in "November," the young man confronts the loss of life itself—like those others, a loss built in to very process of growth. "November" is devoted to a pastoral elegy mourning the death of the young girl, Dido. Her death signifies both an "unnatural" disruption of the natural cycle—coming as it does before the prime of her life—and it also signifies the failure of the cycle itself, which even in the normal course of events, ravages the beauty of spring with autumn and old age. In mourning Dido, "the fairest May. . .that ever went," we mourn the demise of the very ideals of the pastoral of youth—the recreative spirit, the music of invitation and escape: "The mornefull Muse in myrth now list ne maske/ As shee was wont in youngth and sommer dayes." To the young person, mourning the loss of youth means facing the loss of his own life; he experiences the departure of his childhood self as equivalent to personal extinction:

Why doe we longer liue, (ah why liue we so long)
Whose better dayes death hath shut up in woe?
. . .Now is time to dye. Nay time was long ygoe,
O carefull verse.

(72-81)

Dido's death brings the final disillusionment of growing up by revealing the fact of universal mortality. Teaching the frailty and limits of earthly life, it prepares the survivors for their own impending decease.

"December" sharpens and intensifies the feeling of doom. The speaker takes a final retrospective inventory of the year's losses and sees his life as a series of disappointments, failures and falls from Eden:

> Thus is my sommer worne away and wasted,
> Thus is my haruest hastened all to rathe:
> The eare that budded faire, is burnt and blasted,
> And all my hoped gaine is turnd to scathe.
> Of all the seede, that in my youth was sowne.
> Was nought but brakes and brambles to be mowne.
>
> My boughes with bloosmes that crowned were at firste,
> And promised of timely fruite such store,
> Are left both bare and barrein now at erst
> The flattring fruite is fallen to grownd before,
> And rotted, ere they were halfe mellow ripe:
> My haruest wast, my hope away dyd wipe.
>
> (97-108)

In this powerful lyric of despair, Spenser equates Colin with "Eelde," the medieval allegory of old age and saturnine melancholy. The strongest effect of the passage resides in its vision of human aging as an aborted natural process—its imagery of rot preceding ripeness. Spenser quite likely discovered that imagery in "The Reeve's Prologue" of The Canterbury Tales:

> But ik am oold, me list not pley for age;
> Gras tyme is doon, my fodder is now forage;
> This white top writeth myne olde yeris;
> Myn herte is also mowled as myn heris,
> But if I fare as dooth an open-ers,
> That ilke fruyt is ever lenger the wers,
> Til it be roten in mullock or in stree.
> We olde men, I drede, so fare we:
> Til we be roten, kan we nat be rype.[49]

Like the Reeve, Colin finally becomes a "negative senex" who threatens youth with the spectre of its own worst fears of the future—the target of the downward trajectory that the young men have been following since early spring.

Colin has felt like an old man ever since the *Calender's* opening in "Ianvuarie," when as a young herdsman's boy he was just beginning to experience the pains of sexual love—the incongruity between burgeoning desire and barren frustration:

> Such stormy stoures do breede my balefull smart,
> As if my yeare were wast, and woxen old.
> And yet alas, but now my spring begonne,
> And yet alas, Yt is already donne.
>
> You naked trees, whose shady leaues are lost
> Wherein the byrds were wont to build their bowre:
> And now are clothd with mosse and hoary frost,
> Instede of bloosmes, wherewith your buds did flowre:
> I see your teares, that from your boughes doe raine,
> Whose drops in drery ysicles remaine.
>
> Al so my lustfull leafe is drye and sere,
> My timely buds with wayling all are wasted:
>
> (29-48)

The same inversion of youth and age reappears in "Iune," when young Colin replies to old Hobbinoll's recreative invitation with the stern voice of an elder:

> And I, whylst youth, and course of carelesse yeeres
> Did let me walke withouten lincks of loue,
> In such delights did ioy amongst my peeres:
> But ryper age such pleasures doth reproue,
> My fancy eke from former follies moue
> To stayed steps: for time in passing weares
> (As garments doen, which wexen old aboue)
> And draweth newe delightes with hoary heares.
>
> (33-40)

The young man expresses his subjective world-weariness—his feeling of being experienced—with the objective correlative of physical senescence. By "December," this process has become obsessive. From simile he has switched to metaphor, and from metaphor to literal belief. Here Colin presents himself as a full embodiment of the archetype of *senex puer*: the aged boy who appears elsewhere in poems by Shakespeare, Ralegh and Desportes. This archetype of age-in-youth models the self-image of all the young men in the latter half of the *Calender*.

Colin's last words of departure read more like a young person's suicide note than the testament of a real old man:

> The carefull cold hath nypt my rugged rynde,
> And in my face deepe furrowes eld hath pight:
> My head besprent with hoary frost I fynd,
> And my myne eie the Crow his clawe dooth wright.
> Delight is layd abedde, and pleasure past
> No sonne now shines, cloudes han all ouercast.
> . . .
> Adieu delightes, that lulled me asleepe,
> Adieu my deare, whose loue I bought so deare:
> Adieu my little Lambes and loued sheepe,
> Adieu ye Woodes that oft my witnesse were:
> Adieu good *Hobbinoll,* that was so true,
> Tell Rosalind, her Colin bids her adieu.
>
> (134-156)

In contrast to Thenot or Piers or Hobbinoll, the Colin Clout of "December" doesn't convey the impression of being a real old man. The portrait in the accompanying woodcut, the introductory description of a "gentle shepherd (who) satte beside a spring. . .in secreate shade alone. . .(making) of loue his piteous mone," and the delicate, effete style of his complaint all suggest a *senex puer* rather than a literally aged herdsman. In terms of clock time, Colin is just eleven months older than the "Shepherds Boye" who ushered in the year. Indeed, modern psychological studies have noted the connection between youth's experience of itselt as aged and its proclivities for real or attempted suicide:

> Between the ages of sixteen and twenty, suicide is very frequent and less so afterwards. People at that age have very often that strange kind of melancholy sadness and they feel like old people and have an expression in their faces as if they knew all about life and felt very, very old, so what would be the use of playing about with the others, of dancing. . .and they retire in a kind of grandfatherly or grandmotherly attitude toward life.[50]

Numerous commentators have followed E.K. in observing that "December" 's old age elegy imitates Clement Marot's *Eglogue. . .au Roy soubz les noms de Pan et Robin* (1539) just as "November" 's threnody for Dido imitates the French poet's pastoral elegy for the death of the queen mother, Louise.[52] In both cases, Spenser adapted poems about actual old people to create the sense of age-in-youth. Marot's *Eglogue,* written when the poet himself was old, ends not with despair but with gratitude for the king's patronage. "December" abandons Marot's model at line 96, with the introduction of the *adynata* of ripeness and rot. This rhetorical figure is elsewhere associated with premature aging of youth rather than with literal senescence. In *As You Like It,* for instance, Rosalind uses the device to check the know-it-all cynicism of Jaques and Touchstone: "You'll be rotten ere you be ripe, and that's the right virtue of the medlar." (III,ii, 112) The figure also appears in the Daphnis elegy of Theocritus' first *Idyll.* Indeed this very *adynaton* associates the Colin Clout of "December" with the dying young vegetation god known severally as Adonis, Osiris and Tammuz.[52] An ancient Mesopotamian text compares the yearly demise of Tammuz to plants that wither before their time: "tamarisk that in the garden has drunk no water/ whose crown in the field has brought forth no blossom."[53] So young-old Colin moans:

> The fragrant flowres, that in my garden grew
> Bene withered, as they had bene gathered long.
> Theyr rootes bene dryed up for lack of dewe
>
> (109-111)

Though he is the sickest of the sick young men in the *Calender,* Colin nevertheless remains the poem's exemplary character. Not only is he the cynosure of all the other herdsmen who quote his verses and worry over his emotional condition. As an avatar of Daphnis, he takes on some of the heroic qualities of all romantic youth. The melancholy singer who distills music out of his pain will aways be admired—especially for the Wagnerian dirge he sings on his own deathbed, victim of a mysterious love-wound. Colin is somehow blessed in his affliction of youthful morbidity—whether we think of that affliction as the "Elisabethan malady" of neoplatonic genius or as the germanic *Weltschmertz* of the budding *Uebermensch.* His very despair breeds the eloquence that makes him a "mirror" of his contemporaries—their reflection as well as their ideal. In his studies of the Renaissance young men, Luther and Hamlet, Erik Erikson has shown how the extremity of adolescent trials is crucial to the later development of leaders:

> successful ideological leaders are postadolescents who make out of the contradictions of adolescence the polarities of their charisma. . .always convinced that what they felt as adolescents was a curse, a fall, an earthquake, a thunderbolt, in short a revelation to be shared with their generation and many to come.[54]

It is through the repeated falls of Thomalin, Willye, Perigot, Cuddie and Colin that Immerito realizes the perfect pattern of the poet.

Though the tone of the *Calender* seems to spiral downward to darkness as it draws to a close, the work is not, like *Hamlet* or *The Sorrows of Young Werther,* finally a tragedy of youth unable to come of age. In the last four eclogues, a complementary helical movement upward balances the entropic descent, suggesting redemptive possibilities of rejuvenation and rebirth. Spenser accomplishes this reversal of tone with explicit pastoral conventions of closing and also with a trick of design that is less obvious but more integral to the structure and affective strategy of the poem as a whole.[55]

The poetry of anti-pastoral complaint often ends with tentative reversals of feeling—expressions of solace and hope that attend the conclusion of a grief cycle. Spenser follows this modal pattern first in "November," when, after eleven stanzas of "carefull verse," Colin modulates to the "ioyfull verse" affirming a new life after death in "fields aye fressh, the grasse aye greene." And in "December," Spenser offers a final reply to Colin's inventory of the wasting forces of time with an appended emblem and *envoi* asserting the time-transcending qualities of art. These appendices may at first appear, like a Chaucerian retraction, somewhat gratuitous and uncalled-for by the overall tone and structure of the poem. But in fact Spenser prepares for the reversals early along in the sequence. While the young shepherds pass from spring's recreation to wintry gloom in the last half of the year, the old herdsmen who appeared in the early months as antagonists of youth's pleasures and ambitions return in later eclogues as exponents of recreative pleasure and aspiration. While the young characters become fixated on the past, the old characters become oriented toward the future.

For example, the same Thenot who, in "Febrvarie," mocked and threatened Cuddie's attachment to love and who in "Aprill" condemned Colin for being "a foolish boy that is with love yblent," attempts, in "November," to cheer Colin up by urging him to sing "as thou were wont, songs of some jouissaunce." And the same Piers who in "Maye" so vehemently rejected the rites of spring, returns in "October" to exhort Cuddie to aim for the heights and seek delight at the court of the Queen, where songs

> Of love and lustihead tho mayst thou sing,
> And carrol lowde, and leade the Myllers rownde,
> All were *Elisa* one of thilke same ring.
> So mought our *Cuddies* name to Heauen sownde.
>
> (51-54)

The reversals coalesce in a pattern: as the year proceeds, youth ages and dies, while age itself becomes more youthful.

What does this signify? If, as I have argued, all the characters of the *Calender* speak with the voices of a single Young Man, the pattern of youth aging and age becoming youthful represents Immerito's childhood passing away and his maturity coming to birth. Employing the pastoral debate's relativity of perspectives in a subtle but concrete way, Spenser moves us in the course of the year from the child's entropic view of the life cycle to the adult's understanding of aging as advance. This shift in self-perception is the subjective counterpart of physical and social maturation.

Spenser achieves this effect through a serial use of the debate genre. By showing the antagonists disengaging from their allegorical roles and reversing positions in later encounters, he extends the conventions of the *conflictus* to communicate a sense of the personality's growth in time, to communicate, that is, the paradoxical interaction of constancy and change which defines human identity.[56] Such a conception of personal identity as a unity of opposites realized through growth in time prefigures the principle of "dilated being" that Spenser formulates explicitly as a verdict of his last pastoral debate at the conclusion of *The Faerie Queene*:

> I well consider all that ye haue sayd,
> And find all things stedfastnes doe hate
> And changed be: yet being rightly wayd
> They are not changed from their first estate;
> But by their change their being doe dilate:
> And turning to themselues at length againe,
> Do worke their owne perfection so by fate:
> Then ouer them Change doth not rule and raigne;
> But they raigne ouer change, and doe their states maintaine.
>
> (VII,vii, 58)

At this juncture, one may wonder why, if Spenser intended *The Shepheardes Calender* to record youth's coming of age, did he end the work with such a bleak prospect as "December" 's?

Why, among the several young men he portrays, did he not find one individual who managed to fly with some success? Why, indeed did he give no indication within the text that by the time the book was published in his twenty seventh year, he himself had weathered most of the storms it recounts? For in that year of 1579, the "new Poete" had attained a position with good prospects as secretary to the Bishop of Rochester, had apparently resoved his differences with Rosalind and married her and had proved his mettle as an up and coming man of letters.[57]

First of all, Spenser wrote, or at least conceived his eclogues in the years before 1579, while he was still struggling with the problems of maturation and identity.[58] But more important, he fashioned the whole *Calender* to comply with literary conventions that precluded any simply resolved closure. The debate of youth and age has no end; its generic function is to demonstrate the limitations of human perception at any moment in time. And pastoral poetry, conceived as the writer's juvenilia, is thereby restricted to youth's own circumscribed and contradictory view of itself as seen from within. Only once that stage of life has passed does hindsight reveal the nature of its struggles as the shaping growth of individual identity. As is true of the *Bildungsroman* in general, the rough crossing chronicled in the *Calender* doesn't reach calm waters until the book is over. The moment of arrival is in fact announced by an epilogue, recorded in the cautious but confident and satisfied tone of Immerito's *envoi*:

> Goe lyttle Calender, thou hast a free passeporte,
> Goe but a lowly gate emongste the meaner sorte.
> Dare not to match thy pype with Tityrus hys style,
> Nor with the Pilgrim that the Ploughman playde a whyle:
> But followe them farre off, and their high steppes adore,
> The better please, the worse despise, I aske nomore.

With the added perspective of several more years and from the stable vantage point of the full-fledged adult, the same narrative persona, Immerito, looks back at his earlier pastoral stage of life. In it, he recognizes the prelude to his emergence as the triumphant "I" who proclaims his identity at the opening of *The Faerie Queene*:

> Lo I the man, whose Muse whilome did maske,
> As time her taught, in lowly Shepheards weeds,
> Am now enforst a far vnfitter taske,
> For trumpets sterne to chaunge mine Oaten reeds.
>
> (I, i, 1)

Seen from this later moment, the death that Colin greets at the end of "December" is even less of a permanent doom than Dido's. Instead it appears as the dramatic projection of the experience of "the discontinuity between youth and adulthood" enacted in primitive rites of passage by "symbolic death as children and rebirth as adults":[59]

> the central moment of every initiation is represented by the ceremony symbolizing the death of the novice and his return to the fellowship of the living. . .But he returns to life a new man, assuming a new mode of being.[60]

Seen as part of such a process of initiation, Colin's rapid demise makes sense. His death, though real, is not to be confused with the death of Immerito or Spenser, but rather is to be identified as the death of their youth. The experience of initiation is not limited to primitive rites; according to Mircea Eliade, it "lies at the core of every human life."[61] As the climax of what Erikson called the identity crisis, what Jung called the process of individuation and what William James called the conversion of the twice-born, the initiatory ordeal takes place at the borderline of mental illness and creativity. Eliade's account provides an apt commentary on the direct relevance of the *Calender's* concluding painful recognitions:

> . . .any genuine human life implies profound crises, ordeals suffering, loss and reconquest of self, "death and resurrection.". . .whatever

degree of fulfillment it may have brought him, at a certain moment every man sees his life as a failure. This vision does not arise from a moral judgement made on his past, but from an obscure feeling that he has missed his vocation; that he has betrayed the best that was in him. . .This means. . .dreams of a new, regenerated life fully realized and significant.[62]

Just as Immerito is resurrected after the symbolic aging and dying of the young people in the *Calender,* so young Daphnis and his vegetable-god predecessors are reborn after passing through the darkness of winter. By timing Colin's death to coincide with the close of the year, Spenser hearkens back to the origins of the calender itself. Initiatory rites conducting children into adulthood usually take place during periods of New Year celebration, like Rosh-Hashonah-Yom Kippur or Christmas-Epiphany.[63] The litany of past faults and failures that Colin intones in "December" resembles the confession and atonement rituals that form part of such calendrical festivals and that enble the whole society to purify and regenerate itself.

During rites of passage and during New Year's festivals, time stops and reverses direction. The young adult succeeds the old child; the infant new year grows out of the one which is old and dying. At these "liminal" points of the life cycle and seasonal cycle, all sorts of normally ordered polarities get scrambled.[64] Just as adolescent Colin grows unnaturally senescent in December, young and old exchanged roles during the winter solstice celebrations of the Roman Saturnalia. Such ritual reversals express a "rekindling of hope for the abolition of past time."[65] The "descent into the chaos of blurred distinctions and broken forms" and the consequent rebirth and emergence of embryonic form reenact in the present the creation of the cosmos out of the chaos which is imagined to have taken place "in the beginning."[66] The original purpose therefore of all calendars was to transcend time rather than to quantify it. Whether Roman, Mesopotamian or Aztec, they were divided to mark and predict the occurrence of liminal festivals and thereby to make possible the repeated experience of "Eternal

Return." The *Janninya Upanishad Brahmana* states that "the gate of the world of Heavenly Light" is to be found "where sky and earth embrace" and the "ends of the year" are united.[67] According to Buddhist scripture, Winter is the symbol of the great release, combining death with birth.[68] And E.K. assures us that Christian doctrine distinguishes itself with what is in fact an identical conception of the yearly cycle:

> we mayntaine a custome of coumpting the seasons from the moneth Ianuary, vpon a more speciall cause, then the heathen Philosophers euer coulde conceiue, that is, for the incarnation of our mighty Sauiour and eternall redeemer the L. Christ, who as then renewing the state of the decayed world, and returning the compasse of expired yeres to theyr former date and first commencement, left to vs his heires a memoriall of his birth in the ende of the last yeere and beginning of the next.
>
> (p. 13)

Standing by the gate of the other world, where the ends of the year are united at the end of "December," Spenser as Immerito concludes his pastoral with an avowal:

> Loe I haue made a Calender for euery yeare,
> That steele in strength and time in durance shall outweare:
> And if I marked well the starres reuolution,
> It shall continewe till the worlds dissolution.

From this point, he looks forward to the time when youth and age no longer will debate, for time itself will be no more.

But it is not only in the apocalyptic framework of the "Great Sabaoth" or Last Judgement that *The Shepheardes Calender* alludes to an anagogical level of meaning. Spenser's double cycle of aging and rejuvenation also presents itself in the "too much loved nature" that all pastoral sets forth. As the wheel of the year revolves, the fresh greenery of last spring shrivels and dries, while the germs of next year's blossoms sprout from old and toughened twigs. When these opposing orientations of natural process converge in the mind of the beholder, like opposing phases of a wave movement they cancel each other out—leaving behind a momentary epiphany of timelessness. Heraclitus, "the heathen Philosopher," declares:

> as the same thing there exists in us living and dead and the waking and the sleeping and young and old; for these having changed round are those, and those having changed round are these.[69]

Whether we imagine it as the "backstretched connexion" ordering natural cycles or as the core of personal identity, this nameless "same thing" remains the final generic intimation of the pastoral debate of youth and age.

NOTES

[1] *The Works of Edmund Spenser: A Variorum Edition: The Minor Poems,* eds. Charles Grosvenor Osgood and Henry Gibbons Lotspeich (Baltimore: Johns Hopkins Press, 1943), I, 113. All later references are to this edition.

[2] Paul Alpers, "The Eclogue Tradition and the Nature of Pastoral," *CE,* 34, 1972, pp. 364-5.

[3] William Nelson, *The Poetry of Edmund Spenser* (New York: Columbia University Press, 1963), p. 39.

[4] *The Kalendar of Shepherdes,* ed. H. Oskar Sommer (London, 1892).

[5] Lawrence Babb, *The Elisabethan Malady* (East Lansing: Michigan State University Press, 1951), pp. 10-11, 134; also "On the Nature of Elisabethan Psychological Literature," *John Quincy Adams Studies,* pp. 509-522.

[6] These critical disputes are amply represented in the commentaries of the Variorum edition, particularly on pp. 600-609.

[7] Alpers, p. 365. Also Patrick Cullen, *Spenser, Marvell and Renaissance Pastoral* (Cambridge: Harvard University Press, 1970), p. 32; William Nelson, p. 46. And see Isable McCaffrey, "Allegory and Pastoral in *The Shepheardes Calender,*" *ELH* 36 (1969), p. 105.

[8] See chapter four of this study

[9] Cullen, p. vii.

[10] Chapter four, above

[11] Fragment 212 in *The Presocratic Philosophers,* ed. G. S. Kirk and J. E. Raven (Cambridge: Cambridge University Press, 1960), p. 193.

[11a] Though it has been considered risky to identify the "implied author" of any work with the actual person who wrote the book, I join several recent commentators in assuming that the conflicts chronicled in the *Calender* were in fact experienced by the real author, that the various young men in the *Calender* are aspects of himself, and that the discreet voice of Immerito that frames the work is also Edmund Spenser's. See, for instance Richard Helgerson, "The New Poet Presents Himself: Spenser and the Idea of a Literary Career," *PMLA* 93 (1978) 895-6.

[12] William Nelson makes the crucial observation that Spenser explores "the principal subject of the *Calender*. . .time and man. . .not to expose Mutability but to examine human states in terms of their past and future." (p. 37) However, I don't agree with his inference that the structure of the work is essentially cyclical and contains no forward moving plot line. I shall argue that the work's repeated juxtapositions of past and future result from the particularly Janusfaced character of youth as a transitional period in the life cycle

[13] My approach in what follow bears a number of resemblances to that in A. C. Hamilton's classic essay, "The Argument of *The Shepheards Calender*" (*ELH*, 23, 1956, 171-82). Hamilton sees the calendar as essentially tied to the "ritual source of pastoral" (174) in the poet's lament for himself as a dying and reborn being. He states that "the poem's major theme becomes the attempt to find himself." (174) Hamilton sees the plotline or "argument" of the poem as a series of encounters leading to "the rejection of the pastoral life for the truly dedicated life in the world." (181). I see the plot movement and the rejection of pastoral and consequent affirmation of the *vita activa* as ultimately attributable to the passage from youth to maturity, a passage which Hamilton doesn't emphasize. Other writers however have remarked in passing upon the association of pastoral with *Bildungsroman*:

> *Arcadia* is a story of a young man's temporary withdrawel from his normal milieu, his ardent dedication of poetry and his return to the world from which he had exiled himself. In that way it is a *Bildungsroman.*

See Ralph Nash, ed. *Arcadia and Piscatorial Eclogues* by Jacopo Sannazaro, (Detroit: Wayne State Press, 1960), Introd. p. 24. The generic relationship among pastoral, *Bildungsroman* and debate bears further examination. *In Season of Youth: The* Bildungsroman *from Dickens to Golding* (Cambridge, Harvard University Press, 1974) Jerome Hamilton Buckley lists these principal elements of the *Bildungsroman*: childhood, conflict of generations, provinciality, larger society, self-education, alienation, ordeal by love, search for vocation and worthy philosophy. (p. 18) All these themes are also prevalent in pastoral. Wilhelm Dilthey's definition of the *Bildungsroman* also fits the *Calender*: "the regulated development of life is observed; each stage has intrinsic value and at the same time forms a basic for a higher stage. Dissonances and conflicts of life appear as necessary growth points through which the individual must pass on his way to maturity and harmony." *Das Erlebnis und die Dichtung* (Leipzig and Bern, 1934) p. 394, cited in Martin Swales *The German* Bildungsroman from Wieland to Hesse, (Princeton: Princeton Univerity Press, 1978), p. 3. A more recent essay, that came to my attention after this chapter was written, makes the observation of *SC's* relation to the *Bildungsroman* its central point. Bruce R. Smith also affirms that the essential theme of the work is the author's discovery of his own identity. Though he correctly connects Spenser to his successors, Smith doesn't show the sources of *Bildungsroman* in the preceding pastoral tradition. "On Reading *SC*" in *Spenser Studies*, ed. Patrick Cullen and Thomas Roche (Pittsburgh: U. of Pittsburgh Press, 1980), pp. 89 ff.

[14] Dilthey observes that the *Bildungsroman* portrays the tension between "the *Nebeneinander* of possible selves within the hero and the *Nacheinander* of linear time and practical activity." Cited by Swales, p. 29.

[15] *The Complete Writings of William Blake,* ed. Geoffrey Keynes (London: Oxford University Press, 1966), p. 149. Patrick Cullin, in *Spenser, Marvell and Renaissance Pastoral,* discusses the *Calender's* texture of contraries at great length. He describes them as the perspectives of winter vs. spring, Arcadian vs. Mantuanesque literary traditions, tragic vs. comic modes:

> The *Calendar* is organized around recurring juxtapositions of the perspectives of winter (withdrawal, chastity, asceticism, self denial, age) and the perspectives of spring (Participation, love, indulgence, self-assertion, youth). . .the natural year. . .represents the unstable world that man must adapt to and ultimately triumph over, and it symbolizes in its own precarious balances of winter and spring the balance-in-opposition necessary for man and pastoral society within the natural world. (p. 123)

Youth vs. Age is one way of looking at the polarity, but Cullen doesn't think of it as also signifying stages of a process. This avoidance of the dialectical character of all of Spenser's polarities leads to unfortunate omissions in what is otherwise a brilliant interpretation. For instance, Cullen sees "December" as proof of Colin's failure, "demonstrating. . .the penalty of the promise extended man," as opposed to "November," which demonstrates the reward. In his discussion of "December," Cullen conspicuously fails to quote from the Kalendar of *Shepherds,* whose description of the correspondences of the months and ages informs his discussion of the other eclogs. *The Kalendar's* December emphasizes that the darkest month of the winter solstice is also the month of reversal and rebirth, when the days again start getting longer—i.e., the month of Christmas. By entering and taking sides in the old critical controversy about whether or not Colin "fails," Cullen loses some of the advantage gained in this perception of the balance of both sides in the *SC's* debates. They do present morally untenable extremes of attitude, as Cullen points out; these extremes are shown not *in vacuo* however; but as relative to stages of development. Colin doesn't fail; he is outgrown.

[16] Kaspar D. Naegele, "Youth and Society: Some Observations," in *Youth: Change and Challenge,* ed. Erik H. Erikson (New York: W. W. Norton, 1963), p. 46.

[17] From a study by William Perry cited by Kenneth Kenniston in "Youth': A New Stage," *The American Scholar,* Winter, 1970, p. 646.

[18] From studies by Jerome Bruner and Jean Piaget, cited by Kenniston, p. 647.

[19] S. I. Eisenstadt, *Generation to Generation: Age Groups and Social Structure* (Glencoe, III.: The Free Press, 1956), p. 30.

[20] Ibid. p. 31.

[21] Ibid.

[22] Victor Turner, "Variations on a Theme of Liminality," in *Secular Ritual,* ed. S. Moore and Barbara Meyerhoff (Amsterdam, 1977), p. 37.

[23] See discussion of "Febrvarie", in chapter four.

[24] Erik H. Erikson, "Youth: Fidelity and Diversity" in *Youth: Change and Challenge,* p. 11; also *Young Man Luther,* second edition (New York: W. W. Norton, 1962), pp. 14 ff.

[25] *Young Man Luther,* p. 43. Erikson introduced his concept of youth's "moratorium" in connection with Luther's stay in a monastery.

[26] Erikson, "Youth: Fidelity and Diversity," p. 20; *Young Man Luther,* pp 41-2.

[27] In *Birth and Rebirth: Religious Meanings of Initiation in Human Culture,* trans. Willard Trask (N. Y.: Harper, 1958), Mircea Eliade defines "initiation" as:

> The body of rites and teachings whose purpose is to produce a decisive alteration in the religious and social status of a person. . .as a result of a basic change in his existential condition. . .the novice has become *another*. . . (p. 10)

See also, Terence Turner's discussion of how the transformational condition of youth attains a "transcendant" and "cybernetic" relationship to the whole social structure. "Transformation, Hierarchy and Transcendence: A Reformulation of Van Gennep's Model of the Structure of Rites of Passage," in *Secular Ritual* ed. S. Moore and Barbara Myerhoff.

[28] On the traditional association between the *topoi* of the Battle of Ancients and the Moderns, The World Upside Down, and the Debate of Age and Youth, see Ernst Robert Curtius, *European Literature and the Latin Middle Ages,* trans. W. R. Trask (New York, Bollingen Foundation, Pantheon Books, 1953), pp. 94-101; 251-6.

[29] Eisenstadt, p. 33.

[30] *The Aspiring Mind of the Elisabethan Younger Generation* (Durham: University of North Carolina Press, 1966), p. xiii. This book applies the generational theories of cultural history developed by Dilthey, Karl Mannheim, Henri Peyre, Ralph de Toledano, Ortega y Gasset to the specific case of Tudor England. See also Julian Marías, *Generations: A Historical Method,* trans. Harold C. Raley (University of Alabama Press, 1970). Esler's work is also cited by Louis Adrian Montrose in "The Perfecte Patterne of a Poete: The Poetics of Courtship in *SC*," *TSLL* 21, 1 1979, p. 36. Montrose follows a parallel approach to mine, showing how many of the conflicts portrayed in the moral eclogues reflect ideological issues dividing Spenser's society.

[31] Esler, p. 67 ff.

[32] "The Ruines of Time," lines 449-453.

[33] The debate of youth and age is central to *The Canterbury Tales*—it dominates the "Miller's Prologue and Tale," "Wife of Bath's Prologue and Tale," the "Pardoner's Tale" and the "Merchant's Tale."

[34] Curtius points out that the theme of the decline of standards in education is a medieval topos often associated with the debate of youth and age. p. 94.

[35] *The Poetry of Sir Phillip Sidney,* edited by William Ringler (Oxford: The Clarendon Press, 1962), pp. 27-8.

[36] An analogous debate about youth, education and pleasure finds its way into the conversation of younger and older brothers in Milton's *Comus.*

[37] *The Scholemaster* (1570) ed. by Lawrence V. Ryan (Ithaca: Folger Shakespeare Library, 1967), p. xxvi-xxix.

[38] Lawrence Stone, *The Family, Sex and Marriage in England,* 1500-1800 (London, 1977), p. 375.

[39] Stone, p. 163.

[40] David Hunt, *Parents and Children in History* (New York, 1977), pp. 149 ff.

[41] S. R. Smith, "Religion and the Conception of Youth in Seventeenth Century England," *History of Childhood Quarterly,* II, 1975, p. 497.

[42] C. L. Barber, "Holiday Custom and Entertainment," in his *Shakespeare's Festive Comedy: A Study of Dramatic Form and its Relation to Social Custom* (New York: Meridian, 1963), p. 30 ff.

[43] James Morrell Swan, "Courtesy and Rent: Some Versions of Pastoral and History," in "Pastoral, History and Desire: A Psychoanalytic Study of English Renaissance Literature and Society," Diss. Stanford, 1974, pp. 108-196.

[44] Leah Sinaugoulou Marcus, *Childhood and Cultural Despair* (Pittsburgh: University of Pittsburgh Press, 1978).

[45] Erikson, "Youth: Fidelity and Diversity," pp. 15-16.

[46] Marie-Louise von Franz, *The Problem of the Puer Aeternus* (Zurich: Spring Publications, 1970), p. I-3.

[47] Ibid., p. I-4.

[48] Erik H. Erikson, *Childhood and Society,* second edition (New York: W. W. Norton, 1963), p. 262.

[49] *The Works of Geoffrey Chaucer,* ed. F. N. Robinson (Boston: Houghton Mifflin, 1957), p. 55. Paul Alpers says that December's Colin neither expresses despair nor confesses failure, but rather that his is "the traditional act of the old shepherd who submits to the nature of things. ("The Eclogue Tradition and the Nature of Pastoral,") pp. 365-6. But there is a sense of regret here that can hardly qualify as consolation. Its expression is typical of another tradition of old age elegy centering on unmitigated despair. See, G. L. Colffman, "Old Age from Horace to Chaucer," *Speculum* IX, 1934, pp. 249-278. Chaucer's Reeve utters a succinct *adynaton* of unripe-rottenness that aptly expresses what Erikson calls the typical disgust of old age (*Childhood and Society,* p. 268-9). The "open-ers" that the Reeve uses to identify "we olde men" is defined by the OED as "open-arse. . .an old name of the medlar, fruit and tree." The medlar fruit "resembles a small brown-skinned apple, with a large cup-shaped "eye" between the persistent calyx lobes. It is eaten when decayed to a soft pulpy state."

[50] Marie-Louise von Franz, III-19.

[51] Variorum edition, pp. 417-424.

[52] Thomas Perrin Harrison, *The Pastoral Elegy: An anthology* (Austin: University of Texas Press, 1939), p. 1; Frank Kermode, *English Pastoral Poetry* (New York: Barnes & Noble, 1952); Northrop Frye, "Levels of Meaning in Literature," *KR* 12, (1950): 258.

[53] Sir J. G. Frazer, *The New Golden Bough,* ed. Theodore Gaster (New York, 1959), pp. 284-5.

[54] "Youth: Fidelity and Diversity," p. 22.

[55] This reversal is noticed but not accounted for by Patrick Cullin in *Spenser, Marvell and Renaissance Pastoral,* p. 9. In an essay published after this chapter was written, Harry Berger covers some of the same ground. He too observes the pattern of exchange of posture and role between youth and age. But he sees the reversals primarily as symbolic of the failure of both youth and age to break free from the nostalgic illusions of what he calls "the Paradise Principle." Berger does not, as I do, also consider this reversal as redemptive. See "The Aging Boy: Paradise and Parricide in Spenser's *SC,*" in Maynard Mack, ed. *Poetic Traditions of the English Renaissance* (New Haven: Yale University Press, 1982), pp. 25 ff.

[56] Spenser was neither the only nor the first writer to use the debate of youth and age in a serial manner to create a sense of character changing over time. In "The Wife of Bath's Prologue," Chaucer's Alison narrates her autobiography as a sequence of such battles, in which she gradually switched sides from youth to age. And Sidney's Geron, after engaging in battle with young Phillisides, makes peace between his young and his old dog from an intermediary perspective and then argues *against* the position of old age presented by Mastix in the following poem.

[57] Alexander C. Judson, *The Life of Edmund Spenser* (Baltimore: John Hopkins Press, 1945), pp. 45-8.

[58] According to his biographer, the period between young Spenser's departure from Cambridge in 1574 and his employment by the Bishop of Rochester in 1578 remains "obscure years," during which his whereabouts are unknown. (Judson, p. 46). This might have been an interval of retreat, experimentation or "moratorium."

[58a] Both Helgerson and Montrose emphasize the likelihood that Spenser himself was quite uncertain about the outcome of his pioneering commitment to the poet's vocation. Bruce Smith notes that tentativenes and doubt are characteristics of the typical *Bildungsroman's* ending.

[59] Eisenstadt, p. 32.

[60] Mircea Eliade, *Birth and Rebirth,* p. xiv.

[61] Ibid., p. 135.

[62] Ibid., p. 135.

Montrose similarly interprets Colin's demise, though without reference to his passage from childhood to adulthood: "Colin's end is the end of Spenser's beginning. . ." p. 61

[63] Mircea Eliade, *The Myth of Eternal Return* trans. Willard Trask (New York: Pantheon, 1954), p. 52.

[64] According to Victor Turner, "liminality" is a condition—outside the socially defined matrix of status and role—that a person enters during any "non-worldly" experience, be it erotic passion, consciousness alteration, or the passage from one state to another. "Variations on a Theme of Liminality" in *Secular Ritual*, ed. S. Moore and Barbara Myerhoff (Amsterdam, 1967), pp. 36-52). Also *Ritual Process* (Chicago, 1969). "I was so much older then, I'm younger than that now" goes the chorus of Bob Dylan's "My Back Pages."

[65] Eliade, *Myth,* p. 62

[66] Ibid. p. 54.

[67] Ibid., p. 65.

[68] Manly P. Hall, "The Four Seasons of the Spirit," (Los Angeles: Philosophical Research Society, 1965), p. 23.

[69] Heraclitus, Fragments 212, 205, *The Presocratic Philosophers,* pp. 192, 195.

BIBLIOGRAPHY

Alighieri, Dante. *The Purgatorio*. Trans. John Ciardi. New York: New American Library, 1961.

Alpers, Paul. "The Eclogue Tradition and the Nature of Pastoral." *CE* 34 (1972), 353–371.

———. *The Singer of* The Eclogues: *A Study of Virgillian Pastoral*. Berkeley: University of California Press, 1979.

Altman, Joel. *The Tudor Play of Mind: Rhetorical Inquiry and Elizabethan Drama*. Berkeley: University of California Press, 1978.

Aries, Phillipe. *Centuries of Childhood: A Social History of Family Life*. Trans. Robert Baldick. New York: Alfred A. Knopf, 1962.

Aristotle. *Poetics*. Trans. Ingram Bywater. New York: Modern Library, 1954.

———. *Rhetoric*. Trans. W. Rhys Roberts. New York: Modern Library, 1954.

Ascham, Roger. *The Scholemaster* (1570) Ed. Lawrence V. Ryan. Ithaca: Folger Shakespeare Library, 1967.

Auden, Wystan Hugh. *The Age of Anxiety*. New York, 1947.

——— and Chester Kallman. *An Elizabethan Song Book*. London: Faber and Faber, 1957.

Ault, Norman. *Elizabethan Lyrics*. New York: William Sloane, 1949.

Babb, Lawrence. *The Elizabethan Malady: A Study of Melancholia in English Literature from 1580 to 1642*. East Lansing: Michigan State University Press, 1951.

Barber, Cesare Lombardi. *Shakespeare's Festive Comedy: A Study of Dramatic Form and its Relation to Social Custom*. Cleveland: Meridian, 1966.

Barkan, Leonard. *Nature's Work of Art: The Human Body as an Image of the World*. New Haven and London: Yale University Press, 1975.

Berg, William. *Early Vergil*. London: The Athlone Press, 1974.

Berger, Harry. "The Renaissance Imagination: Second World and Green World." *Centennial Review* 9 (1965), 36–79.

———. "The Aging Boy: Paradise and Parricide in Spenser's *SC*." *Poetic Traditions of the English Renaissance*, ed. Maynard Mack. New Haven: Yale University Press, 1982. pp. 25 ff.

Blake, William. *The Complete Writings*. Ed. Geoffrey Keynes. London: Oxford University Press, 1966.

———. *Songs of Innocence and Experience: Showing the Two Contrary States of the Soul*. Facsimile edition by Geoffrey Keynes. New York: Orion Press, 1925.

Bloomfield, Morton. *The Seven Deadly Sins*. East Lansing: Michigan State University Press, 1952.

Blyth, R. H. *Zen in English Literature and Oriental Classics.* Tokyo, 1942; rpt. New York: Dutton, 1960.

Boas, George. *The Cult of Childhood.* London: The Warburg Institute, 1966.

Bossy, M. R. "The Prowess of Debate." dissertation. Yale 1970.

Bronson, B. H. "The Dialog song or Proteus Observed." *PQ*, 54, 117–136.

Brown, Norman O. *Life Against Death: The Psychoanalytic Meaning of History.* New York. Modern Library Paperback, 1959.

Buckley, Jerome Hamilton. *Season of Youth: The Bildungsroman from Dickens to Golding.* Cambridge: Harvard University Press, 1974.

Castiglione, Baldassare. *The Courtier.* Translated by Sir Thomas Hoby (1561) in *Three Renaissance Classics.* Ed. Burton A. Milligan. New York: Scribner's, 1963.

Chaucer, Geoffrey. *Works.* Ed. F. N. Robinson. Boston: Houghton Mifflin, 1957.

Chew, Samuel C. *This Strange Eventful History.* New Haven: Yale University Press, 1962.

Cicero, Marcus Tullius. *Cicero on the Art of Growing Old (De Senectute).* Trans. H. N. Couch. Providence: Brown University Press, 1959.

Cody, Richard. *The Landscape of the Mind: Pastoralism and Platonic Theory in Tasso's Aminta and Shakespeare's Early Comedies.* Oxford: The Clarendon Press, 1969.

Cohn, Norman. *The Pursuit of the Milennium: Revolutionary Messianism in Medieval and Reformation Europe and its Bearing on Modern Totalitarian Movements.* New York: Harper Torchbooks, 2nd ed., 1961.

Coffman, G. R. "Old Age from Horace to Chaucer." *Speculum* IX (1934), 249–278.

Colie, Rosalie. *Paradoxica Epidemica.* Princeton: Princeton University Press, 1966.

______. *The Resources of Kind: Genre Theory in the Renaissance.* Berkeley: University of California Press, 1973.

Congleton, J. E. *Theories of Pastoral Poetry in England, 1684–1798.* Gainesville: University of Florida Press, 1973.

Coveney, Peter. *The Image of Childhood: The Individual and Society; A Study of the Theme in English Literature.* Baltimore: Penguin Books, rev. ed. 1967.

Cullen, Patrick. *Spenser, Marvell and Renaissance Pastoral.* Cambridge: Harvard University Press, 1970.

Curtius, Ernst Robert. *European Literature in the Latin Middle Ages.*Trans. Willard Trask. New York: Pantheon Books, 1953.

Davis, Natalie Z. "Youth Groups and Charivaris in 16th Century France." *Past and Present*, 50 (1971), 50–55.

Diderot, Denis. *Supplement au Voyage de Bougainville.* Ed. Gilbert Chinard. Baltimore: Johns Hopkins Press, 1935.

Donne, John. *Selected Poetry.* Ed. Marius Bewley. New York: Signet, 1965.

Doran, Madeleine. *Endeavors of Art: A Study of Form in Elizabethan Drama.* Madison: University of Wisconsin Press, 1954.

Drayton, Michael. *Works.* gen. ed. J. W. Hebel. Vol. V. Ed. Kathleen Tillotson. Oxford: Oxford University Press, 1961.

Dryer, Adolf. *Der Peripatos ueber das Greisenalter.* Paderborn: F. Schoningh, 1939. New York: Johnson reprint Corp., 1968.

Eggers, Graydon, Trans. *The Owl and the Nightingale.* Durham: University of North Carolina Press, 1955.

Eisenstadt, Schmuel I. *Generation to Generation: Age Groups and Social Structure.* Glencoe, Ill.: The Free Press, 1956.

———. "Archetypal Patterns of Youth." In *Youth: Change and Challenge,* ed. Erik H. Erikson. New York: Basic Books, 1963.

Eliade, Mircea. *The Myth of the Eternal Return.* New York: Pantheon, 1954.

———. *Birth and Rebirth: The Meanings of Initiation in Human Cultures.* Trans. Willard R. Trask. New York: Harper, 1958.

———. *Yoga: Immortality and Freedom.* Trans. Willard R. Trask. Princeton: Princeton University Press, 2nd. ed., 1969.

Empson, William. *Some Versions of Pastoral.* London, 1935; rpt. New York: New Directions, 1960.

Erikson, Erik H. *Young Man Luther.* 2nd ed. New York: W. W. Norton, 1962.

———. *Childhood and Society.* 2nd ed. New York: W. W. Norton, 1963.

———. "Youth: Fidelity and Diversity." In *Youth: Change and Challenge.* Ed. Erik H. Erikson. New York: Basic Books, 1963.

———. "Reflections on Dr. Borg's Life Cycle." In *Adulthood.* Ed. Erik H. Erikson. New York: W. W. Norton, 1978.

Esler, Anthony. *The Aspiring Mind of the Elisabethan Younger Generation.* Durham: University of North Carolina Press, 1966.

Fish, Stanley. *Self-Consuming Artifacts.* Berkeley: University of California Press, 1972.

———. *The Living Temple: George Herbert and Catechizing.* Berkeley: University of California Press, 1972.

Forsythe, R. S. "The Passionate Shepherd and English Poetry." *PMLA* 40 (1925), 692–742.

Frazer, Sir James G. *The New Golden Bough.* Ed. Theodore Gaster. New York: Criterion Books, 1959.

Fraenger, Wilhelm. *The Milennium of Hieronymus Bosch: Outlines of a New Interpretation.* Trans. Esther Wilkins and Ernst Kaiser. Chicago: University of Chicago Press, 1951.

Friedman, Donald. *Marvell's Pastoral Art.* Berkeley: University of California Press, 1970.

Frye, Northrop. *Anatomy of Criticism: Four Essays.* Princeton: Princeton University Press, 1957.

Gabelentz, Hans v.d. *Die Lebensalter u.d. menschliche Leben in Tiergestalt.* Berlin, 1938.

Garcilasso de la Vega. *Works.* Trans. and ed. J. H. Wiffen. London: 1823.

Gardner, E. G. *Dante and the Mystics.* London, 1913.

Giamatti, A. B. *The Earthly Paradise and the Renaissance Epic.* Princeton: Princeton University Press.

Gombrich, E. H. *The Heritage of Apelles: Studies in the Art of the Renaissance.* Ithaca: Cornell University Press, 1976.

Googe, Barnabe. *Eglogs, Epytaphes, and Sonettes,* ed. E. A. Arber. London, 1871.

Gow, A. S. F. *The Greek Bucolic Poets.* Cambridge: Cambridge University Press, 1953.

Grant, W. Leonard. *Neo-Latin Literature and the Pastoral.* Chapel Hill: University of North Carolina Press, 1965.

Greg, W. W. *Pastoral Poetry and Pastoral Drama.* London: Sidgewick and Jackson, 1906, rpt. New York: Russell and Russell, 1959.

Gubrium, Jaber. "Alternatives to Disengagement: The Old Men of the Highland Druze." In *Time, Roles and Self in Old Age.* Ed. Jaber Gubrium. New York, 1976.

Guillen, Claudio. *Literature as System: Essays Toward the Theory of Literary History.* Princeton: Princeton University Press, 1971.

Haessler, Hans. "*The Owl and the Nightingale* und die literarishen Bestrebungen des 12. und 13 Jhts." Frankfurt-am-Mein, 1942.

Hall, Manly P. "The Four Seasons of the Spirit." Los Angeles: Philosophical Research Society, 1965.

Hamilton, A. C. "The Argument of *The Shepheardes Calender.*" *ELH* 23 (1956), 171–82.

Hanford, James Holly. "Classical Eclogue and Medieval Debate." *Romanic Review* 2 (1911), 16–31, 129–143.

Harrison, Thomas Perrin. *The Pastoral Elegy: An Anthology with Introduction, Commentary, and Notes.* Austin, 1939.

Heberg, Betty Nye. "The *Bucolics* and the Medieval Poetical Debate." *Transactions and Proceedings of the American Philological Assn.* 75 (1944), 47–70.

Helgerson, Richard. "The New Poet Presents Himself: Spenser and the Idea of a Literary Career." *PMLA* 93 (1978) 895 ff.

Henrysson, Robert. *The Poems and Fables of Robert Henrysson.* Ed. H. Harvey Wood. Edinburgh: Oliver and Boyd, 1933.

Herrick, Robert. *The Complete Poems.* Ed. J. Max Patrick. New York: Doubleday-Anchor, 1963.

Hillman, James. "Puer and Senex." In *Puer Papers,* ed. Cynthia Giles. Irving, Texas: Spring Publications, 1979.

Hirsh, E. D. *Innocence and Experience.* New Haven: Yale University Press, 1964.

Homer. *The Odyssey.* Trans. Robert Fitzgerald. New York: Anchor-Doubleday, 1963.

Huizinga, Johan. *The Waning of the Middle Ages.* New York: Anchor-Doubleday, 1954.

Hunt, David. *Parents and Children in History.* New York, 1977.

Hunt, John Dixon. *The Figure in the Landscape: Poetry, Painting and Gardening during the Eighteenth Century.* Baltimore: Johns Hopkins Press, 1976.

Johnson, Samuel. "Pastoral Poetry I." *Rambler* #36, July 21, 1750. In *Eighteenth Century Critical Essays.* Ed. Scott Elledge. Ithaca: Cornell University Press, 1961.

Jonson, Ben. *The Complete Poetry.* Ed. William B. Hunter Jr. New York: Anchor Seventeenth Century Series, 1963.

Jones, W. P. *The Pastourelle.* Cambridge: Harvard University Press, 1931.

Judson, Alexander C. *The Life of Edmund Spenser.* Baltimore: Johns Hopkins Press, 1945.

Jung, Carl Gustave. "The Stages of Life." In *The Portable Jung,* ed. Joseph Campbell. New York: The Viking Press, 1971, rpt. Penguin, 1976.

______. *Symbols of Transformation.* Trans. R. F. C. Hull. *Collected Works.* Vol. V. Bollingen Series XX. Princeton: Princeton University Press, 2nd ed., 1967.

______. "The Psychology of the Child Archetype." In *Archetypes of the Collective Unconscious.* New York: Pantheon, 1959.

Kakar, Sudhir. "The Human Life Cycle: The Traditional Hindu View and the Psychology of Erik H. Erikson." *Philosphy of East and West,* XVIII: 3 (1968).

Kalstone, David. *Sidney's Poetry: Contexts and Interpretations.* Cambridge: Harvard University Press, 1965.

Kennedy, C. J. *Rhetorical Norms in Renaissance Literature.* New Haven: Yale University Press, 1978.

Kenniston, Kenneth. " 'Youth' as a 'New' Stage of Life." *American Scholar,* 1970, pp. 636–650.

Kermode, Frank. *English Pastoral Poetry from its Beginnings to Marvell.* New York: Barnes and Noble, 1952.

———. "The Argument of Marvell's Garden." In *Seventeenth Century English Poetry.* New York: Oxford University Press, 1962.

Kirk, G. S. and J. E. Raven. *The Presocratic Philosophers.* Cambridge: Cambridge University Press, 1960.

Kronenfeld, Judy Zahler. "The Treatment of Pastoral Ideals in *As You Like It:* A Study of Traditional Renaissance Dichotomies." Diss. Stanford, 1971.

Lambert, Ellen Zetzel. *Placing Sorrow: A Study of the Pastoral Elegy Convention from Theocritus to Milton.* Chapel Hill: University of North Carolina Press, 1976.

Lampe, D. E. "Middle English Debate Poems." Diss. Minnesota, 1969.

Layard, John. *The Virgin Archetype.* New York and Zurich: Spring Publications, 1972.

Leach, Eleanor Winsor. *Vergil's* Eclogues: *Landscapes of Experience.* Ithaca: Cornell University Press, 1974.

Lerner, Laurance. *The Uses of Nostalgia: Studies in Pastoral Poetry.* New York: Schocken Books, 1972.

Levin, Harry. *The Myth of the Golden Age in the Renaissance.* Bloomington: Indiana University Press, 1969.

Lewis, Clive Stapleton. *English Literature in the 16th Century Excluding Drama.* Oxford: Clarendon Press, 1944.

Lifton, Robert Jay. *The Broken Connection: On Death and the Continuity of Life.* New York: Simon and Schuster, 1979.

Lidz, Theodore. *The Person: His or Her Development Throughout the Life Cycle.* Revised ed. New York: Basic Books, 1976.

Lloyd, G. E. R. *Polarity and Analogy: Two Types of Argument in Early Greek Thought.* Cambridge: Cambridge University Press, 1966.

Lodge, Thomas. *Rosalynde, or Euphues' Golden Legacy.* Ed. Edward Chauncy Baldwin. Boston: Ginn and Co., 1910.

Longus. *Daphynis and Chloe.* Trans. Paul Turner. Harmondsworth: Penguin, 1968.

Lovejoy, A. O. and George Boas. *Primitivism and Related Ideas in Antiquity.* Baltimore: Johns Hopkins Press, 1935; rpt. 1965.

Lovelace, Richard. *Poems.* Ed. C. H. Wilkinson,. Oxford: Clarendon Press, 1925.

Manuel, Frank E. *Utopias and Utopian Thought.* Cambridge: Houghton Mifflin, 1966.

Mantuanus, Baptista. *The Eclogues of Baptista Mantuanus.* Edited with an Introduction by Wilfred P. Mustard. Baltimore: Johns Hopkins Press, 1911.

Marcus, Leah Sinanoglou. *Childhood and Cultural Despair: A Theme and Variations in Seventeenth Century Literature.* Pittsburgh: University of Pittsburgh Press, 1978.

Marias, Julian. *Generations: A Historical Method.* Trans. Harold C. Raley. University of Alabama Press, 1970.

Marlowe, Christopher. *The Complete Works.* Ed. Fredson Bowers. Cambridge: Cambridge University Press, 1973.

Marot, Clement. *Oeuvres Lyriques.* Ed. C. A. Mayer. London, 1964.

Marvell, Andrew. *Poems and Letters.* Ed. H. M. Margoliouth, revised by Pierre Legouis, 2 Vols. Oxford: Clarendon Press, 1971.

Marx, Janet Howell. "The Marriage of Man and God: Solomon's *Song of Songs* and Resurrection in *The Divine Comedy.*" Thesis, Columbia, 1969.

McCaffrey, Isabel. "Allegory and Pastoral in The Shepheardes Calender." *ELH* 36 (1969) pp. 105ff.

McCanless, Michael. *Dialectical Criticism and Renaissance Literature.* Berkeley: University of California Press, 1975.

Miller, Robert P. "The Scriptural Eunuch and Chaucer's Pardoner." In Schoek and Taylor, *Chaucer Criticism.* Terre Haute: Notre Dame University Press, 1960.

Milton, John. *The Complete Poems and Major Prose.* Ed. Merritt Y. Hughes. New York: The Odyssey Press, 1957.

Mirandola, Pico della. *On the Dignity of Man.* Trans. Charles G. Wallis. Ed. Paul J. W. Miller. New York: Library of Liberal Arts, 1965.

Montaigne, Michel de. *The Complete Essays of Montaigne.* Trans. Donald Frame Stanford: Stanford University Press, 1965.

Montrose, Louis Adrian. "The Perfecte Patterne of a Poete: The Poetics of Courtship in *SC.*" *Texas Studies in Language and Literature* 21 1 (1979) 36ff.

Moore, Tom. "Artemis and the Puer." *Puer Papers.* Ed. Cynthia Giles. Irving Texas: Spring Publications, 1979.

Naegele, Kaspar D. "Youth and Society: Some Observations." In *Youth: Change and Challenge.* Ed. Erik H. Erikson. New York: W. W. Norton, 1963.

Nelson, William. *The Poetry of Edmund Spenser.* New York: Columbia University Press, 1963.

Offord, M. Y. *The Parlement of the Thre Ages.* London: Early English Text Society. Oxford University Press, 1959.

Paden, W. D. "The Medieval *Pastourelle:* A Critical and Textual Reevaluation." Diss. Yale, 1971.

Panofsky, Erwin. "*Et in Arcadia Ego:* Poussin and the Elegaic Tradition." In *Meaning and the Visual Arts.* New York: Anchor, 1955.

Parry, Adam. "Landscape in Greek Poetry." *Yale Classical Studies* XV (1957), 29ff.

Patch, H. R. *The Other World According to Descriptions in Medieval Literature.* Cambridge: Harvard University Press, 1950.

Perret, Jacques. "The Georgics." In *Vergil: A Collection of Critical Essays.* Ed. Steele Commager. Englewood Cliffs: Prentice-Hall, 1966.

Petrarch, Francisco. *Petrarch's Secret or the Soul's Conflict with Passion.* Trans. William H. Draper. London, 1911.

Plato. *Plato's Phaedrus.* Ed. W. C. Helmbold and W. G. Rabinowitz New York: Liberal Arts Press, 1956.

______. *The Republic of Plato.* Trans. and ed. Francis M. Cornford. New York: Oxford University Press, 1945.

Pope, Alexander. "Pastoral Poetry." Guardian #40 (1713) in *The Tatler and The Guardian Complete in One Volume.* Edinburgh: William P. Nimmo and Co., 1880.

Poggioli, Renato. The Oaten Flute: *Essays on Pastoral Poetry and The Pastoral Ideal.* Cambridge: Harvard University Press, 1975.

Putnam, Michael. *Vergil's Pastoral Art: Studies in the Eclogues.* Princeton: Princeton University Press, 1970.

Puttenhame, George. *The Arte of English Poesie.* Ed. Gladys Doidge Wilcock and Alice Walker. Cambridge: Cambridge University Press, 1936.

Ralegh, Sir Walter. *The Poems of Sir Walter Ralegh.* Ed. Agnes Latham. Cambridge: Harvard University Press, 1962.

Richardson, Bessie. *Old Age among the Ancient Greeks: The Greek Portrayal of Old Age in Literature, Art and Inscriptions.* Baltimore: Johns Hopkins Press, 1933.

Robertson, D. W. *A Preface to Chaucer: Studies in Medieval Perspectives.* Princeton: Princeton University Press, 1962.

Roheim, Geza. *Animism, Magic and the Divine King.* London: Kegan and Paul, 1930.

Rollins, Hyder Edward. *England's Helicon.* 2 vols. Cambridge: Harvard University Press, 1935.

———. *A Paradise of Dainty Devices.* Cambridge: Harvard University Press, 1927.

Rosenmeyer, Thomas. *The Green Cabinet: Theocritus and the European Pastoral Lyric.* Berkeley: University of California Press, 1969.

Roszak, Theodore. *The Making of a Counter-Culture: Reflections on the Technocratic Society and its Youthful Opposition.* Garden City: Doubleday, 1969.

Sanford, Charles. *The Quest for Paradise: Europe and the American Moral Imagination.* Urbana: University of Illinois Press, 1961.

Sannazaro, Jacopo. *Arcadia and Piscatorial Eclogues.* Trans. Ralph Nash. Detroit: Wayne State University Press, 1960.

Segal, Charles. "*Tamon Cantabitis, Arcades:* Exile and Arcadia in Eclogues One and Nine." *Arion* 4(1965), 243–265.

Segal, Muriel. *Virgins, Reluctant, Dubious and Avowed.* New York: Macmillan, 1977.

Shakespeare, William. *The Complete Works of William Shakespeare.* Ed. George Lyman Kittredge. Boston: Ginn and Co.

Sidney, Sir Phillip. *The Prose Works of Sir Phillip Sidney.* Four Volumes. Ed. Albert Feuillerat. Cambridge: Cambridge University Press, 1962.

———. *The Poems of Sir Phillip Sidney.* Ed. William Ringler. Oxford: Clarendon Press,

Smith, Bruce C. "On Reading *SC.*" *Spenser Studies,* ed. Patrick Cullen and Thomas Roche. Pittsburgh: University of Pittsburgh Press, 1980. pp. 89 ff.

Smith, Hallett. *Elizabethan Poetry: A Study in Conventions, Meaning and Expression.* Cambridge: Harvard University Press, 1952.

Smith, S. R. "Religion and the Conception of Youth in Seventeenth Century England." *History of Childhood Quarterly,* II(1975) 497ff.

Sommer, H. Oskar. *The Kalendar of Shepherds.* London, 1892.

Sorenson, Robert. *Adolescent Sexuality in Contemporary America.* New York: World, 1973.

Spenser, Edmund. *The Works of Edmund Spenser: A Variorum Edition.* Six Volumes. Ed. Edwin Greenlaw, et. al. Baltimore: Johns Hopkins Press, 1932–42.

———. *The Minor Poems.* Two Volumes. Ed. Charles Grosvenor Osgood and Henry Gibbons Lotspeich. Baltimore: Johns Hopkins Press, 1943.

———. *The Shepheardes Calender,* edited and with an introduction by S. K. Heninger Jr. Delmar, New York: Scholars' Facsimiles and Reprints, 1979.

Spevak, Marvin. *The Harvard Concordance to Shakespeare.* Cambridge: Belnap Press, 1973.

Stevens, Wallace. *The Collected Poems.* New York: Alfred A. Knopf, 1961.

Stewart, Stanley. *The Enclosed Garden.* Madison: University of Wisconsin Press, 1966.

Stone, Lawrence. *The Family, Sex, Marriage in England, 1500–1800.* London, 1977.

Swales, Martin. *The German* Bildungsroman *from Wieland to Hesse.* Princeton: Princeton University Press, 1978.

Swan, James Morrell. "Pastoral, History and Desire: A Psychoanalytic Study of English Renaissance Literature and Society." Diss. Stanford, 1974.

Tayler, Edward, William. *Nature and Art in Renaissance Literature.* New York: Columbia University, 1964.

Theocritus. *The Poems of Theocritus.* Trans. Anna Rist. Chapel Hill: University of North Carolina Press, 1978.

Tolliver, Harold. *Pastoral Forms and Attitudes*. Berkeley: University of California Press, 1971.

Trimpi, Wesley. "The Quality of Fiction: The Rhetorical Transmission of Literary Theory." *Traditio* XXX(1974).

Turner, Terence. "Transformation, Hierarchy and Transcendance: A Reformulation of Van Gennep's Model of the Structure of Rites of Passage." In *Secular Ritual*. Ed. Barbara Myerhoff and S. Moore. Amsterdam, 1977.

Turner, Victor. "Variations on a Theme of Liminality." In *Secular Ritual*. Ed. Barbara Myerhoff and S. Moore. Amsterdam, 1977.

Varagnac, Andre. *Civilisation Traditionelle et les Genres de Vie*. Paris: Editions Andre Michel, 1948.

Vaux, Thomas Lord. *The Poems of Lord Vaux*. Ed. Larry P. Vonalt. Denver: Alan Swallow, 1960.

Vergil (Publius Vergilius Maro) *The Georgics*. Trans. K. R. Mackenzie. London: Folio Society, 1969.

Wagenknecht, David. *Blake's Night: William Blake and the Idea of Pastoral*. Cambridge: Harvard University Press, 1973.

Walther, Hans. *Das Streitgedicht in der lateinischen Literatur des Mittelalters*. Meunchen: C. H. Becksche Verlag, 1920.

Walton, Izaak. *The Complete Angler or the Contemplative Man's Recreation of Izaak Walton and Charles Cotton*. Ed. James Russell Lowell. Boston: Little Brown and Co., 1891.

Warburg, Aby. "Sandro Botticellis 'Geburt der Venus' and 'Frueling'." *Gesammelte Schriften*. I, 1–45. Leipzig, 1932.

Watson, Wilbur H. and Robert J. Jaxwell. *Human Aging and Dying: A Study in Sociocultural Gerontology*. New York: St. Martin's Press 1977.

Williams, Raymond. *The Country and the City*. New York: Oxford University Press, 1973.

Winters, Yvor. "The Sixteenth Century Lyric in England." In *Forms of Discovery*. Denver: Alan Swallow, 1967.

Wordsworth, William. *The Poetical Works of William Wordsworth*. Ed. Thomas Henry Hutchinson and Ernest de Selincourt. London: Oxford University Press, 1959.

Yeats, William Butler. *The Collected Poems of William Butler Yeats*. New York: Macmillan, 1956.

Richard Wakefield

ROBERT FROST

and the Opposing Lights of the Hour

American University Studies: Series IV, English Language and Literature.
Vol. 16
ISBN 0-8204-0152-8 238 pp. hardcover/lam. US $ 27.70
recommended prices - alterations reserved

Robert Frost's early poems establish a philosophy that became, in his later work, more explicit but seldom more powerfully expressed. He believed that activity has meaning only when it is an exertion against opposition, that we establish ourselves, virtually create ourselves, in the range of movement allowed us by external constraints. Speech, as activity, likewise takes on character when placed in opposition to the mechanical rhythms of poetry - and thus for Frost did a philosophy of life cohere with a theory of poetry.

Contents: Voice against rhythm - Self against nature - Self against society- Self-preservation against the re-definition of romantic love - The necessity of discovering the range in which meaningful activity can take place.

PETER LANG PUBLISHING, INC.
34 East 39th Street
USA - New York, NY 10016

Edward Trostle Jones

FOLLOWING DIRECTIONS

A Study of Peter Brook

American University Studies: Series IV, English Language and Literature. Vol. 3
ISBN 0-8204-0116-1 220 pp. hardcover/lam. US $ 25.65
recommended prices – alterations reserved

This critical study of Peter Brook attempts a comprehensive survey of the director's long and distinguished career in theatre and in film from his early years as boy wonder of the commercial British stage through his inventive years as a Shakespeare director and innovative film-maker to his recent Parisian collective experimentations where he seeks to enlarge the boundaries of theatre for performers and audiences alike. The hallmark of Brook's work has been his imaginative eclecticism and his unwillingness to rest satisfied with his own successes. By considering his techniques, theatrical and cinematic, his favored thematic content, and factors of innovation over the years, we can appreciate the way Brook combines the pragmatic and the prophetic as a world-class director whose aesthetics have changed modern theatre.
Contents: A comprehensive critical survey and evaluation of Peter Brook's work in theatre and in film from his beginnings in the nineteen forties until the present, with emphasis upon his eclecticism.

PETER LANG PUBLISHING, INC.
34 East 39th Street
USA – New York, NY 10016